The Hindu Religious Tradition

THE RELIGIOUS LIFE OF MAN
Frederick J. Streng, Series Editor

Understanding Religious Man
Frederick J. Streng

The House of Islam
Kenneth Cragg

Japanese Religion: Unity and Diversity
H. Byron Earhart

Chinese Religion: An Introduction
Laurence G. Thompson

The Buddhist Religion
Richard H. Robinson

The Way of Torah: An Introduction to Judaism
Jacob Neusner

The Hindu Religious Tradition
Thomas J. Hopkins

forthcoming:

Primitive Religions
Charles H. Long

The Hindu Religious Tradition

THOMAS J. HOPKINS

Franklin & Marshall College

DICKENSON PUBLISHING COMPANY, INC.

Encino, California and Belmont, California

To Fran, Kathy, Susan, Nick and Patrick

Library of Congress Catalog Card Number: 74-158118

Printed in the United States of America

3 4 5 6 7 8 9 10

Table of Contents

Foreword

The Religious Life of Man series is intended as an introduction to a large, complex field of inquiry—man's religious experience. It seeks to present the depth and richness of religious concepts, forms of worship, spiritual practices, and social institutions found in the major religious traditions throughout the world.

As a specialist in the language and culture in which a religion is found, each author is able to illuminate the meanings of a religious perspective and practice as other human beings have experienced it. To communicate this meaning to readers who have had no special training in these cultures and religions, the authors have attempted to provide clear, nontechnical descriptions and interpretations of religious life.

Different interpretive approaches have been used, depending upon the nature of the religious data; some religious expressions, for instance, lend themselves more to developmental, others more to topical studies. But this lack of a single interpretation may itself be instructive, for the experiences and practices regarded as religious in one culture may not be the most important in another.

The Religious Life of Man is concerned with, on the one hand, the variety of religious expressions found in different traditions and, on the other, the similarities in the structures of religious life. The various forms are interpreted in terms of their cultural context and historical continuity, demonstrating both the diverse expressions and commonalities of religious traditions. Besides the single volumes on different religions, the series offers a core book on the study of religious meaning, which describes different study approaches and examines several modes and structures of religious awareness. In addition, each book presents a list of materials for further reading, including translations of religious texts and detailed examinations of specific topics.

We hope the reader will find these volumes "introductory" in the most significant sense: an introduction to a new perspective for understanding himself and others.

Frederick J. Streng
Series Editor

Preface

This book expresses a personal and academic interest in the Hindu religious tradition that began some fifteen years ago at Yale University. Norvin Hein started the process. Paul Thieme and Charles Heimsath at Yale and Norman Brown at Penn added to it during my years of graduate study; Milton Singer, Ed Dimock and J. A. B. van Buitenen at Chicago have contributed much to it since. Periodic caucuses with Bob Lester, Dan Smith and John Carman—fellow graduate students and continuing friends—have raised new questions and opened new areas of study. Gary Tarr has taught me most of what I know of Hindu art.

My students have been major catalysts in shaping my thinking over the past ten years. They have asked many questions I could not answer, forcing me to learn more and find better ways of explaining a complex tradition to those who confront it for the first time. They have come also with personal and practical concerns, pushing me to understand the tradition in human terms: what it has meant and can mean to those whose lives are shaped by it.

For answers to many of these questions I am indebted to numerous Hindu friends and teachers: to T. K. Venkateswaran of Madras; Narmadeshwar Prasad of Patna; A. R. Subramanyaraj Urs, K. Gnanambal of the Anthropological Survey of India, and the Swamiji of the Parakala Maṭh in Mysore; Manohar Bangalorekar, Master Kale and his disciples, devotees at the Pāpamaharāj Maṭh, and the thousands of pilgrims in Pandharpur; the priest in Kumbakonam who chanted the thousand names of Vishnu for me in the courtyard of a Rāma temple at midnight, and the bronze-caster who showed me the care with which devoted craftsmen make images. From them I have learned something of the variety of the tradition and the many meanings it has for those who share it.

I owe a major debt to Fred Streng, the editor of this series, who encouraged me to write this book and has borne with great patience the slow evolution of the text. Norvin Hein, who read the first draft, gave his usual sage advice on many points. Greg Beck, my student assistant and astrology consultant, gave valuable aid in preparing the manuscript, as did Dan Jackson in the final stages. Florence Staman suffered through the typing, aided by Graceann Rohrer. My wife, of course, did all the worst jobs under the greatest pressure.

Most authors express thanks and regrets to their families for their writing, and it is easy to see why. My family has endured more of the pain than the pleasure of bringing forth this book, and I owe them more than the usual debt of gratitude. I hope their long wait for the struggle to end is repaid in the result: a beginner's guide to a great religious community by a sympathetic outsider.

Thomas J. Hopkins
Lancaster, Pa.

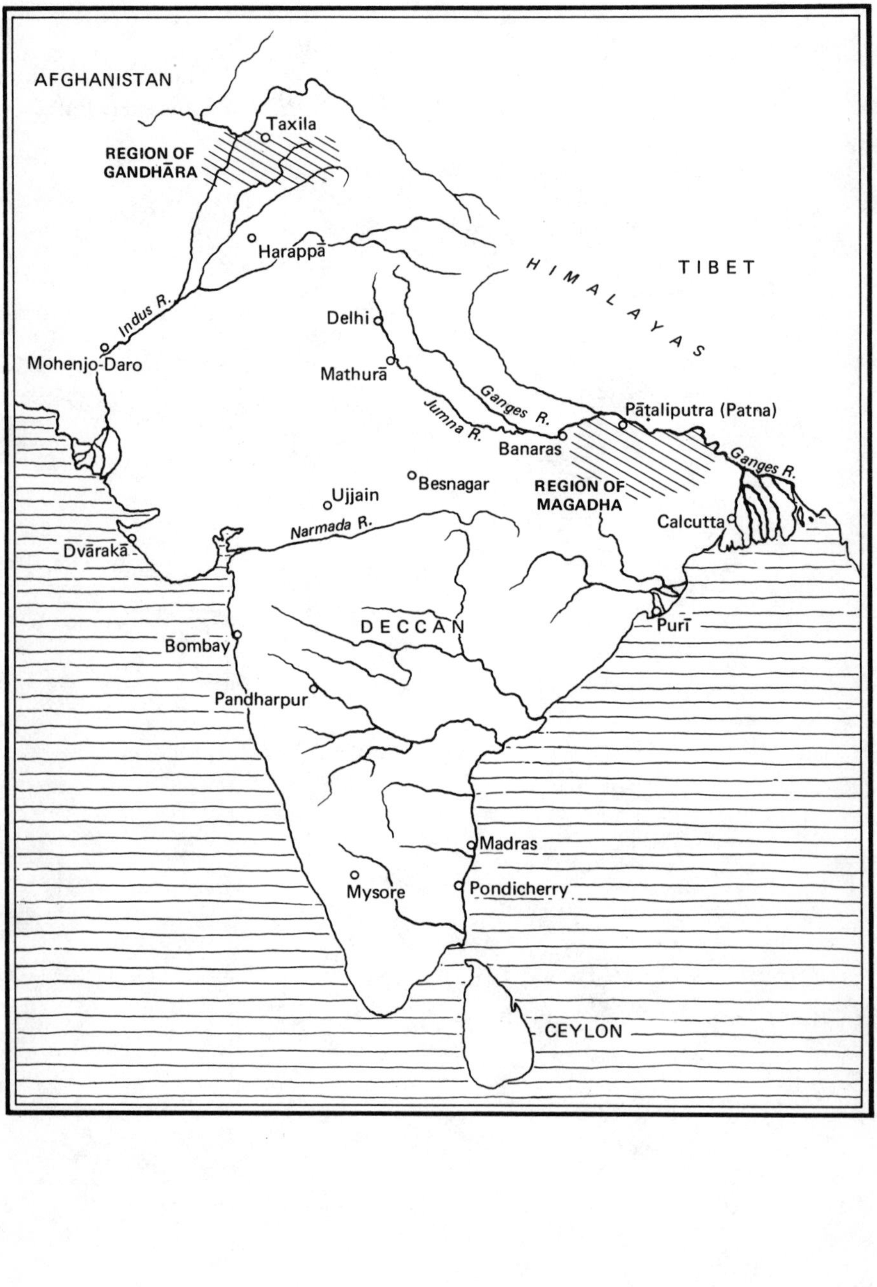
AFGHANISTAN
Taxila
REGION OF GANDHĀRA
Harappā
Indus R.
Mohenjo-Daro
HIMALAYAS
TIBET
Delhi
Mathurā
Ganges R.
Jumna R.
Pāṭaliputra (Patna)
Banaras
Ganges R.
Besnagar
Ujjain
REGION OF MAGADHA
Calcutta
Narmada R.
Dvārakā
DECCAN
Purī
Bombay
Pandharpur
Madras
Mysore
Pondicherry
CEYLON

Introduction

Stand by a street in an Indian city and watch the endless variety of people who pass: men in slacks and sport shirts or Western suits; men in loosely wrapped dhotis with a cloth draped over bare shoulders; women in saris, some of rough peasant cloth and some silk, in constantly changing colors and styles; a few boys, some in blue jeans, with a Beatles record; a holy man in loincloth and sandals and long tangled hair; a Sikh, with turban and beard; a group coming from a nearby temple, with flowers in hand and fresh spots of red powder on their foreheads; priests from the Rāmakrishna Mission in long saffron robes; a funeral party, led by drummers, carrying a corpse on a palanquin; a beggar. Go to another city nearby and the pattern is the same, but subtly different. Go to another part of the country and the variety is still there but the styles and types of people have changed; what you were learning to identify is no longer seen, and there is much that is new and never seen before.

This is the horizontal pattern: city differs from city, region from region, east from west, north from south. If you take one region or group and trace it back in time, the complexity is no less. Centuries or millennia of changing customs and rituals, accumulation of myths and legends, stories and scriptures, new rulers and new people, new contacts and new alliances, new conflicts.

If you know a family, there are more questions. The mother, a widow, is a devout worshiper of Śiva; her sister-in-law, equally devout, follows the teachings of Rāmakrishna; the eldest son is an engineer trained in England, a worshiper of Śiva but not as knowledgeable or dedicated—at least not yet—as his mother and younger brother; his wife's father worships Krishna, as does all her family.

The family priest or *purohit* is learned and conservative; he is prepared to converse in Sanskrit, but not English. He conducts regular services in the family worship room and advises the family on the time for special rituals; he also draws up horoscopes and serves as the family astrologer. The *purohit* of their relatives is younger and more liberal, though no less learned; he conducts morning worship services for the family before he goes to his full-time job in a business office.

The family worships Śiva in the home; they go to a temple of the Goddess Cāmuṇḍā or Durgā for special occasions; they visit a temple and teaching center dedicated to Vishnu; they sing devotional songs to Krishna. There are ties to all these, family traditions that connect them and personal preferences that make each family member unique. Another family would have a different pattern; a third would have yet another.

How can you sort out all these patterns—family, regional, historical—and come to a simple understanding of the whole? The answer quite simply is: you cannot. No one can, or has, or perhaps ever will. The patterns keep shifting; and, as you understand more, you have more questions. The discussion that follows is, hopefully, a guide to better understanding and, doubtless, also to more questions. The approach, as far as possible, is historical and chronological; this seems the minimum requirement to sort out the strands of accumulating tradition. It is also selective, since scholars, too, have their personal preferences. The subject is the thoughts, values, and practices of roughly one fifth of the world's population: where they came from, how they developed, what they are now, and where perhaps they are heading.

1.
The Aryans and Early Indian Culture

What we know of Hindu beginnings comes from two radically different sources: the remains of the great ancient Indus Valley civilization and the religious literature of the Aryans. The first of these carries our knowledge back to the third millennium B.C. by means of material artifacts; the second presents in ritual hymns the religious life of Aryan tribes that entered India in the second millennium B.C. Both of these sources are incomplete, but it is here that we must begin a study of Indian religion, moving from a sketch of the non-Aryans to a more detailed portrait of their Aryan conquerors.

The Indus Civilization

Early Aryan hymns express disdain for the pre-Aryan Indians. The non-Aryans they describe are dark and snub-nosed, immoral by Aryan standards, with customs that arouse Aryan contempt—a people whose characteristics link them with the demons and evil spirits of Aryan myth. By this evidence, Aryans met only a native population devoid of cultural achievement.

Somewhat inconsistently, early hymns also refer to heroic Aryan struggles against fortified opponents. Indra, the favorite Aryan god, is called the "fortress-splitter" and is praised for his destruction of citadels. Fortified cities seem out of place in a primitive culture. Until recently, therefore, scholars interpreted references to citadels and conquered fortresses as Aryan self-praise couched in poetic hyperbole, or as imagery dealing not with historical but with mythological events.

This interpretation may still be true in part. The hymns do praise the Aryans' prowess and celebrate their gods' control over nature and demonic powers; they do contain elements of hyperbole and myth. They were meant to glorify the Aryans and their gods against all rivals. But in light of recent evidence, they also come much closer to fact than historians had supposed.

A revised view of the whole pre-Aryan question began to emerge less than fifty years ago with the excavation of two mound sites in western India: Harappā, on an upper tributary of the Indus River, and Mohenjo-daro several hundred miles downstream (see map). It was soon evident that a great and hitherto unknown civilization had been discovered. The two major mounds at Harappā and Mohenjo-daro each covered citadels set on man-made hills adjacent to a major city. Throughout the Indus Valley and beyond smaller communities were found that shared the same culture, and new sites are still being discovered.

From the first excavated site and greatest area of concentration, this entire cultural complex has been designated as the Harappan or Indus Civilization. Ages of the various sites differ, but the major cities flourished from around 2500 B.C. to 1500 B.C. At least one pre-Harappan city has been dated as early as 3000 B.C., several centuries after the development of Sumerian culture in Mesopotamia but roughly contemporary with the founding of the first Egyptian dynasty. The known distribution of Harappan sites extends along 800 miles of the Indus River and along the coast of the Arabian Sea for another 800 miles, making it larger in area than either ancient Egypt or Mesopotamia.

Clearly this was one of the great early civilizations, and it is all the more frustrating that we know so little about it. The few brief inscriptions left by the Indus people have not yet been deciphered. No literary or intellectual products can be traced back to the Indus Civilization, and interpretation of the culture from material remains alone has proved difficult and inadequate. It is not known how or when the culture was developed, whether the creators of the culture were indigenous or not, or what relation they had to the dark snub-nosed people described in Aryan hymns. All we know is that the culture flowered suddenly with the building of Harappā and Mohenjo-daro, which contain most of the clues we have for understanding the Indus Civilization as a whole.

The Indus Cities

Both great Indus cities consist of a "lower city" about three miles in circumference with a walled citadel mound on the western side. The size and similarity of the cities, their commanding positions in the northern and southern portions of the Indus Valley, the citadels and extensive grain storage facilities—all indicate that they were the major political and economic centers of the extensive Indus system. Culturally they were no less important, so it is from them that we must develop our interpretation of Indus religion.

The single most important feature of the cities is the planning and control evident even in the oldest levels. There is no indication of random growth. Instead, the Indus cities were apparently built with all their mature features present in the beginning and then, as remarkably, were preserved with little observable change for almost a thousand years.

The city plan at Mohenjo-daro, the best preserved of the cities, is representative of the Indus pattern. The city is laid out with a rectangular grid of main streets dividing the city into 1200- by 800-foot blocks about the same size as the citadel mound. The baked brick walls along the main streets are blank, with lanes providing access to dwelling units built around courtyards within the block. Residences range in size from small barrack-like units to two spacious complexes tentatively identified as a palace and a hostel. All the buildings remained unchanged in basic plan over the centuries; when units were rebuilt, old walls served as foundations for new construction.

Temples had major importance in other ancient civilizations, but evidence for their existence in Mohenjo-daro is inconclusive. One or the other of two massive buildings may have been a temple, but either might have served other purposes. Where the rulers no doubt had religious as well as secular authority, many public buildings might have had religious elements such as the stone sculptures and the enclosure for a posited "sacred tree" found at one of the sites. No other possible temples have been found, and we have no further evidence that there ever was one in the Indus cities. Whatever the reasons for this, the absence of identifiable temples makes even more important the most unique feature of the Indus cities: the elaborate system of bathing and drainage facilities found in both the "lower city" and the citadel.

Each residence or dwelling group throughout the city was provided with a well and a bathing room or bathing floor with provision for drainage. There were also built-in latrines, with examples even of seat latrines. Waste from the bathing areas and latrines flowed through chutes into an extensive system of enclosed brick drains built into the otherwise unpaved streets. This system is not only impressive in itself as an example of large-scale organization and maintenance but is unique in the ancient world. It suggests not only an advanced concern for hygiene, but also a special cultural or cultic emphasis on bathing and personal purity. This assumption is supported by the most significant structure on the Mohenjo-daro citadel, the building called the Great Bath.

The central feature of the Great Bath is a large lined tank sunk in the floor of an open courtyard, with steps leading down into the tank at each end. Special rooms for private bathing in an adjacent building apparently relate to the purpose of the main tank. The complex as a whole has the appearance of a center for ritual bathing and must have had an important role in citadel activities. What that role was is unclear, as is so much else about the Indus cities; but, together with the bathing and drainage system of the "lower city," the Great Bath is an essential key to understanding some obviously important Indus values and practices.

Indus Art

Other keys are found in Indus art, which presents a different and varied body of data for interpreting Indus religion. In contrast to the massive architecture of the cities, Indus art was on a small scale. A few stone and bronze sculptures have been found, but the items of greatest religious interest are the numerous clay figurines and carved stone seals that show the variety of life in the cities.

The liveliest Indus art was made of clay, the medium of the common people. Terra-cotta figurines in particular reveal the popular interests. The favorite figurine subject is male animals, most frequently humped bulls. Female animals seem to have attracted little interest, and no figurines of cows have been found.

Human figurines by contrast are mostly female, the usual type being a rather crude standing woman with a wide girdle, a necklace, and an elaborate headdress. Occasionally a lump of clay representing an infant is placed at the breast or on the hip, and the figures sometimes show signs of pregnancy—evidence perhaps that they expressed a concern for fecundity.

Rivaling clay folk art in quantity, but even more important as a source of cultural information, are the carved stone stamp seals found throughout the civilization. These seals with few exceptions are flat square sections of soapstone from ¾ to 1¼ inches on a side, engraved on the front with a group of signs in the Indus script, a drawing or design, or a combination of these. The bulk of the surviving examples of Indus script are found on these seals. Since they were apparently used to mark property in the manner of a signet ring, each seal had a distinctive combination of symbols, a fact that has created great obstacles to deciphering the script.

The main information so far provided by the seals comes from their engraved designs. Some of these designs are purely linear patterns, but most of them are pictures. As is true of clay figurines, the favorite subjects are male animals. Many of these are animals drawn from nature: short-horned bulls, humped bulls with heavy dewlaps, one-horned rhinoceroses, tigers, elephants, antelopes, and crocodiles. The animal most frequently shown, however, is apparently mythical and appears only on the seals: an oxlike beast whose single horn, erect and often inclined forward, has given it the nickname "unicorn."

An object always shown in front of the "unicorn," or under its nose, has been interpreted as a "sacred manger" or "sacred brazier." It apparently has religious or cultic significance, since one seal shows an image of a "unicorn" being carried in procession alongside one of these objects. Similar "sacred mangers" are occasionally shown with other animals, raising the likelihood that these animals—perhaps all the animals shown on the seals—were considered sacred or were objects of veneration. The same conclusion is suggested by a scene of a buffalo facing a line of prostrate men and another of some kind of leaping or vaulting over bulls reminiscent of ancient Minoa. The details of these scenes can be variously interpreted; but the prostration before a buffalo is almost certainly a ritual, and both scenes probably refer to cultic practices.

Although animals are skillfully detailed in the seal drawings, humans are little more than stick figures. Their crudeness makes it hard to distinguish between scenes of secular and cultic activities, or even to tell whether the figures represent men or divinities. In a few scenes, however, there is no doubt about either the cultic character of the activities or the divinity of the main figure.

One such scene, repeated with slight variation on three seals, shows a male figure seated on a low stool with knees pointed to the sides, feet together at his groin, and bangle-clad arms resting on his knees. On his head is a horned headdress, and in two examples of this scene he has faces on the sides as well as the front of his head. One of the seals shows the seated figure attended by an elephant and a tiger on his left and a rhinoceros and buffalo on his right, with smaller horned animals—antelopes or goats—beneath his stool. The unique representation of this figure and the sense of quiet authority he conveys strongly suggest that he is either a priest or a god, more likely the latter. This is further emphasized by his association with a variety of animals, perhaps as Lord of Creatures, and the fact that in some instances he is shown with an erect penis, symbol of both maleness and fertile power.

Trees as well as animals seem to have had a place in the Indus cult. In a scene repeated on several seals, a nude figure with flowing hair and a horned headdress similar to the seated figure is shown standing between the upright branches of a pipal tree. Another figure with flowing hair and a tall headdress, perhaps of the same type but seen from the side, is kneeling at the base of the tree with a huge goat behind and towering over him. A line of seven robed attendants faces these figures at the bottom of the scene. The familiar figure in the horned headdress is shown squatting in the center of a scene on one seal with a group of animals on his left and on his right a tiger looking upward at a tree in which a man is seated. Although again the full meaning of these scenes is unclear, the trees and the figures in them must certainly have cultic significance.

Other scenes might be added to this list: two cobras back a pair of worshipers kneeling beside a seated figure; a human figure holds back two rearing tigers with his outstretched arms; a horned tiger is attacked by a monster half bull and half man. In these as in other scenes and figures, we have glimpses of rituals, of episodes from myth and story, of gods and heroes, and of animals powerful and perhaps divine. Yet here as elsewhere we have no context, nothing to which we can refer these isolated glimpses to give them substance or relate them to the broader life of the society.

This is true in general not only of the seals but of the whole range of Indus art. Yet, taken together, the art does give us valuable evidence to set alongside the massive yet unpeopled remains of the citadels and cities. Here at least we have visual evidence of those elements of daily life, cultic practices, myth, and legend important enough to inspire artistic expression.

Animals were clearly a primary interest of the Indus people. Some of the animal portraits on seals are miniature masterpieces, and even the cruder terracotta animals were often vigorously and realistically conceived. Since wild as well as domestic animals are portrayed, we can assume that their attraction stemmed from more than their economic value or their familiarity in daily life; it must rather have derived from a fascination with the natural powers their animal qualities represent.

From the seals it appears that many animals had sacredness and cultic value. The predominantly male seal animals and animal figurines are, for the most part, either those noted for their physical and sexual power—bulls, rhinoceroses, elephants, and tigers—or, as is true of snakes and crocodiles, are animals widely regarded as symbols of sexuality, fertility, or longevity. On horned animals, the horns—symbols of power, especially sexual power—are strongly emphasized; in one scene even a tiger is shown with horns. The "unicorn," the animal most clearly granted special status on the seals, combines male physical power with a single erect horn that almost certainly has sexual connotations.

The emphasis on natural powers, especially powers of life and fertility, is not confined to animal images. It is likely that the "sacred tree" on several seals represents the same concern. The male in a horned headdress, himself a symbol of potency with his horns and erect penis, is linked with both trees and animals. The importance given to males as symbolic of generative power seems further supported by the discovery at Indus sites of a number of polished stone *lingams,* replicas of the erect phallus, mostly small but ranging up to two feet in height. Whatever their use, and whether or not they were the direct objects of cultic worship, these phallic images epitomize the natural powers that the Indus culture recognized in animals, in sacred trees, and in man himself.

In contrast to the variety of male symbols, female representations are limited to a few basic types. Cult scenes on the seals are dominated by male figures, and both individual animals on the seals and the bronze and terra-cotta animal sculptures are primarily male. The only female images found in large numbers are the roughly formed terra-cotta human figurines, whose widespread distribution indicates their importance at the popular level and points up by contrast the rarity of female figures of all kinds at other levels of Indus art.

The Continuation of Indus Culture

The Indus cities, so impressively stable for nearly a millennium, began in their later years to show increasing signs of disorder. As control broke down further, the great material culture that depended on urban wealth and centralized power came to an end. We do not know why the civilization collapsed. Poor conservation, population movements foreshadowing the coming of the Aryan tribes, or geological changes that altered the flow of the Indus River all have been suggested as possible causes. Whatever the explanation, by the time the Aryans arrived, the great urban centers of the Indus were dead or dying.

The Aryans, however, did not enter a cultural vacuum. Cultural patterns nurtured in the Indus cities survived long after the cities themselves were gone. Preserved in continuing village cultures, carried southward and into the Ganges Valley by late extensions of the Indus Civilization, maintained in the traditions of a conquered non-Aryan population, they gradually merged with Aryan culture in a great and growing synthesis.

Indus culture was by no means the only non-Aryan influence on this synthesis, nor was its influence, for the most part, direct. Much of the cultural merger occurred centuries after Indus culture had lost its identity, and involved not only the successors of Indus culture but other independent non-Aryan traditions. Nevertheless, the Indus Civilization as the highest achievement of the early non-Aryans provides the most complete evidence we have of a cultural tradition that the Aryan tribes could alter but could not destroy.

The most obvious feature of the Indus culture in its heyday is the enormous control exercised by the ruling elite. There is an almost compulsive concern for order, purity, and structural stability evidenced in the provisions for bathing and in the city plan itself. The masculine ascetic quality evidenced in the cities appears also in the male figure with the horned headdress depicted on the seals, with his characteristics of both sexuality and self-discipline. Even—perhaps especially—the stone *lingams* convey an ascetic purity despite their obvious sexual symbolism. One gets the clear impression that this was not a self-indulgent culture, but rather one that revered power only in conjunction with rigor and orderliness.

The masculine emphasis of Indus elitist culture is not so evident at the popular level, where female terra-cotta figures are found in significant numbers. These figures have an aura of propriety, however, when compared to the more exuberantly sexual females in much other ancient art, and there are no figures with such symbolic features as the exaggerated genitals found in Mother Goddess images elsewhere in the world. The absence of female figures in the cult scenes on seals, and the prominence of male animal figures at all levels of Indus art, indicate that females were not given major cultic or artistic importance. If the female figurines had any cultic importance, possibly as symbols of fecundity, it was probably in a loosely structured household cult.

Generalized interest was reserved for male powers, which appear in a variety of symbols at every cultural level. Male powers are seldom represented by human figures, but are expressed instead by male animals such as bulls, male buffaloes, and the "unicorn." The only anthropomorphic male sexual figure is the "horned god," who significantly is not an ordinary human. While women were apparently suitable for expressing the limited role of female powers, men seem to have been considered inappropriate, or perhaps inadequate, for expressing the more important male powers. This may indicate that only animals were believed to have enough strength and vitality to stand as male symbols, and for this reason were given sacred status, while men could only appropriate these natural powers through ritual or conserve them through restraint and purification.

Indus religious interests seem, in summary, to have revolved around the worship of male animals raised to sacred status, the parallel worship of a horned male figure represented as Lord of (male) Creatures, worship of the *lingam* as the supreme symbol of male powers, and a conservative emphasis on order, restraint, and purification by bathing. Worship of the female powers of fertility and fecundity may have constituted a subsidiary cult at the popular or domestic level.

We can hardly be wrong in seeing some of these elements in the cult of

Śiva that was absorbed into the Aryan tradition a thousand years after the death of the Indus cities. Śiva is the Lord of Creatures as well as the great ascetic, and is often shown seated in a manner similar to that of the "horned god" of the Indus seals, and at times with penis erect. His universal symbol is the *lingam,* his animal companion is Nandi the bull, and a bull serves as the *vāhana* or "vehicle" on which he rides. And, although he is one of the great gods of the later Aryan synthesis, he has no secure place in the early Aryan Vedic writings unless, ironically, we see in the Vedic criticism of "those who worship the phallus" a reference to his early Indus cult.

Less certainly, we may identify other Indus features in the later tradition. Purification with water becomes, though it was not originally, a prominent feature of the Aryan cult. Though this might be simply a natural development, there must surely be some significance in the fact that special tanks on the order of the Great Bath are used for ritual bathing at the site of most major temples. And in the later caste system, a rigid social hierarchy based on levels of purification and pollution, we might see a further outcropping of the concern for structure and purity found in the Indus cities. We need not emphasize these points, however, to be sure that much of the non-Aryan culture of the Indus did not die with the Indus cities, but continued in a variety of ways to affect later Indian civilization.

The Coming of the Aryans

Unlike the settled Indus farmers, the Aryans were pastoral nomads, one of the many Indo-European tribes that migrated outward from the steppes of eastern Europe in the second millennium B.C. Other tribes moved into western Europe, Italy, Greece, and the Middle East, and a closely related group of tribes settled in Iran. The Aryans continued across the mountains of Afghanistan into northwest India, the end of the Indo-European trail. The culture they brought was sharply different from that of the declining Indus Civilization.

If the Indus peoples were typified by their cities, the Aryans were typified no less by their two-wheeled horse-drawn chariots, the mark of both their mobility and their militarism. Indus strength was based on agriculture and trade administered from urban centers, with little evidence of military concerns except for defensive citadels. Aryans by contrast were warriors, winning their way like other Indo-European tribes by means of military prowess. Held together by a patriarchal tribal structure, skilled in bronze metallurgy and weaponry, and equipped with their highly effective fighting chariots, the Aryans were a formidable force when they entered India.

Aryans made their first contacts with the Indus peoples in warfare, in a series of pitched battles against the last strongholds of non-Aryan resistance. Though they probably did not cause the collapse of Indus Civilization, they ended any chance of its recovery. Certainly they had no interest in preserving what they found, either the cities or the agriculture. Instead, they continued to move eastward across the northern Indian plain, developing their own culture in relative isolation.

Isolation is a key factor in Aryan development in India. Except for the declining Indus system, the Aryans encountered no high cultures of the sort found across Iran to the west in Mesopotamia, Egypt, and Crete. Contacts with Mesopotamia stopped with the end of Indus trade, and the wall of the Himalayas cut off influence from the expanding high culture in China. The Aryans were thus free to develop on their own and work out accommodations with the other people of the Indian subcontinent on their own terms.

The successors of the Indus civilization had abandoned many of the more sophisticated elements of that culture, including the Indus script. Himalayan culture and the village cultures of the plains were preliterate and only loosely organized. Outside religious influences on the Aryans came mostly from primitive traditions in which magic and myth were important elements. The Aryan response was first to ignore these traditions, then gradually to adopt elements that could be accommodated into the Aryan religious system. The result was a high culture fundamentally Aryan in structure but with many local and non-Aryan beliefs and practices within it. It could expand at many levels, either by more refined intellectual development or by appropriating more popular and primitive elements. Many such expansions can be seen in the transition from early Aryan religion to the later Hindu tradition.

The Gods of the Early Aryans

Our knowledge of early Aryan religion comes from collections of Aryan hymns called Vedas. The term *veda* means "knowledge" or "body of knowledge." The earliest of the collections, the *Rig Veda,* is "the body of knowledge concerning verses of praise (*ṛig*)." It is here that we can see most clearly the characteristics of what is called early Vedic religion, the religion of the early Vedic hymn collections.

Early Vedic religion centered around divine powers or gods called *devas.* The number of *devas* was sometimes reckoned as 33, though more than this number are mentioned in the *Rig Veda* and other Vedic collections. Numbering of the gods was, in any event, arbitrary, as the Vedic texts themselves state. More important were the functions and powers of the gods and their association with natural phenomena. These gave the *devas* their basic identity, and on this basis they were divided into three classes, celestial, atmospheric, and terrestrial, depending on which of the three "worlds" (sky, atmosphere, or earth) was their primary location and realm of activity.

The division of *devas* into these categories indicates their close association with the powers of nature. The natural world for the Aryans was a realm of powers that affected and controlled their lives. These powers were personal, manifestations of personal will. Indus peoples seem also to have worshiped natural powers, but the personal forces of nature were apparently for them manifested mainly in animals. For the Aryans it was the *devas* who represented and controlled the forces of nature, and the powers that first attracted their interest and inspired their awe were cosmic: the sky, the sun, and the order of nature itself.

Interest in the cosmic powers of nature was an Indo-European heritage, most evident in the Aryan celestial gods. The oldest of these gods was probably Dyaus Pitṛi, "Sky Father," who corresponds to the Greek god Zeus and the Roman god Jupiter. More important to the Aryans, however, was Varuna, another Indo-European god corresponding to the Greek Ouranos and to an Iranian god later known as Ahura Mazda.

Varuna's primary characteristic was his role as guardian of cosmic order and overseer of moral action. He created the world and ruled it by the standard of *ṛita,* "the course of things" and thus by extension "the *proper* course of things." The term *ṛita* embodies most of the meanings of the English word "right" and extends into the area of "rite" or ritual as well. As the guiding principle of Varuna it was the standard for cosmic, moral, and liturgical order, the basis for what is true and in its proper place, for proper movement and for what is correctly said or done.

Varuna and *ṛita* provided a structure for other celestial powers or *devas.* Many of these were associated with the sun, celebrated as the source of life and light. The solar *deva* Mitra, corresponding to the Iranian sun god Mithra, was Varuna's chief assistant as well as the friend and benefactor of man. His solar role was shared with other *devas* such as Sūrya, who represented the physical aspect of the sun, Savitṛi, representing the sun's ability to stimulate life, and Pūṣan, the guide of men and animals and bringer of prosperity.

Of the remaining celestial *devas,* the most notable was the benevolent Vishnu. Though he also was associated with the sun, Vishnu's connection with natural phenomena was less emphasized than that of other celestial gods. His main distinction in the Vedas was the oft-mentioned three strides by which he traversed earth and atmosphere and reached "the highest step," "the highest place of Vishnu," beyond the flight of birds or the knowledge of men. From this he was known as "wide-striding" and was uniquely associated with "the highest place," his special heaven, both significant factors in his later rise to prominence as one of the major Hindu gods. Despite these qualities, however, he remained a subordinate figure in the early Vedic period, his powers largely overshadowed by his role as friend and ally of the far more important god Indra.

Indra as thunder god belonged to the class of atmospheric gods that included Vāyu the god of wind, Parjanya the god of the rain cloud, a troop of storm gods called the Maruts, and Rudra the father of the Maruts. Most of these gods were closely connected with their respective atmospheric phenomena and seldom achieved independent personification. Only Rudra and Indra, for different reasons, were given importance in their own right.

Rudra gained stature from his complexity as the representative of ambiguous primal powers of nature. He was feared for his malevolent destruction and anxiously invoked with the hopeful epithet *śiva* ("auspicious"), yet was often praised for his ability to bestow healing remedies and protect his petitioners from destruction. Even with this, however, he remained rather vaguely defined in personal terms and achieved his prominence only later. Rudra in the *Rig Veda* was, like Vishnu, a minor deity overshadowed by Indra.

Indra stood alone among the atmospheric gods, and indeed among the Vedic gods in general, as a figure of paramount prestige and popularity. The key to his character was a myth describing his conquest of the demon Vṛitra, a serpentine monster who blocked the flow of life-giving waters. Numerous hymns refer to this story and praise Indra as the victorious benefactor who released the pent-up streams and rivers. Most of Indra's epithets relate in some way to this great battle against the enemy of man.

His great popularity, however, depended more on his personal qualities than on his mythical feat itself. As a god famous for successful warfare, he was the special champion of the Aryan warrior and the model of what a warrior should be. In contrast to the detached cosmic sovereignty of Varuna, Indra engaged in active personal struggle with his foes. Besides slaying the mythic enemy Vṛitra, he is at times said to have fought the human enemies of the Aryans, the dark-skinned people called Dāsas or Dasyus. The tawny Indra, belly full of exhilarating Soma juice, beard agitated, brandishing his glittering thunderbolt, boasting of his prowess and eager to join battle with the enemy, clearly reflects the Aryan warrior's self-image.

As the Aryans' closest divine ally, Indra thus became the greatest of the Rig Vedic gods. Varuna, whose cosmic functions and divine sovereignty seem more important in description, declined in interest and in the end was celebrated in far fewer hymns. The two gods were, however, in a sense complementary. Each dominated his own class of gods, and together they represented divine monarchy in both its passive and active forms: eternal universal order, and active intervention to overcome obstacles and bestow bounty on man. Yet the celestial and atmospheric gods did not constitute a complete religious system in themselves. Already in the *Rig Veda,* and increasingly in later Vedic writings, interest shifted away from these gods and was focused on the third class of divine beings, the terrestrial *devas,* dominated by the divinized elements of the fire sacrifice: Agni, fire itself and the god of fire; Bṛihaspati, Lord of Prayer and the divine cultic priest; and Soma, the most important libation in the sacrificial ritual.

The importance of these gods depended entirely on the fire sacrifice. Both fire and the Soma plant existed on their own apart from man, but their special value derived from their role in the cultic ritual. Man does not create the heavens or the storm clouds, however much he may think he can influence them. Man can and does build fires, press out the juice of Soma plants, and recite ritual prayers. These elements may be seen as gods, but their importance depends on man's use of them. Here we see clearly the interest in human control that marks the development of the fire sacrifice.

The Aryan Fire Sacrifice

Fire is a key element in human culture, and it is not surprising that fire has a place of honor in many myths and religious practices. Among some peoples, including the Indo-Europeans, it received divine status. Various branches of the Indo-Europeans preserved sacred fires, paid reverence to the fire of the home hearth, and gave offerings of food to the fire as to a personal deity. Among the Iranians and Aryans, these practices were organized into a fire sacrifice administered by priests.

At its simplest and probably earliest level, the Indo-Iranian sacrifice was a hospitality rite to the gods. Gods of special concern to the worshiper were invited to a celebration in their honor centered around a fire built on a special altar. The attendant gods seated themselves on grass strewn around the altar as a place of honor, and there received offerings as guests. The most important offerings were placed in the fire and were conveyed to the other gods by Agni, the god of the fire. It was around these offerings that the Vedic ritual developed.

The divine guests were honored not only with food and other gifts but with hymns of praise recited by a poet-priest. Drawing allusions from Aryan myth, the poet-priests wove together statements in lyric style appropriate to the gods being honored, the purpose of the sacrifice, and the particular divine qualities or functions relevant to that purpose. A typical sacrificial hymn contained an invocation in a tone of friendliness, reverence, or fear depending upon the god and the poet's relation to him; praise of those great qualities and actions of the god called to mind by the occasion; and a request, either implicit or direct, that the god use his powers for the benefit of the sacrificer. Within this general framework, the poet demonstrated his skill in combining mythical reference, figurative or symbolic allusions, and metrical form to create a statement that captured both the truth about the god and the spirit of the occasion.

By Vedic times the composition of hymns was confined to a small number of highly skilled poet-priests who were considered inspired. The earliest hymns in the *Rig Veda* were the product of a few families of such priests who passed down their hymns and poetic skills from one generation to another. The hymn collections of these families were eventually brought together to make up the core of the *Rig Veda,* the so-called family books (Books II–VII). Other groups of hymns were added to form Books I and VIII, and then most of the hymns to Soma were taken from these earlier sections to make Book IX, a special collection for use in the Soma ritual. A late collection of hymns was finally added to form Book X and complete the *Rig Veda Saṃhitā,* the collection (*saṃhitā*) of the Veda of stanzas.

The formation of the *Rig Veda Saṃhitā* was paralleled by changes in the Vedic priesthood and in the ritual tradition. Priests did not have a monopoly on religious ritual or even on the performance of sacrifices, since even in later times Aryan householders performed many domestic ceremonies on their own. The early Vedic priests concentrated instead on certain specialized sacrifices, gradually elaborating them with new hymns and more complex ritual practices. By the time the *Rig Veda Saṃhitā* was completed, there was general agreement on the form of these special rituals within the community of priests. By this time also, priests had become skilled professionals.

Individual householders performed sacrifices and ceremonies for themselves and their families, but the more elaborate priestly sacrifices were performed for wealthy patrons in exchange for gifts and other payments. The sacrificer—that is, the patron of the sacrifice—was promised material rewards on earth and in heaven in return for his sacrifice to the gods and his gifts to the priests. Only the gods could give health, long life, a prosperous family with many sons, and wealth in cattle, but priests were the agents whose skill induced the gods to grant human requests. Those who could afford it thus sought far and wide for priests whose skill was generally acknowledged and whose sacrificial services would most likely be effective.

It was common practice for at least the most renowned priests to travel long distances to serve such patrons. Other priests gathered at their sacrifices to observe and occasionally participate, and priests often competed for honors in the skill of their sacrificial performances. Innovations in the sacrifice, additional details and embellishments, and new ritual skills were readily adopted by fellow professionals to increase the effectiveness and value of their own services. The more prominent priests were also sought as teachers by fledgling members of the priesthood who often went to distant places in search of qualified instruction. Acquired bodies of hymns, details of ritual procedure, and training in the performance of sacrifices passed in this way from one generation to another, creating normative patterns for the priestly community as a whole.

The distinction between the hieratic or priestly cult and domestic ceremonies was gradually obscured as the priestly ritual became more elaborate. A wide variety of popular religious practices was added to the priestly rituals, while domestic ceremonies were altered to conform to priestly standards. The result was increased involvement of priests in the religious and ritual life of the Aryan community as the great arbiters of both cultic and domestic ritual. A formal distinction was maintained between *Śrauta* rites (rites using the Vedic hymns), which were necessarily performed by priests, and *Gṛiha* ("domestic") rites, performed by the Aryan householder himself; but both the latter and the former were subject to priestly influence. Some domestic rites became almost indistinguishable from the priestly *Śrauta* sacrifices; and, even where older ceremonies were retained, they were usually interwoven with elements of the priestly ritual.

There were, however, built-in limitations on priestly elaboration and control of domestic rites. Domestic ceremonies were limited to rites within the means of the ordinary householder, rites that in most cases he could perform himself. The required daily sacrifices of the Aryan householder remained simple offerings: *homa* sacrifices in which cooked food was offered to Agni and the creator god Prajāpati in the morning and to Sūrya and Prajāpati in the evening; and the *Pañca Mahāyajña,* the "Five Great Sacrifices," in which cooked food was offered in the household fire to the gods, food was offered on the ground in behalf of all beings, water or food sprinkled with water was thrown in the air for the Fathers, food was offered to guests, priests, and beggars, and a verbal offering was made by reciting some part of the Vedic hymns.

Relative simplicity also characterized domestic rituals celebrating the new moon and full moon, the seasons of the year, and the first fruits of the harvest, or marking special family occasions such as the building of a new house, the birth of a son, and the more important stages in the life of a child: his naming, his first solid food, his first tonsure, and the like. The householder and his family had major ritual roles in all these ceremonies, including the important rituals involving priests which marked a child's entry into studentship and marriage. Performed on the domestic fire maintained by pious householders, most of the daily and other domestic rituals were handed down with little change or elaboration from Vedic times to the present.

Unlike domestic ceremonies, the *Śrauta* sacrifices performed by priests became more and more elaborate. The domestic fire was not used for these sacrifices. Instead, a special set of three fires was developed early in the Vedic period solely for use in the *Śrauta* ceremonies. As rituals using these fires became more complex, sacrificial duties were divided among several priests. Priestly training became more specialized, and separate priestly traditions developed to meet the needs of ritual specialists.

Eventually, the meaning of the sacrifice itself began to change. Once a hospitality rite and celebration of the *devas,* the sacrifice came to be viewed as a power in its own right. Centuries of priestly concentration on the sacrificial ritual brought about a new view of reality. With this came also the first stage in a continuing synthesis of Aryan and non-Aryan religion structured around the Vedic tradition.

2.
The Creative Power of the Sacrifice

The Aryan tribes migrated slowly across the plain of northern India to the valley of the Ganges and Jumna rivers. There, between the tenth and seventh centuries B.C., the major elaboration of the fire sacrifice occurred. Indra and other early Aryan gods lost most of their importance as the Aryan world view changed. Aryan religious life was increasingly dominated by the fire sacrifice, the creative source of all the powers of nature and the gods.

Decline of the Vedic Gods

The divine powers or *devas* of early Aryan religion had few fixed attributes or functions. Only certain basic qualities were clearly defined by myths or implied by natural phenomena identified with the gods. Other qualities and acts were ascribed to a variety of gods, and hymns often magnified the god being praised by granting him powers normally applied to other deities.

This tendency toward shifting attributes for a long time largely benefited Indra, who absorbed many of the powers of Varuna and of lesser *devas*. Indra might in time have acquired sole divine status, since the combined powers he acquired were logically those of a monotheistic god. The trend toward monotheism, however, ran counter to developments that centered not on Indra but on the terrestrial gods and beyond them on the sacrifice itself.

As more and more attention was directed toward the sacrificial ritual, only gods directly associated with the ritual retained priestly interest. Indra and other atmospheric and celestial gods only received sacrifices; they had little to do with sacrificial functions. Agni by contrast was the sacrificial fire itself as well as the god of fire, the medium by which men related to the gods. One of the clearest indications of the transformation of the sacrifice is the increased importance granted by the priests to Agni, the central element in the ritual.

The Expanded Role of Agni

As recipient of gifts offered to all the gods, Agni was identified with them even in the early hymns of the *Rig Veda:*

> You, O Agni, are Indra, the bull [strongest] of all that exist; you are the wide-striding Vishnu, worthy of reverence; you, O Lord of the Holy Word (Brah-

maṇaspati), are the chief priest who finds riches [for the sacrificer]; you, O distributer, are associated with munificence. You, O Agni, are King Varuna, whole laws are firm; you are Mitra, the wonder-worker to be revered; you are Aryaman, the reliable lord, of whom I would get enjoyment; . . . . You, O Agni, are Rudra, the Asura of lofty heaven; as the troop of Maruts, you control sustenance. (*Rig Veda* II.1.3, 4, 6)

Here Agni not only stands for the other gods in the sacrifice but *is* all the gods: "In you, O son of strength, are all gods," *Rig Veda* V.3.11 declares.

As the messenger to the gods, Agni linked the worlds of gods and men. He also linked these worlds with nature by the various physical forms of fire. Agni was often compared to the sun, kindled by the gods in heaven as by men on earth. Agni was present in the heavenly waters, from which he was brought down by lightning, and in the aerial or atmospheric waters, where he was referred to as the shining thunder. Brought down from his high abode in rain, Agni was latent in streams and ponds until he passed into plants, from which fire again could be kindled. Completing the cycle, Agni in plants was seen as offering himself to himself in fire, rising again in smoke to the clouds.

Because of his multiple forms, Agni was said to have a triple character related to his existence in heaven, on earth, and in the aerial waters. The distinction between these three characters appears in the symbolism of the sacrificial plot used for the *Śrauta* ritual:

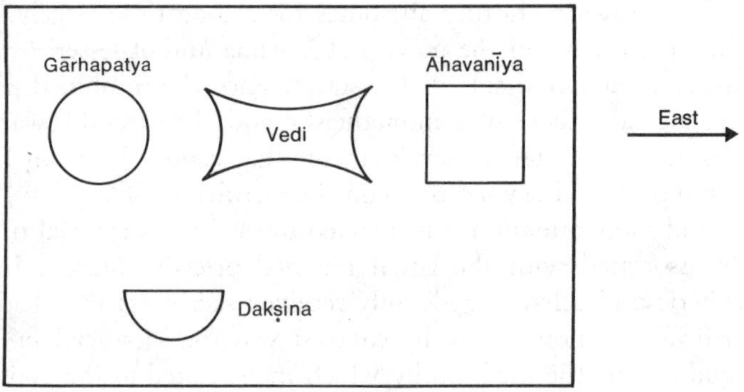

The developed *Śrauta* sacrifice utilized three basic fires, designated as the *Gārhapatya, Āhavanīya,* and *Dakṣina* fires. The *Gārhapatya* fire, the "fire belonging to the lord of the home," was mainly used to prepare food for the sacrifice. Most of the prepared offerings were placed in the *Āhavanīya* fire, the "fire of offering," located to the east of the *Gārhapatya* in the direction of the rising sun, the primary orientation of the sacrifice. The *Dakṣina* or "southern" fire, though less used in major rituals, had the dual function of warding off hostile spirits and receiving special offerings to departed ancestors. Between the two main fires was the *Vedi,* a ritually insulated grass-lined pit in which oblations and sacrificial utensils were placed to preserve their power when not in use.

Each of the three fires rested on an altar with a specified contour: round for the *Gārhapatya,* square for the *Āhavanīya,* and semicircular for the *Dakṣina.* Elaborate altars were at times constructed for special purposes, but the usual altar was a slightly raised mound made of sand, earth, pebbles, and pieces of wood spread in the proper shape. The shape of the altars gives a fundamental identity to each of the fires. The round *Gārhapatya* altar represents the earth (a flat round disc or island); the square *Āhavanīya* altar, the four-directional sky; and the *Dakṣina* altar, the atmosphere between earth and the overarching heavens. Agni on the three altars is present in his three forms as the terrestrial, celestial, and aerial fires, bringing the three worlds together in the sacred sacrificial plot.

The most basic ritual meaning is conveyed by the symbolism of the two main altars, as food cooked on the fire of earth is conveyed to the fire in heaven, the sun. Agni in this sense linked men on earth with heaven, as sacrifices in the *Dakṣina* fire linked them with their departed ancestors. Present in all the worlds and identified with all the gods, Agni as the unifying physical power in the sacrifice was supreme.

The Sounds of the Sacrifice

The basic symbolic power of the three fires led to a search for new symbols and identities. This search was not limited to the fires and fire altars, but was expanded to include other—eventually all—elements of the sacrificial performance. One of the most fundamental of these elements was sound, which had, like fire, a central place in the sacrifice from early times.

Many Vedic hymns contain identities such as "You, O Agni, are Indra," originally intended as statements of praise. In the developing ritual, these came to be considered formulations of the truth in sound. Such ritual formulations were called mantras, formulas which embodied in their sound the special power to bring into reality the truth they expressed. Not only identities but other truths could be established by these formulas, so it became increasingly important for the ritualist to choose mantras that best suited particular ritual needs.

The earlier tendency to unify the functions and powers of many gods in one god was largely replaced by the unification of all things, including the gods, in the sacrifice. The fires, the sacrificial plot, ritual actions, and offerings of various kinds were woven together into an elaborate structure that was heavily dependent on the mantras which established the basic identities and correspondences. Great importance was thus given to speech, particularly the speech or language of the hymns and mantras. Bṛihaspati or Brahmaṇaspati, "Lord of Prayer," became a prominent deity, and under this name or as Vācaspati, "Lord of Speech," was granted priestly status along with Agni. Even speech itself was deified as the goddess Vāc and took its place among the great divine powers of the developed Vedic system.

The speech honored in this manner was the special speech of the sacrifice, the thread of sound that wove the sacrifice together. This speech was Sanskrit, *saṃskṛita* ("well-formed"), and was considered the reproduction in sound of the structure of reality. Sanskrit words were not just arbitrary labels assigned to phenomena; they were the sound forms of objects, actions, and attributes, related to the corresponding reality in the same way as visual forms and different only in being perceived by the ear and not by the eye. The fact that thought can be considered as internalized speech further emphasized the importance of speech, leading to the conclusion that examining the speech used in the sacrificial ritual would reveal the underlying structure of reality.

Words and sounds designate differences between various aspects of reality, but the possibility of identities and correspondences of sounds pointed to an underlying unity. This unity was closely related to *brahman,* the power captured in the sound of the mantras. In the later portions of the *Rig Veda,* the priests of the sacrifice are referred to as *brāhmaṇas* ("having to do with *brahman*"); the term referred not only to their use of prayers and mantras, but more importantly to their knowledge and use of the power of *brahman* contained in ritual sounds and speech. The great importance given to speech, and to the *brāhmaṇas* who know it, is seen in one of the most frequently quoted Vedic verses:

> Holy Utterance (Vāc) is measured as four quarters; wise *brāhmaṇas* know these. The three [quarters] that are set down in secret they do not bring into movement. The fourth [quarter] of Holy Utterance is what men speak. They call it Indra, Mitra, Varuna, Fire (Agni); or it is the heavenly Sun-bird. That which is One [neuter gender] the seers speak of in various terms; they call it Agni, Yama, Mātariśvan. (*Rig Veda* I.164)

Rig Veda I.164 marks a significant stage in the development of the sacrificial tradition. Throughout the hymn, there is a search for the One that has established order and underlies all phenomena—the activities of men and gods, days and nights, the months and the three four-month seasons of the year, earth, atmosphere, and heaven. The central theme of the hymn is the correlation between the elements of the sacrifice and the natural world, especially between the three fires and the forms of Agni in earth, atmosphere, and heaven, and between the seven meters—the various forms of speech—and those aspects of the natural world which they establish.

The gods themselves are said to have performed sacrifices in order to reach their present place in heaven; they, like the seers, know the true basis of things. That basis, in the verses quoted, is found in speech, Vāc, of which three quarters are hidden and the fourth is manifested in sound and words, the names of the One. The gods in this hymn clearly have no ultimate power or control; they are only a part of the manifested world, the world of names. The greater part of the One that constitutes reality is hidden and unmanifested like the secret three quarters of speech. The manifested part, corresponding to "what men speak," is known through the various terms applied to it in the speech of the sacrificial ritual.

This hymn and others such as *Rig Veda* X.7, X.71, and X.125, raised Vāc to the level of a supreme ruler or principle in the universe. The speech of the sacrifice is in them not a form of address to the gods, nor mere statements about the gods; it is the hidden truth that the seers used to name the gods and give them their existence! This truth, expressed in the sacrifice, is the source of knowledge. The sacrifice is thus no longer a ceremony to the gods nor even a symbolic representation of reality. It *is* reality, or the principal manifestation of reality; it is the One expressed in name and sound. Knowledge of the natural world has become secondary to knowledge of holy speech; one does not learn the truth from nature, but learns instead about the phenomena of nature from a knowledge of the truth manifest in the sacrifice.

Creation and the Sacrifice

The power of speech easily accounted for the existence of names, the sound manifestation of reality, but not the manifestation of the One in physical forms. Early hymns had credited various gods with creation, but the gods themselves were now seen to be later than the establishment of order. Creation of the physical universe thus became a puzzling problem to which only tentative answers could be given. Late Vedic hymns reflected this puzzlement, and at times could only pose questions:

> Who truly knows? Who shall here proclaim it—whence they were produced, whence this creation? The gods [arose] on this side [later], by the creation of this [empiric world, to which the gods belong]; then who knows whence it came into being? This creation, whence it came into being, whether it was established, or whether not—he who is its overseer in the highest heaven, he verily knows, or perchance he knows not. (*Rig Veda* X.129.6, 7)

The problem was not so much *what* was accomplished but *who* accomplished it. The physical world is an empirical fact; it is the why and how of its existence that is hard to determine. This why and how is only partially explained by the underlying reality of speech. Speech accounts for, or reflects, the diversity of phenomena in the manifest names of things, and hidden speech provides a substratum on which the multiplicity of things depends. But speech is itself nonphysical. What then was the origin of the forms or appearances, the physical characteristics of things? The older gods could no longer be considered creators of the physical world; they were only a part of it and also must have been created. But by whom, out of what, and by what process?

Various Rig Vedic hymns describe creation as the work of a divine craftsman (X.81) or of a smith (X.72), or as having come forth from a cosmic embryo (X.121). These were not seen as contradictions, but as complementary views of the same fundamental process. Underlying them all, as it underlay all Vedic speculation, was the model of the fire sacrifice.

The creative work of the *deva* Viśvakarman, "the All-Maker," in X.81 and X.82, is compared to a cosmic sacrifice he performed for himself, taking on the functions of other divinized sacrificial elements and creative powers. He is identified with Vācaspati, "Lord of Holy Utterance," and is said to have created heaven and earth by smelting, as Brahmaṇaspati created the gods. Like Vāc, he is "the sole name-giver of the gods" and is "beyond the heaven, beyond this earth"; like Hiraṇyagarbha, "the Golden Embryo," he is "the first embryo which the waters bore."

It is clear from these passages that the fundamental agency in creation is to be found in the fire sacrifice, or *is* the fire sacrifice itself. The lord of creation, "the All-Maker," is lord of speech, lord of *brahman;* he is the embryo evolved from the waters that produced Agni and the sacrifice. Lord of the sacrifice, he creates by the power of the sacrifice. Or, to state the Vedic position more accurately, *the primary act of creation is the creation of the sacrifice; that being created, all else is formed from it.*

One of the best early statements of this view is found in *Rig Veda* X.90, the *Puruṣa Sūkta,* or "Hymn to the Person," where many elements found in other hymns were brought together in an effort to state a careful correlation between the sacrifice and the universe. The hymn consists of two basic parts: a description of the origin and greatness of the cosmic Man or primal Person, the Puruṣa, and a description of the sacrifice of the Puruṣa. The first part, verses 1–5, establishes the basic identity of the Puruṣa and the universe; the second part establishes the more detailed correspondences between the sacrifice and the Puruṣa on the one hand and individual features of the universe on the other. The first three verses declare:

> The Puruṣa has a thousand heads, a thousand eyes, and a thousand feet. He, encompassing the world on all sides, stood out ten fingers' lengths beyond.
> The Puruṣa alone is all this universe, what has been, and what is to be. He rules likewise over [the world of] immortality [viz., the gods], which he grows beyond, by [sacrificial?] food.
> Such is the extent of his greatness; and the Puruṣa is still greater than this. A quarter of him is all beings, three quarters are [the world of] the immortal in heaven. (*Rig Veda* X.90.1–3)

The basic identity is clear: the Puruṣa is the universe, this All, past, present, and future; one quarter is manifested as all beings, animate and inanimate; the other three quarters are the world of the immortal and the upper regions. The conception here is very similar to the statements about Vāc, "Speech," in *Rig Veda* I.164.45: "The three quarters that are set down in secret they do not bring into movement. The fourth quarter of Holy Utterance is what men speak."

The second part of *Rig Veda* X.90 gives a systematic correlation of various features of the universe with the sacrifice. Such correlations were assumed in many hymns from at least as early as I.164, but the correlations in X.90 are distinguished by the completeness and logic of their symbolism. Underlying the presentation is a carefully considered order of relationships which, once stated in this hymn, became a norm for later views of the structure of the universe. The order and structure can be seen in the diagram of verses 6–14 below.

The correlations are of two types: those that relate sets of cosmic phenomena to the sacrifice as a whole, and those that explain distinctions between phenomena by relating them to different parts of the Puruṣa.

In the first type, the sacrifice is viewed as an integrated unit, an offering

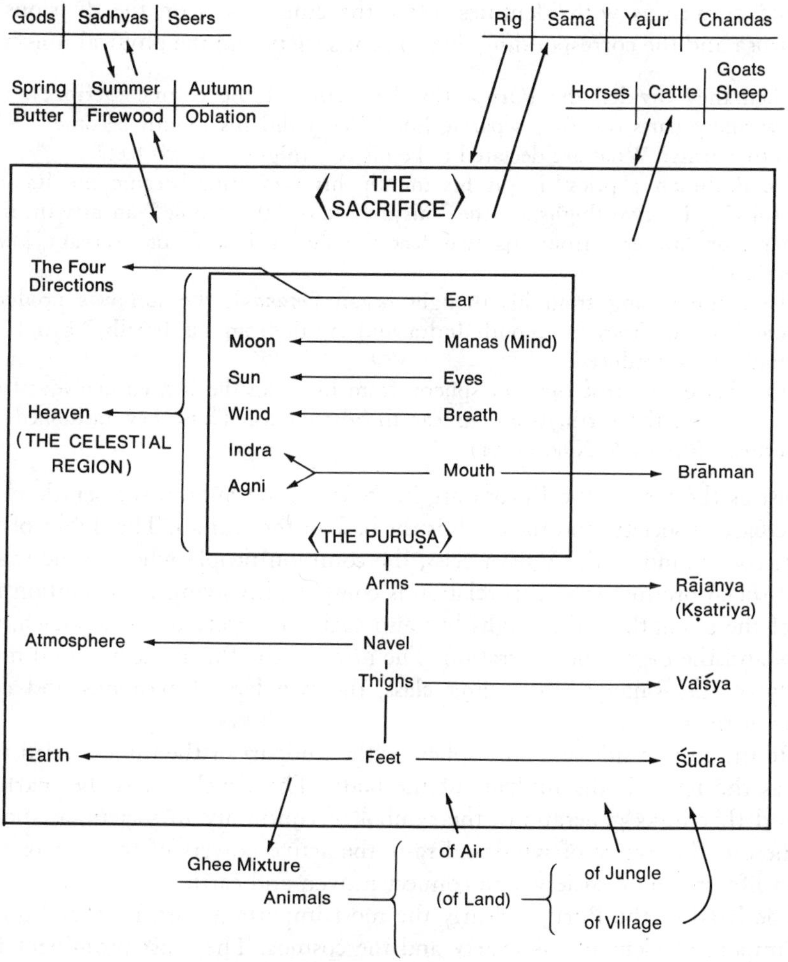

performed by the gods, *Sādhyas* (a class of celestial beings), and *Ṛishis* ("seers"). The seasons are used in this sacrifice as ritual materials: spring as clarified butter or ghee, summer as fuel, and autumn as an accompanying offering. From the cosmic sacrifice thus performed come several products. From the mixture of clarified butter and curds poured into the fire come the classes of common animals: animals of the air and the wild and domestic animals of the ground. The various classes of mantras are produced from the sacrifice, and the more important animals.

These relationships are reciprocal: horses, cattle, sheep, and goats are the primary offerings in animal sacrifices, and mantras are the sound offering in all sacrificial rituals; sacrifices maintain the regularity of the seasons and establish the gods, *Sādhyas,* and *Ṛishis* in heaven. The sacrifice provides the power and structure for transformation in both directions.

The concern in the second type of correlations is with ranking and differentiation as well as with identities. Here the emphasis is on the divisions of the Puruṣa and the corresponding divisions of society and the physical universe:

> When they divided the Puruṣa [as the victim at the cosmic sacrifice], into how many parts did they separate him? What did his mouth become? What his two arms? What are declared to be his two thighs, his two feet?
> The Brāhman ["priest"] was his mouth, his two arms became the Rājanya ["ruler"]; his two thighs are the Vaiśya [one of "the people," an artisan, merchant, or farmer], from his two feet the Śūdra ["serf" or "servant"] was produced.
> The moon sprang from his thought organ [*manas*], the sun was produced from his eye; from his mouth Indra and Agni, from his breath Vāyu ["the wind"] was produced.
> From his navel arose the atmosphere, from his head the heaven evolved; from his two feet the earth, from his ear the directions. Thus they fashioned the worlds. (*Rig Veda* X.90.11–14)

Just as the feet of the Puruṣa are his base, so the Śūdras, the servile class, are the base of society, and the earth is the base of the cosmos. The thighs of the Puruṣa correspond to the Vaiśya class, the common people who are the mainstay of social productivity; this relation is complex, involving a recognition not only of the strength of the thighs but also their proximity to the stomach, the womb, and the organs of generation. The arms of the Puruṣa correspond more directly to the Rājanya, the ruling class, the wielders of weapons and controllers of men.

On the cosmic side, the atmosphere is the midpart of the three-leveled universe as the navel is the midpart of the body. The navel also is the mark of the cord that links generations, the symbol of continuity in society, as the atmosphere is the source of wind and rain, the active powers of the cosmos that sustain life, maintain society, and connect heaven and earth.

The head of the Puruṣa, clearly the most important part, is related to the most important elements of society and the cosmos. The most prominent feature here is the mouth, the organ of speech, related to the *brāhmaṇas* among men and to the two most important gods, Indra and Agni. The connection between speech and fire is again evident. Agni is the mouth of the gods, as he is also their priest; he consumes the food offered to the gods, and, as the central agent in the sacrifice, has a role analogous to that of the human priest who is, by comparison, a god among men.

More important than any single association in this scheme is the total system of correlations it establishes between various levels and types of phenomena. The cosmos, the world of nature, human society, and the sacrifice are seen as parallel orders of reality of equal antiquity and permanence. The four classes of society, listed for the first time in verse 12, are as much a part of the structure of things as earth, atmosphere, and heaven or the gods. The sacrifice of the Puruṣa is a common reference point for all things; it explains their unity and diversity and their relationship to each other, and provides a means of moving from one order of reality to another. The consequence is the belief that knowledge of one order of reality provides knowledge of the others, since they are linked by systematic identities. The sacrifice, the closest and most easily examined of these realities, controls them all; to know the sacrifice is therefore to know and control the universe.

The Creative Power of Heat

Rig Veda X.90 is focused on the sacrifice as the key to creation, but other hymns seek the life force in an even more basic concept: the power of *tapas,* "heat" or "fervor." *Tapas* in various forms was seen as an essential element at all levels of the universe, from human to cosmic. Two late Rig Vedic hymns, X.129 and X.190, see it as the impelling force behind creation itself:

> Nonexistent there was not, existent there was not then. There was not the atmospheric space, nor the vault beyond. What stirred, where, and in whose control? Was there water, a deep abyss?
> Nor death nor immortality [mortals nor immortals] was there then; there was no distinction of night or day. That One breathed without breath by inner power; than it verily there was nothing else further.
> Darkness there was, hidden by darkness, in the beginning: an undistinguished ocean was This All. What generative principle was enveloped by emptiness—by the might of [its own] fervor (*tapas*) That One was born.
> Desire [*kāma,* "creative, or perhaps sacrificial, impulse"] arose then in the beginning, which was the first seed of thought. The [causal] connection of the existent the sages found in the nonexistent, searching with devotion in their hearts. (*Rig Veda* X.129.1–4)

> Cosmic Order (*ṛita*) and Truth (*satya*) were born out of kindled Heat (*tapas*).
> From that night was born, from that the ocean with its waves.
> From the ocean with its waves the year was born, which arranges days and nights and rules over all that blinks [lives].

The Creator [or Ordainer] fashioned in regular order the sun and moon, heaven and earth, the atmosphere and the light. (*Rig Veda* X.190.1–3)

Correspondences were sought that would link this cosmic creative power of *tapas* to other levels or forms of heat. This search eventually focused on two sets of phenomena involving heat in nature, in the ritual, and in man.

The first of these sets brought together parallel relations between heat and liquid. In nature, the heat of the sun draws up water from the earth and produces rain; the fires of the sacrifice heat up ritual cooking vessels, from which liquid boils over or rises as steam; and mental concentration, physical activity, and the heat of fires and cooking vessels heat the sacrificial priest, whose devotional fervor is evidenced by his sweat. The priest who toiled and sweated in the sacrificial performance thus manifested in his own person the same heat, the same *tapas,* that is the effective power of both the sacrifice and the sun, in which he participated ritually by his actions in the sacrifice and physically by his self-generated *tapas.*

The second set of phenomena were associated with the ripening of food by the sun and the cooking of food by fire. In both instances the application of heat makes food suitable for eating, and in both instances such food was called *pakva,* "cooked" or "ripe." Milk also was considered "ripened" or "cooked" as a result of certain cosmic actions of Indra, who was praised in a number of hymns for putting the *pakva* milk suitable for eating into cows that were themselves raw or uncooked.

From concepts such as these, a belief in the independent power of *tapas* gradually developed. *Tapas* or heat was the effective power in the activities credited to Indra, but men could also create *tapas*—in the sacrifice by the fires, and in themselves by devotional fervor. This was not merely symbolic reproduction or paralleling of cosmic phenomena, but actual participation in those phenomena. *Tapas* in the priest or in the ritual was not different in kind or consequences from the related cosmic manifestation of *tapas,* as long as the relationship was understood and the proper ritual connections were made.

The connections—the identities and correspondences between parallel phenomena—were especially important as the ritual came more and more to be seen as a kind of tuning device that brought the various forms of *tapas* into harmonic relationship with each other. Once the parallel forms were tuned, power flowed from one to the other and all were reinforced by the established resonance. The power of *tapas* was thus seen as a natural power, built into the structure of reality. The gods did not create *tapas;* they only knew how to use it.

The power of *tapas* had also been available to the *Ṛishis,* who formed the early hymns. They had seen the truth and set it down in mantras; they had performed the truth in the sacrifice; by their knowledge they had become like gods and won immortality, as they had won heaven by *tapas.* What is more important, they had shown the way to later men who could acquire the same power. As the ritual expressed the knowledge of the *Ṛishis,* so those who sought their power, the creative power of *tapas,* should seek to know the structure and truth of the sacrifice. *Tapas,* more general in its manifestations than fire and closer to the creative qualities of sound, served as a link between the two, between the physical and the mental aspects of the sacrifice, as it were. The emergence of this concept marks one more stage in the evolution of a new world view.

Ritual Magic and the Atharva Veda

The logic of magic is based on a strict causal determinism: if this is done, that will result. Many of the emerging views of the sacrifice were based on similar principles. This trend, combined with the emphasis on ritual correspondences, made the sacrifice resemble more and more a ceremony of mimetic magic.

Mimetic or imitative magic relies on the establishment of identities between the controlling ritual and the natural phenomena to be controlled. A ritual order is created that parallels and simulates the natural order by means of physical, symbolic, or verbal replicas and imitative acts. Ritual operations anticipate a corresponding result in the natural world, brought about by the power of the ritual and the accuracy of established identities.

Popular magic using these principles, such as the use of voodoo dolls, involves relatively simple identities and straightforward operations. The difference between this and the late Vedic sacrifice is largely one of degree. The form and underlying conception of the developed sacrifice were recognizably magical, but the model was the whole universe. This is magic indeed on the largest possible scale, suited only for highly skilled practitioners.

The search for correspondences between the sacrifice and other phenomena may have been influenced from the beginning by principles of mimetic magic. Certainly magic must have been associated with the sacrifice from an early time; and, as the sacrifice became more elaborate, more and more elements of magic were added. Many of the new sacrificial forms were appropriated from popular or domestic rites whose numerous magical elements were preserved when the rites were adapted to the *Śrauta* ritual.

The priests who performed the *Śrauta* sacrifices performed domestic rites as well, for themselves and probably also for others, and were thus by no means isolated from popular religious views. Nor was domestic religion free of priestly influence. The priestly ritual was, after all, the most impressive and powerful institution of the society for a period of centuries and was an obvious source of borrowing and imitation. Ritual forms and mantras thus passed over into popular use for magical ceremonies, and this no doubt in return affected the understanding of these mantras in the *Śrautra* ritual. Priests who used mantras for magic in domestic rites were likely to carry this practice back into the hieratic ritual along with many of the magic rites themselves. The result was a gradual synthesis of popular religious practices and the sacrificial cult, seen perhaps most clearly in the *Atharva Veda.*

The *Atharva Veda Saṃhitā* contains some 565 metrical and prose hymns in nineteen books. Magical and ritual interaction is evident throughout, but the balance of interest varies in the three divisions of the collection. The 433 hymns of the first division are all short, some only a single verse, and are mainly straightforward charms and imprecations. They are clearly intended for use as magical spells to satisfy popular desires: protection from snakes, good luck in gambling, release from demons or witchcraft, riddance of a cough, successful childbirth, success against enemies, success in love affairs, recovery of virility, or destruction of the virility of a rival.

The hymns in the second division are without exception longer and include several extensive semiprose passages. This reflects the different character of the material: the short hymns in the first division are obviously magical charms, even though they often refer to technical features of the priestly ritual; the longer hymns of the second division are more concerned with systematic speculation on the meaning of the ritual. It is in the speculative hymns and the use made of them that we find the clearest influence of magical thinking on the ritual itself.

The purpose of the speculative hymns in general can be briefly stated: to gain knowledge in order to gain power and control. Popular magic was concerned with specific personal needs, but control of the universe itself was possible through control of the sacrifice. This control depended on exact knowledge of the identities and correspondences that established the sacrifice as a ritual replica of the cosmos; the more basic that knowledge was, the greater the control would be. The magical conception of the sacrifice increased the incentive for speculation, with the result that the greatest Vedic speculative hymns are found in the *Atharva Veda*.

The Priest as Ritualist and Magician

Concern for knowledge in the sacrifice was of course not new with the *Atharva Veda*. Knowledge had been essential to the sacrifice from the time of the early poet-priest, whose expression of the truth about the gods had ensured sacrificial success. The *Atharva Veda* represents not an innovation in the search for knowledge but a shift in the type of knowledge sought, a shift reflecting changes in the priesthood and in the understanding of sacrificial power.

The early Rig Vedic poets were believed to have powers beyond those of ordinary men. They were *Ṛishis,* "seers," with the gift of seeing the truth. Their creative power, by which they formulated statements of this truth, was called *brahman*. The term *brahman* was applied also to the hymns, whose words and structure preserved the truth revealed by the seers. Since these were passed down and recited orally, sound came to be considered the special form of *brahman*.

The early Vedic priest had the dual function of reciting hymns to the gods and making the sacrificial offerings, e.g., pouring the melted butter or the Soma juice. From the latter function he was called the Hotṛi, "the Pourer," but although the name remained, the ritual activity of the Hotṛi priest was gradually altered. The manual jobs in the sacrifice, including the offering and pouring of oblations, were taken over by a priest called the Adhvaryu.

The Hotṛi remained the most important priest as long as the sacrifice was centered on the hymns as statements to the gods, since as reciter of the hymns the Hotṛi provided the *brahman* or truth power that made the sacrifice effective. Elaboration of the ritual, however, and increased emphasis on the sacrificial performance as a whole, gradually shifted importance to the chief ritual actor, the Adhvaryu. Hymns came to be seen as ritual formulas or mantras, important more for their appropriateness in the ritual than for their qualities as poetry of praise. The Hotṛi, as this happened, was reduced to a ritual adjunct, a reciter of mantras to accompany the main ritual action and a specialist in ritual sounds.

The value of the hymns as mantras was the fact that they were properly formulated expressions of *brahman*. Individual words, phrases, and verses of the hymns were believed to have *brahman* power to no less a degree than did entire hymns. It thus became common practice to abstract from hymns those portions especially relevant to a particular ritual because of the gods addressed, the divine characteristics emphasized, or the meter in which they were written. Selection of proper meters was especially important, since metrical pattern largely determined the sound characteristics of hymns and thus their ritual efficacy.

Concern for sound in the sacrifice reached its logical conclusion in the Soma sacrifices, where special priests were employed to sing verses to accompany the actions of the Adhvaryu priest and the chanting of the Hotṛi. Verses chosen for musical presentation were usually taken from the Rig Vedic hymns, but were often altered to fit the melodies used. In these songs, called *Sāmans,* form and melody were the overriding considerations; the meaning of the original verses was secondary, and in their transposition to a new form only the sounds of the original words were preserved.

The *Sāmans* sung in the Soma ritual consisted in general of a prelude introduced by the sound *huṃ;* the main body of the *Sāman,* the *Udgītha,* introduced by the sound *oṃ* and sung by the Udgātṛi priest; a response also introduced by *huṃ;* and a finale. As the most important of the several *Sāman* singers, the Udgātṛi became a ritual specialist concentrating perhaps even more than the Hōtṛi on the presentation of proper sound in the ritual. With increased emphasis on this aspect of the sacrifice, Udgātṛi priests came to constitute a third major priestly group alongside the Hotṛi and Adhvaryu priests.

Specialization of ritual functions led to a separate collection of mantras for each of the three priestly groups. The *Rig Veda Saṃhitā,* the original collection of hymns, became the special mantra collection of the Hotṛi priest. Probably by analogy, the *Sāman* songs were brought together as the *Sāma Veda Saṃhitā* for use by the Udgātṛi priest.

The Adhvaryu's main ritual contribution was manual rather than oral, but he also had a body of prose and verse mantras to make his actions more effective. These formulas, called *yajus,* were muttered by the Adhvaryu in a low voice as he went about his duties, and were not a part of the public offering in the same way as the loud chants of the Hotṛi and the songs of the Udgātri. They were nevertheless essential to the sacrifice and were brought together in a collection called the *Yajur Veda Saṃhitā.*

The mantra collections of the Hotṛi, Udgātṛi, and Adhvaryu priests remained for a long time the only recognized Vedas. Later writings regularly refer to the *trayī vidyā,* the "triple knowledge" contained in the *Rig, Sāma,* and *Yajur Vedas,* with no mention of a fourth class of mantras. Priests used mantras later found in the *Atharva Veda,* but seemed unwilling to grant status to a fourth Veda. Acceptance of the *Atharva Veda* required priestly champions who would establish the collection on a formal basis and use it as their Veda alongside the *trayī vidyā.* This occurred only when the sacrifice had reached a high degree of elaboration and the Hotṛi, Udgātṛi, and Adhvaryu priests were supplemented by a supervisory priest called the Brahman.

The name of the Brahman priest reflects his primary function: to ensure sacrificial success by maintaining and protecting the *brahman,* the power of the mantras, and that of the sacrifice. The Brahman's job was that of an overseer or conductor who followed the details of the ritual performance and counteracted any mistakes made by the other priests. He himself had no active part in the ceremony, but sat in a special place near the main fire altar performing his functions of prevention and correction by meditation and by silent recitation of appropriate mantras.

To perform his task properly the Brahman priest had to know the *Rig, Sāma,* and *Yajur Vedas,* but he used as his special mantras those collected as the *Atharva Veda.* The function of these mantras as magical formulas was transferred to the ritual sacrifice, and the transformation of the sacrifice was completed. It now was a magical performance of cosmic proportions, with the Brahman as chief magician and overseer of ritual potency. The *Atharva Veda* now moved to a central place in the tradition: its magical charms protected and enhanced the sacrificial performance, and its speculative hymns, going beyond even the hymns of the late *Rig Veda,* provided new knowledge of *brahman,* the effective power and underlying reality of the sacrifice.

This development further enhanced the status of the ritual performers, since all priests participated to some extent in the knowledge and use of *brahman* and thus had access to cosmic powers unavailable to other men. The magical view of the sacrifice rationalized these powers and brought them under the control of those who knew their secrets. Ritual knowledge became even more important than before, and with this came a greater concern to protect it from misuse by rigorous training and high standards of purity for priests.

Knowledge and Ritual Purity

The speculative trends of the late Vedic hymns were continued in priestly commentaries on the sacrificial ritual. These texts, called Brāhmaṇas, all had a common concern: the knowledge and control of *brahman* as it was manifested in the *Śrauta* rituals. A frequent refrain in the Brāhmaṇas is the statement that one who "knowing thus" performs a ritual gets the desired benefit. Knowledge alone could unlock the power of the ritual. Without proper knowledge, as a later text stated, the sacrifice was no better than an offering poured on dead ashes.

The ritual was not only sterile without knowledge, but was potentially dangerous. Ritual actions and mantras had inherent power that, if used improperly, could have disastrous results. As we have seen, the mantras of the *Atharva Veda* and the supervision of the Brahman priest were used to correct errors in the sacrifice that might turn the ritual against the sacrificer. The Brāhmaṇas carried this concern to its logical extreme, placing each element of the ritual in a context which ensured that everything would be in its proper place and that that place would be understood. To establish this context, extensive use was made of myths and legends, etymologies, and any other relevant information that could confirm the identities and correspondences linking the microcosmic ritual with the macrocosmic universe.

Special care was taken with the performers of the ritual. They were the repository of ritual knowledge and their fitness was essential for ritual effectiveness. Not only were they given careful education and training, but they were expected to maintain high standards of ritual purity. Only a person purified and ritually prepared could be entrusted with the *brahman* power.

Most of the rituals were performed by priests, who were expected to maintain a permanent condition of purity. For certain sacrifices, however, laymen also were required to undergo extensive ritual preparation. This was especially true of the Soma sacrifice, for which there was a special consecration ceremony. This ceremony, called the *dīkshā,* illustrates the nature and the importance of ritual purity in the *Śrauta* ceremony. It also gives us details of at least one means by which that purity could be attained, and indicates the degree to which principles of mimetic magic had been absorbed into the sacrificial tradition.

The consecration ceremony for the Soma sacrifice was essentially a ritually enacted birth, or rebirth. The sacrificer was bathed and had his hair cut, and was anointed with fresh butter to signify his embryonic state. He was then conducted to "the hut of the consecrated": "the hut of the consecrated is the womb of the consecrated" (*Aitareya Brāhmaṇa* 1.3). In this symbolic womb, a hut near the sacred fire, he was covered with a garment which was "the caul of the consecrated"; over this was placed a black antelope skin representing the placenta. He had to keep his hands closed, for "verily closing its hands the embryo lies within; with closed hands the child is born." He was fed only cooked milk while in this condition and was required to stammer when he spoke. If he itched he was forbidden to scratch himself directly with his bare hands, but had to use an antelope horn with which he was provided.

These details from various Brāhmaṇas and later ritual texts make clear the nature of this rite as a symbolic gestation period. Further details indicate that it was more than just that. The nearness of the fire, confinement in the hut, and the enclosing garment and skin all tended to produce heat in the sacrificer. It was expected that sweating would occur, but he was not to be given water or bathed for the duration of the ritual. Though other elements were present, the central concern was the increase of heat (*tapas*) which accompanied or brought about an increase in the ritual potency of the sacrificer. The body of the sacrificer was filled with special power. He should touch himself only with a nonconducting material, the antelope horn, and could not be bathed because water also would spoil or remove the special condition.

The elaborate preparation represented by the consecration ceremony was necessary because of the great power of the sacrifice. The knowledge and use of *brahman* and the acquisition of *tapas* were only for those who were ritually pure and fit, since these powers raised men to the status of gods and gave them control over the gods. More than that: the powers available in the sacrifice ultimately gave men control over the universe itself. This claim, implicit throughout the sacrificial tradition, is made explicit in the *Śatapatha Brāhmaṇa* by a comprehensive identification of the fire sacrifice and the universe.

The Ritual as Creator and Preserver of the Cosmos

Almost a third of the *Śatapatha Brāhmaṇa* is devoted to the theory and construction of an altar for the Soma sacrifice built in the shape of a hawk with outstretched wings and tail. The building of this altar is related by a complex symbolism to the creation of the universe by Prajāpati, "Lord of Offspring," the main creator god of the late Vedic hymns and Brāhmaṇas. The account of this dual creation brings together a number of earlier mythological themes and relates them in a connected way to the Brahmanical theory of the sacrifice. The resultant conception, if not all the details, remained an important theoretical base for the later tradition.

Echoing *Rig Veda* X.129, the *Śatapatha Brāhmaṇa* account begins with a statement that "this universe was nonexistent in the beginning." There was only nonexistence, the unformed, made up of the "vital airs" or *prāṇās,* the breaths or vital powers of life. These vital airs created seven separate persons (*puruṣas*), which then came together to make one Person (Puruṣa). The initial process of formation concludes with a basic identity: "That same Person became Prajāpati [Lord of Generation]. And that Person which became Prajāpati is this very Agni [fire altar] who is now to be built" (*Śatapatha Brāhmaṇa* VI.1.1.5).

The now unified Prajāpati exerted himself ("heated *tapas*") and created the universe with all its parts, the various classes of gods, and finally mortal creatures. Then, having created creatures, Prajāpati "became relaxed"—literally, began to fall to pieces or become disjointed—and the vital breaths departed from him. He called to Agni to restore him, promising Agni that in return he would be called by Agni's name. Agni agreed and restored him: "Therefore, while being Prajāpati, they called him Agni" (*Śatapatha Brāhmaṇa* VI.1.2.13).

The restoration of Prajāpati is then described in terms of the building or piling of the fire altar, the five layers of which are identified with the five bodily parts of Prajāpati (hair, skin, flesh, bone, and marrow). Prajāpati is also said to be the year, and the five layers the five seasons; he is the wind, and the five layers the five regions of space. When the altar has been built the fire that is laid down on it is the sun: "That same Agni is indeed raised on the altar and that just because Agni had restored him [Prajāpati]."

This account is obviously not a "scientific" explanation of creation, nor was it ever intended to be. It is a ritual myth, the purpose of which is to tie together the elements of the ritual with the universe. The myth includes most of the Vedic creative principles, but the key element is the fire sacrifice, identified with Prajāpati and Agni and related to them both by the power of *tapas*.

Prajāpati creates by means of *tapas*. His practice of *tapas,* the heating up of his own *tapas,* is necessary for his creative activity. The creative power or energy which came from his own *tapas,* however, was used up in creating the universe. Prajāpati had to be restored. He was restored by Agni, fire, which is both the source of *tapas* and its primary earthly manifestation.

But Agni, in the most basic identity, is the fire sacrifice, so it is ultimately the fire sacrifice that restores Prajāpati. The maintenance of the entire universe can then be said to depend on regular performance of the fire sacrifice, which provides the *tapas* that sustains the continual process of creation. Prajāpati first created Agni, but is now so dependent on what he created that he is identified with it: "While being Prajāpati they call him Agni."

The Place of Man in the Cosmos

There could be no higher claim for ritual power than is made in the *Śatapatha Brāhmaṇa,* that the fire sacrifice is identical with the universe, and that the creation and maintenance of the universe depend upon the continued performance of the sacrificial ritual. The lasting contribution of the Brāhmaṇas was the development of a comprehensive theory and a consistent world view to support this claim. The effectiveness of mantras, the magical potency of ritual actions and speech, and the creative power of *tapas* all were comprehended within the Brahmanical system.

The structure of this system was an elaborate set of identities and correspondences binding together the cosmos, the sacrifice, and man. The sacrificial ritual was the central and unifying factor in this system. It provided both the conceptual tools by which man could understand the universe and the practical means by which he could control it. Those who had access to the "triple science," to *brahman,* knew where they stood in relation to the cosmos and knew what had to be done to make their life and afterlife successful.

The priest as ritualist clearly had both enormous power and a great responsibility. By his knowledge of *brahman* and by his supervision of the ritual he preserved the universal order. Knowledge and purity were essential for his role. He was under obligation to speak the truth, since his very words had creative power. As a participant in the great ritual drama that reproduced the order of the cosmos, he largely defined man's place in the cosmos. Set apart from other men, he alone had access to the means by which all men might obtain their desired goals.

Those goals for the Vedas and Brāhmaṇas were wealth, power, health, prosperity, and success during one's lifetime—which, it was hoped, would be long—and after death, immortality in heaven. The priest and sacrificer, raised in the ritual to the status of gods, anticipated in a temporary way the permanent reward that could be won by repeated sacrifices. Ritual action, *karma,* properly performed and continued throughout a person's lifetime, would result in his passage after death to the world of the fathers or to the world of the gods, there to live free of his mortal body. This prospect, even more than the immediate worldly benefits that the sacrifice provided, was the main incentive to sacrificers and priests alike.

It was assumed at first that immortality once gained was a permanent state. In the later Brāhmaṇas, however, the fear arose that even this state was not free from death, that the effects of past ritual actions might run out and death and dissolution again occur. This "redeath" did not in its earliest conception involve rebirth and a return to earthly struggles. The prospect was nevertheless frightening, and the universe, once so secure, no longer seemed such a pleasant place. The conclusion was slowly reached that the phenomenal world, brought forth and maintained by ritual speech and action, might in the end be a trap in which man no less than the rest of nature was caught up in continuing cycles of creation and destruction. And if this was so, then what was the value of the material rewards of the sacrifice or of a longer-lasting but ultimately impermanent afterlife in heaven?

A new understanding of man was needed to meet these concerns. The earlier Vedic tradition had paid little attention to the nature of man. The ritually based Brahmanical world view saw the phenomenal world as a creation brought forth by the power of *tapas* and the impulse of desire. Man was a part of this created world, and had access through the ritual to the powers that created and controlled it. Controlling *tapas* and the sacrifice, man could satisfy his own desires; within the created world he was a creative agent in his own behalf.

But if the ritual did not bring permanent satisfaction of desires, if not only death but redeath brought an end to its benefits, then the whole Brahmanical system was called into question. Priestly authority rested on the assurance of ritual effectiveness. The ability of the ritual to bring results was never questioned, but the value of those results was increasingly uncertain. Material gains could not survive death, either here or in the hereafter. Was there then some higher goal, some true state of immortality that was not ruled by death and could not be eroded by time? And if so, how might it be obtained? How could man, created and characterized by desire, transcend his finite condition?

3.
The Upanishads

The late Vedic hymns and Brāhmaṇas viewed the universe from the perspective of the sacrificial ritual as a creation of inherently magical powers. The phenomenal world, the world of thought and action, was neither permanent nor self-existent; it was a manifestation of names and forms brought forth by the creative powers of *brahman* and *tapas*. Later attempts to understand man and transcend human limitations were not confined to ritualistic or even Vedic principles and assumptions, but almost all were influenced by this general world view. This was due in no small part to the first and formative attempts, which grew directly out of the Vedic ritual.

The Search for the Self of Man

It was generally assumed in the Brāhmaṇas that proper ritual action was as important as proper knowledge for the success of the sacrifice. At times, however, the Brāhmaṇas claimed that knowledge alone would bring the desired results *without* ritual actions. By the end of the Brāhmaṇa period (*ca.* 800 B.C.), the independent effectiveness of ritual knowledge was widely acknowledged. The concept of ritualism was extended to include mental as well as physical performance, based on the belief that ritual sounds and actions could be internalized, converted into thought, without a loss of potency. For those who were properly qualified, private mental performance of the ritual was as effective as external public performance.

In line with the elitist tradition of the priesthood, high qualifications were established for this advanced ritual practice, and the necessary knowledge was passed down as restricted or secret teachings. A distinction was gradually made between the main body of ritual texts and those that emphasized only the meaning of rituals without assuming that the rituals would be physically performed. Collections of these teachings were called Āraṇyakas, "Forest Books," because their contents were taught and put into practice in forest retreats.

The Āraṇyakas gave a new status to the individual person. Perfected knowledge, though derived from the sacrificial ritual, did not depend for its effectiveness on the elaborate paraphernalia of the sacrifice; mental ritual performance could bring the same results. The performer was thus raised in power and importance to the level of the sacrifice itself. A person of advanced training and knowledge became a creator in his own right; like the Brahman priest he could meditate on the meaning of the sacrifice, search out its hidden truths, and control the universe by the power of his mantras alone.

This development led to a conclusion that was only slowly recognized: if the individual person had the power of the sacrifice, then in the most basic sense he *was* the sacrifice. He was then also by identity the Puruṣa, creator of the cosmos, who had brought forth his own form by his inherent creative power. Phenomenal man by this reasoning was but an extension of his own inner nature, his own essential self.

But what *was* the essential self of man? The term introduced into Vedic inquiry was the common word for "self," *ātman,* used generally as a reflexive pronoun. From this general usage, *ātman* was given a more specific meaning as the essential part of man, his basic reality. At times this was taken to be the body or the trunk of the body as distinguished from the limbs. Gradually, however, the *ātman* was distinguished from the gross physical body; it was the *inner* self, the principle or entity that gave man his essential nature.

Throughout the Vedic period there were many suggestions made as to what the nature of that self might be. Some of the most fruitful suggestions are found in the speculative hymns of the *Atharva Veda,* where an extensive search is carried out to discover the nature of the One that underlay phenomenal existence. *Tapas,* speech, breath, the abstract primal being Skambha ("the Support") and the creator god Prajāpati all are discussed as creative powers. The most important hymns, however, focus on *brahman.*

Even in the early hymns of the *Atharva Veda, brahman* often was treated as not just the power of the mantras or of the sacrifice but as a basic cosmic principle. Thus in hymn 4.1 of the first division of the *Atharva Veda, brahman* is said to have lowest and highest forms and to be "the womb of both the existent and the nonexistent." In 10.2 it is said that "by *brahman* the earth was disposed, as *brahman* the sky was set above, as *brahman* this atmosphere, the wide expanse, was set aloft and crosswise" (10.2.25), and (in 10.2.29 and 33) that *brahman* also enters into this citadel (*pur*) which is man (*puruṣa*).

In a figure that frequently recurs in later writings, the unity or binding force of the world is represented as "the thread stretched out on which these creatures are strung together," while the underlying reality is seen as the thread of the thread: "Who knows the thread of the thread, he would know the great *brahman* power" (10.8.37). The culmination of this hymn sets forth an even more important claim: that within the human body—the "lotus with nine gates covered over with three strands"—is "the prodigy . . . which consists of self (*ātman*)" known by *brahman*-knowers (10.8.43). *Brahman* is not only the basic principle of the cosmos; it is also the self of man.

The older meanings of *brahman* as the Vedic mantras or as the power of the sacrifice have been replaced in these passages by a more comprehensive understanding of *brahman* (or, in its universal form, Brahman) as the ultimate or absolute reality of the universe. This is a logical development from the ritual tradition: the sacrifice is the universe; *brahman* is the sustaining power of the sacrifice; therefore *brahman,* or Brahman, is the sustaining power or reality behind the universe. All things come from Brahman and are supported by Brahman; to know Brahman is to know all, since Brahman *is* "this All," this universe. And, as *Atharva Veda* 10.8.44 implies, the person who knows this Brahman as his *ātman* has no need to fear death, for this *ātman* is complete in itself, self-existent, wise, and immortal.

But what is it that is known? What can be the nature of *brahman*—or by identity of *ātman*—that it can be at the same time the underlying principle of the universe, the sacrificial ritual, and man? How one can know it depends on what it is; the method of knowledge must fit what is to be known. As long as *brahman* was considered only in terms of the ritual, then ritual knowledge gave a sufficient understanding of this reality. But if *brahman* is universal and, moreover, is present in man as his "self," then ritual knowledge alone is not sufficient, though it may be necessary. The human person cannot be fully comprehended by ritual knowledge. Despite attempts to relate him to the sacrificial ritual by identities and correspondences, the individual in his dynamic processes goes beyond the structure of the ritual.

The attempt to understand Brahman as the reality of *both* man and the cosmos thus also had to go beyond purely ritual speculation. Identification of Brahman and *ātman* led to investigation of human experience in order to describe the "self" in empirical terms. This investigation is a central theme of the last group of Vedic writings, the Upanishads, which carry Vedic speculation to its highest level.

Speculation in the Early Upanishads

The development of Upanishadic thought can be seen most clearly in the two oldest Upanishads, the *Bṛihadāraṇyaka* and *Chāndogya*. Both begin with topics developed in the earlier Brāhmaṇas and Āraṇyakas: identifications between elements of the sacrifice and the cosmos. The *Bṛihadāraṇyaka,* an Upanishad of the Adhvaryu priests, takes up the theme of the Vedic horse sacrifice and identifies the parts of the sacrificial horse with the sun, the wind, the year, and so on. The *Chāndogya,* an Upanishad of the Udgātṛi priests, begins with a discussion of the sound syllable *oṃ,* the *Udgītha,* with which the Udgātṛi priest began each of his songs: it is the quintessence of essences; it is the sun; it is space, the final goal; it is the immortal fearless sound knowing which and entering which a person becomes immortal.

The focus in both Upanishads soon shifts away from such narrowly ritual concerns to more general speculative questions. Numerous discussions are carried out on the nature of Brahman, continuing and refining earlier Vedic speculation. Brahman is viewed as the One, the totality of the existent and the nonexistent. It is the underlying truth of all that exists, the reality on which all name and form depend. Brahman itself is beyond specification, beyond name and form, identifiable with only one other reality: the *ātman* or self of man.

The greatest innovations in the *Bṛihadāraṇyaka* and *Chāndogya* are in the investigation of this identity and the investigation of the self. With what in man can Brahman be identified? What, it is asked, is most essential in man, what most permanent? What in man corresponds to the place of Brahman in the ritual and the cosmos? Many suggestions are made, only to be rejected as partial or dependent on other entities. At the end of one such series of suggestions, the sage Yājñavalkya remarks: "That self is not this, not that (*neti neti*). It is incomprehensible for it is not comprehended. It is indestructible for it is never destroyed. It is unattached for it does not attach itself. It is unfettered. It does not suffer. It is not injured" (*Bṛihadāraṇyaka* 3.9.26). Few things could be found that met this set of qualifications.

It was suggested in both early Upanishads that the most important thing in man might be his breath. A person can continue to exist without speech, sight, hearing, or even mind, but when breath departs all the senses depart with it. Breath, however, was both too closely connected to the body and too physical to serve adequately as an ultimate principle in man. It became increasingly clear that the search for *ātman,* like the search for Brahman, had to go beyond physical phenomena.

One of the more important early efforts to find a nonmaterial essence of life is found in a teaching ascribed to Prajāpati in the *Chāndogya Upanishad.* He teaches first that the self is the body, but this is clearly inadequate; the self then would suffer all the changes of the body. Prajāpati teaches next that the self is "he who moves about happy in a dream"; but the dream self experiences not only happiness but also unpleasantness and pain. Perhaps, then, it is said, the self is when a man is asleep, composed, serene, knows no dream. But in that state there is no awareness even of personal existence; such a one "has gone to annihilation" (*Chāndogya* 8. 11.1).

Prajāpati then offers a final explanation: the body, which is mortal, is only the support of the deathless, bodiless self. Freed from the body, the self rises up and reaches the highest life where he appears in his own form as "the supreme person." There he moves about, laughing, playing, and rejoicing, without remembering the appendage of the body. "As an animal is attached to a cart, so is life attached to this body." It is the sense organs that see, smell, utter sound, hear, and think; the self perceives, but is not attached to the organs of perception (*Chāndogya* 8. 12.4–5).

This explanation established several points basic to the view of the Upanishads: the self is essentially free of the body, though supported by the body while incarnate; in its freed state it is bodiless and, though perceptive, is independent of the active agents of bodily perception; and in its own form it is the supreme person. The approach used in this teaching is also significant: the elimination of inadequate definitions of the self in a progressive movement from external phenomena to internal states. Applied more thoroughly, this approach was used by the sage Yājñavalkya in the *Bṛihadāraṇyaka* to develop one of the most important of all Upanishadic teachings.

The Teaching of Yājñavalkya

The teachings of Yājñavalkya represent a significant shift away from the analysis of ritual speech and action found in the Brāhmaṇas. Ritual concerns are not absent, but emphasis is on the functions and dynamics of the human person. Earlier attempts to parallel the ritual and the person, the *puruṣa,* did not deal with the mental and psychological states of man, nor did they take into account the changes that occur in a person in the course of time. These had become crucial in the effort to discover the self of man which, unlike the cosmic Brahman, had to be related to human psychophysiological processes.

Yājñavalkya asserts that the true self is the person (*puruṣa*) consisting of intelligence, the inner light within the vital breaths (*prāṇās*), within the heart. It illumines all actions of men but is itself self-illuminated. "With the self indeed as the light one sits, moves about, does one's work, and returns (*Bṛihadāraṇyaka* 4. 3.6). This inner person has two states, the state of this world and the state of being in the other world. Between these states is an intermediate or twilight state, the state of dream, through which the self passes from one state to the other and in which both other states can be seen; in dream both the evils of this world and the joys of the other world are experienced.

The self in this "twilight state" is the creator, self-illuminated, the agent who creates wagons, teams, roads, pools, rivers, and lakes, joys, delights, and pleasures, where none otherwise existed. The person in dreaming sleep "takes along the material of this all-embracing world with all its contents, himself tears it apart, himself builds it up"; by his own light he dreams. The self in the dream state is demonstrably free of the body and of the sense organs, whose function during sleep does not affect the activities of the self. The body, guarded by the vital breath, is left behind by the temporarily released and self-illumined self.

In a third state, that of "deep sleep," the self is free even from the appearance of activity. In both the waking and dream states it might be thought through ignorance that the self is affected by what happens to the forms or to the body; thus there is pain, fear, and craving. In the state of deep sleep, however, these apparent attachments are removed and the self is seen in its true condition of freedom.

> This verily is his form which is free from craving, free from evils, free from fear. As a man when in the embrace of his beloved wife knows nothing without or within, so the person when in the embrace of the intelligent self knows nothing without or within. That verily is his form in which his desire is ful-

filled, in which the self is his desire, in which he is without desire, free from any sorrow. (*Bṛihadāraṇyaka* 4. 3.21)

This is not a state of unconsciousness, but, as the analogy to sexual intercourse indicates, a state of totally unified consciousness in which there is no awareness of difference. The self in this condition maintains its character as a perceiver, but there is nothing else separate from it that it could perceive. In this state, free of all fear and desire and conscious only of oneness, the self experiences the highest bliss, *ānanda,* the bliss of the world of Brahman. But this state is not attained permanently in deep sleep, and there is an inevitable return to the states of dream and waking. The state of deep sleep is only a precursor of the desired permanent condition of release.

Yājñavalkya then goes on to describe the self at the time of death and the final attainment of Brahman. Here, as in sleep, speculation is tied to observation. When a person approaches death, his senses cease to function properly. They are withdrawn from the outside world, gathered in, so that one by one the person loses external sense contact. With the senses withdrawn, the unified self departs from the body and the senses or life breaths depart with it. The self becomes merely consciousness or intelligence, and what likewise has intelligence—the vital powers—depart with him. The body, now lifeless, is left behind.

In the view of the earlier Vedic tradition, the self or person would at this point depart on a long path to the world of the fathers. Yājñavalkya neither rejects nor supports this view, but states instead a more general proposition: when the self departs, "his knowledge and his work take hold of him as also his past experience" (*Bṛihadāraṇyaka* 4. 4.4). This principle is then developed more completely into a teaching with enormous consequences for the later tradition, the doctrine of rebirth on the basis of past actions:

Just as a grass leech [or caterpillar] when it has come to the end of a blade of grass, after having made another approach [to another blade] draws itself together towards it, so this self, after having thrown away this body, and dispelled ignorance, after having another approach [to another body] draws itself together [for making the transition to another body].

And as a goldsmith taking a piece of gold turns it into another, newer and more beautiful shape, even so does this self, after having thrown away this body and dispelled its ignorance, make unto himself another, newer and more beautiful shape like that of the Fathers or of the *gandharvas,* or of the gods or of Prajāpati or of Brahmā or of other beings (*Bṛihadāraṇyaka* 4.4.4–5).

This self, Yājñavalkya continues, is Brahman. It is everything that is, but what it becomes in any specific situation is the result of the individual's past action: "According as one acts, according as one behaves, so does he become. The doer of good becomes good, the doer of evil becomes evil. One becomes virtuous by virtuous action, bad by bad action" (*Bṛihadāraṇyaka* 4. 4.5). This causal condition applies both to the present and to the future life. Good actions increase goodness and merit in one's present life and also determine the form or body the self shapes for itself in its future life.

Actions are necessarily performed by the body and do not alter the basic nature of the self. The self is nevertheless clearly related in some way to the actions of its created form, since its future condition is controlled by the consequences of these actions. The connection which Yājñavalkya designates is *desire,* the attachment of the mind or thought to a desired object. A person, he says, consists simply of desire. As he desires, so he resolves; as he resolves, so is the deed he does; as is the deed he does, so is that to which he attains. The person attached to objects of desire goes at death to that upon which his thought is most intent, carrying with him his accumulated actions, his *ḳarma.*

Rebirth as a consequence of actions applies only to one who is desirous. Desire (*ḳāma*) causes the will to act, and actions (*ḳarma*) determine the embodied condition of the self. It is the same thing to say that a man is as he acts or that he is as he desires; it is his desires and actions that distinguish a person *as an individual person.* The self in its own nature has none of the characteristics of men or even of the gods; it is one without a second, pure subject without the consciousness of an object different from itself. It is desire that leads to birth and rebirth, desire that leads to the creation of individual forms and bodies that contain the self in this world and in the heavenly world as well.

Bound by accumulated *ḳarma* and the desire to create new forms, the self of a desirous person is not freed even at death. Though one body may be left behind, the effects of past actions and continuing attachments remain as an ongoing causal force that brings about a new embodied state. But, Yājñavalkya continues, it is not so for "the man who does not desire, who is without desire, whose desire is satisfied, whose desire is the self" (*Bṛihadāraṇyaḳa* 4. 4.6). Such a person, being just Brahman, goes to Brahman at his death. When desire is eliminated, rebirth is eliminated; there is no further embodiment of the self.

The means to this result is knowledge: not ordinary knowledge or even ritual knowledge, but the knowledge, the full awareness, that the self and Brahman are one. "Being just that, even that we become. Dire disaster comes to him who knows it not! Those who know it become immortal; the others attain naught but suffering" (*Bṛihadāraṇyaḳa* 4. 4.15). The self is what Brahman is: the one beyond all natural and cosmic processes. In it there is no diversity; it is unborn, great and constant, without impurity. One who sees diversity in the self attains death after death, but one who knows it as the one great Brahman is free of endless death and rebirth.

Knowledge of the self for Yājñavalkya brings an end to rebirth because it brings an end to desire for anything other than the self. The self is the one true source of all that has value, and thus the only true object of desire. Only ignorance of the self could bring desire for anything else; when one knows the self, there is nothing more that he could desire. Nothing else need be loved or held dear, because all else is only a manifestation of the self: "When the self is seen, heard, reflected on and known then all this is known" (*Bṛihadāraṇyaka* 4. 5.6).

Being Alone Exists

The *Chāndogya Upanishad,* like the *Bṛihadāraṇyaka,* contains a wide variety of teachings. One of the most important of these, and the one most often referred to in later times, is the instruction given by the Brāhman householder Uddālaka to his son Śvetaketu. The central theme of this instruction is the difference between the underlying reality and the modifications in that reality that give rise to manifold names and forms.

Uddālaka explains to his son that the truth (*satya*) of anything made of clay is clay, copper is the truth of what is made of copper, and iron the truth of all things made of iron. So is it also, he says, with the universe. The universe in the beginning was Being or the Existent (*sat*) alone, One without a second; from that the plurality of existent entities was born by successive modifications of the One. The One created or emitted heat, heat created water, and water, food. The highest power, Being itself, entered by means of the living self (*ātman*) into the three created potencies (heat, water, and food), causing them to combine in various threefold ways and become differentiated in name and form. In this way, though it was in truth the one sole origin and highest self, the Existent became also the self of all individual created beings.

For Uddālaka, as for Yājñavalkya, the relation of created beings to the Existent can be inferred from the phenomena of sleep and death. Of the two, Uddālaka places much more emphasis on death as an example of union with the underlying reality. Sleep is a temporary return to oneness, but at death all the created potencies return to the Existent, the resting place of all creatures: "When man here is dying, his speech enters into his thought organ, thought organ into life breath, life breath into heat, heat into the supreme potency [the Existent]" (*Chāndogya* 6. 8.6). This description of death, like Yājñavalkya's, is based on empirical observation. When a man dies, his consciousness or thought persists after speech is gone, and breath survives after consciousness ceases. When breath leaves, the body gradually loses its heat until only the cold corpse remains.

What is other than the body, the self of the individual, then passes to another state. That state is ordinarily reincarnation, the creation of a new body and the beginning of another life. Human actions are a part of nature; and even when the body is totally dispersed, the lingering consequences of actions remain. The effects of all actions are stored up, as it were, in the universal causal network where they become the determining factors in a new personal existence. They bring about the embodiment of the self in a new form and determine the characteristics of that form. The basic principle is stated explicitly in an earlier portion of the *Chāndogya:*

> Those whose conduct here has been good will quickly attain a good birth [literally, womb], the birth [or womb] of a Brāhman, the birth of a Kṣatriya, or the birth of a Vaiśya. But those whose conduct here has been evil will quickly attain an evil birth, the birth of a dog, the birth of a hog, or the birth of a Caṇḍāla. (*Chāndogya* 5. 10.7)

Fundamental to this view is the creative power of desire and thought. Just as the One, the primal Person, satisfies his desire by creating the form of the cosmos, so the individual, in satisfying his desires, continually recreates his bodily form. By actions resulting from his desire he binds himself into the universal process of cause and effect. As long as the effects of individual action remain, so must individual existence remain. When one bodily form dies, another form is produced to carry on the effects of past actions and past desires.

Is there escape from this? And if so, how? The answer, for Uddālaka, lies in knowledge. This entire phenomenal universe was in the beginning "the Existent" only, "One alone without a second." Though this original One was manifested into many, differentiated by name and form, all the differentiated individual beings remain in essence only the original one reality.

The underlying reality, however, is not recognized and known. Men consider themselves different from each other and from the One because their thinking cannot get beyond names and modifications. They think of themselves in terms of body, form, name, and other individual characteristics instead of thinking of their true self—what alone is most true in themselves and in all others—as identical with the self of the universe. Since all things are ultimately the Existent, individual differences are no more significant than are the individual rivers that in the end all flow together to make the single ocean. When all beings finally come to the One, they will no longer remember or care about their individual existences; they will know only That, they will become fully That, because they always have been and only can be That.

The Real, the self, is in all manifested things as sap is in every part of a tree, giving it life, or as salt is in salty water, giving it a saline taste; it is like the subtle essence in the seed of a banyan tree from which the great tree grows. Only the effects and not the subtle essence itself can be perceived. So it is with the Existent, That Brahman that is the reality of all things. "While no doubt you do not perceive the Existent here," Uddālaka concludes, "it is not to be doubted that it is here just the same. What that subtle essence is, a state of having That as its nature, is this universe; That is the real, That is the self, *That art thou,* Śvetaketu!" (*Chāndogya* 6. 13).

Man's basic problem is thus, according to Uddālaka, a lack of knowledge. Man ascribes reality to individual entities in the world, not realizing that they are only names and forms; the underlying Real is not known and its presence in all things as their essence is not recognized. So also men ascribe reality to their own existences as defined by name and form, not knowing the one Reality present in them as their selves. Though they enter the One in deep sleep and at the time of death, they do not know it, and final merger does not occur.

The ignorant person in the world, Uddālaka points out, is like a man brought into a desert blindfolded and then turned loose to find his way home. Not knowing how he came there or where to look for what he seeks, he wanders aimlessly until a guide or instructor gives him the right direction. "There is delay for him only as long as he is not freed [of ignorance]; then he will arrive home" (*Chāndogya* 6.14.1,2). Home for man is the Existent, present everywhere as the self of the world and of man. Ignorance is destroyed for one who knows where it is and how to reach it; setting aside the distraction of names and forms, he can recognize and quickly attain his final goal.

The Final Goal of the Upanishads

The teachings of Yājñavalkya and Uddālaka are the best developed statements of the early Upanishads. Together they exerted an enormous influence on the later tradition, not least because they represent a basically pragmatic concern. Their attempts to locate and define the self were not exercises in abstract thought or philosophy for its own sake. Their goal was salvation, defined as the release of the self from its continued bondage to rebirth.

They are agreed that the ultimately real, the One without a second, is Brahman, and that Brahman is present in the phenomenal world as the self of man. They are further agreed that the knowledge that brings release is knowledge of the unchanging Brahman, and that this knowledge is obscured by the condition of the embodied self. They differ, however, in their assessment of this condition, expressed in their views of how the self is caught up in the world of phenomena and how it can eventually be freed from transmigration.

The self that transmigrates is not, for Yājñavalkya, the pure self alone, identical with Brahman, but that self along with the vital breaths and the knowledge, work, and past experience that it has accumulated (see *Bṛihadāraṇyaḳa* 4. 4.2). This self is called by later commentators the *lingātman,* the "subtle self" or "characteristic self," the self encumbered by the characteristic qualities acquired in particular embodied states.

Release is impossible as long as this "subtle self" continues to function. Mind, the "characteristic mark" of the subtle self, stores up past impressions, desires, and purposes and carries them—and the subtle self along with them—from one waking state to the next and from one life to the next. It and the other vital breaths that cling together around the self provide the continuity from one particular existence to another because their basic distinguishing feature is their particularity: *this* body, *this* life, *this* set of memories, experiences, and impressions from the past. The subtle self is thus bound together by the conviction that the continuity of *this* self is important and that there is something to be gained by maintaining its existence.

Release can therefore be effected only by knowledge that counteracts the self-perpetuation of the embodied self. There is only one such knowledge, according to Yājñavalkya and the Upanishads in general: knowledge that the true self is Brahman. If one knows that the self of man is Brahman only and that Brahman includes within itself the entire universe, past, present, and future, then what is to be gained, what purpose could be served, by maintaining a particular individual existence? "If a person knows the self as 'I am this,' then wishing what and for desire of what should he suffer in the body?" (*Bṛihadāraṇyaka* 4. 12).

The ignorance that leads to continued rebirth is not at any time a characteristic of the true self, which is never anything other than Brahman, Reality itself. Ignorance is a quality of the subtle self which is preserved by, and in turn causes, continuing particularity. The knowledge that brings release thus must also be acquired by the embodied self, to replace the previous ignorance. This knowledge can be pointed out by others, but to be finally effective it must be personally appropriated. Once obtained, it becomes the only knowledge worth preserving. It ends the clinging to individual experiences, destroys the value of all particular worldly knowledge and perception, and eliminates the cause of the continuing existence of the subtle self.

The subtle self, once its false knowledge has been fully replaced by the one true knowledge, terminates its existence when the body dies. Knowledge destroys all worldly desires, the mind and the vital breaths do not draw together around the self at the time of death, and the true self is released from bondage: "Being just the Brahman, unto the Brahman he (the self) arrives" (*Bṛihadāraṇyaka* 4. 4.8).

The final goal of man is thus, as Yājñavalkya explains it, to dissolve the subtle or phenomenal self. Uddālaka's teaching presents a rather different approach to the problem. He assumes no separate individual selves, but instead sees the entire universe as a progressive manifestation of the Real (*sat*). One only in the beginning, the Real or the Existent propagated itself into the many, creating first heat, from heat water, and from water food. From these "potencies" the manifest world was then created.

The entire phenomenal universe was for Uddālaka produced from combinations of the three "potencies" emitted in series from the Existent. Each of these potencies has as its "root" the one emitted before, and the Existent is the "root" or cause of all. Not only is it both material and efficient cause, however, but it also is an imperceptible "fineness" or "subtle essence" pervading all things as their life-force, causal potency, and flavor.

When a person dies, his bodily functions devolve back into the "supreme potency," the Existent, from which they have come. This assumption of a progressive devolution *in series* is quite different from Yājñavalkya's description of the vital powers or life breaths "gathering together unto the self at the time of death" (*Bṛihadāraṇyaka* 4.3.44). In Yājñavalkya's view, there is no merger with Brahman except for the released self, and then the merger is permanent. The transmigratory self remains separate from Brahman, still bound to phenomenal existence by the influence of past actions carried along with the self.

If Uddālaka then assumes no continuing subtle self, what is the cause of transmigration? In Yājñavalkya's teaching the vital powers are directly involved in bodily activity and carry the effects of that attachment with them in the "knowledge and past deeds and memory" that take hold of the subtle self. No such positive influence is evident in Uddālaka's statements, and actions as such seem a less important factor in rebirth. The emphasis is instead more directly on the absence of knowledge. All bodily manifestations devolve back into the Real at the time of death, but the merger is not complete unless there is prior knowledge of the Real. Only a person who knows that Brahman is his own reality remains in the condition of union, since only his knowledge is sufficiently purified of all false understanding. Only such a person has no doubts, and can enter the merger with the One with assurance that this is his final resting place.

Others, who have not attained the quiet acceptance of union that comes from the knowledge that "That art thou," still cling at death to phenomenal existence. They resist the cessation of life in the empirical world, and retain their perceptions of names and forms. With their knowledge defiled by the continuation of discriminations and distinctions, they do not realize that they have reached the condition of pure Being, Reality itself. Retaining the perception of duality, they must return again to a manifested state until they are finally cleansed of all ignorance and have at death only the pure knowledge of the self.

The Religious Implications of Upanishadic Teaching

Although the teachings of Yājñavalkya and Uddālaka differ in their theoretical analysis of the self's relation to the body and the mechanism of release, there is little difference in the implications of their teaching. The goal of man for both is release from "rebirth," from the perpetual recreation of a new bodily form after the death of each previous body. Whether the perpetuation of embodied existence is caused by desire or by ignorance, both agree that it can only be ended by proper knowledge.

Rebirth is inevitable for one who through ignorance is desirous of worldly goals and performs actions directed toward those goals. The relative quality of successive lives is improved by good actions and diminished by bad; but, as long as there is desire for anything other than the self alone, there can be no release. The desire that binds men to the world can only be destroyed by the knowledge that the only true reality is to be found in the self; knowing this, one has no wish or desire for anything other than the self and no reason why he should be further concerned with the body. Renouncing worldly desires and thus the desire for bodily existence, such a one attains Brahman.

The knowledge that brings release cannot be purely theoretical knowledge.

What is required is not a knowledge that ignorance causes attachment but *an elimination of ignorance,* not a knowledge that desire must be eliminated but *an actual elimination of desire.* Saving knowledge is knowledge that is lived in every thought and action. A person with such knowledge is transformed; indeed he *must* be transformed in order to have such knowledge. True knowledge of Brahman is inseparable from purification and an altered way of life. This is evident in a statement by Yājñavalkya that not only summarizes the Upanishadic teaching but shows its broader implications:

> Now it is this Self that is the controller of all, the lord of all, the sovereign of all; it governs all this universe, whatever is at all. It becomes not greater by good deed, nor less by evil deed. It is overlord of creatures; it is the lord of the world(s); it is the guardian of the world(s); it is the dyke that holds apart these worlds, lest they should crash together [i.e., it keeps the world order from falling into chaos]. This it is which they seek to know through repetition of the Vedas, through celibate life, through asceticism, through faith, through sacrifice, and through fasting. When one knows this he becomes a *Muni* ["silent sage"]. This it is which wandering ascetics seek as their heavenly world when they wander forth as ascetics.
>
> Therefore those *Brāhmaṇas* of old, learned and wise, desired no offspring, thinking: What shall we do with offspring, we who possess this Self, this [equivalent of the] Heavenly World [which is the traditional object of begetting sons]?—Abandoning both the desire for sons and the desire for possessions and the desire for heaven, they wandered forth abegging. For the desire for sons is the same as the desire for possessions, and the desire for possessions is the same as the desire for heaven; for both are nothing but desires.
>
> This Self is [simply described as] "Not, not." It is ungraspable, for it is not grasped. It is indestructible, for it is not destroyed. It has no attachment, and is unfastened; it is not attached, and [yet] is not unsteady. For it, immortal, passes beyond both these two states [in which one thinks] "For this reason I have done evil," "For this reason I have done good." It is not disturbed by good or evil things that are done or left undone; its heaven is not lost by any deed. This is meant by this verse:
>
> This is the constant greatness of the *Brāhmaṇa* ["the knower of Brahman"]; he increases not nor becomes less by deed. This [greatness] it is, the basis of which one should seek to find; having found it, one is not stained by evil deed.
>
> Therefore one who knows this, becoming pacified, controlled, at peace, patient, full of faith, should see the Self in the Self alone. He looks upon everyone as it. Everyone comes to be his Self; he becomes the Self of everyone. He passes over all evil; evil does not pass over him. He subdues all evil; evil does not subdue him. He is free from evil, free from age, free from hunger, free from thirst, a Brāhman, whoso has this knowledge. (*Bṛihadāraṇyaka* 4.4.24–28.)

Ritual knowledge only becomes effective through performance, through expression in actions, sounds, or thoughts. This is no less true of the knowledge of Brahman, but the results and thus the expression are quite different. Ritual knowledge is in behalf of worldly gain; the knowledge of Brahman requires giving up worldly gain, the elimination of all desires except desire for the self or Brahman. Actions, speech, and thoughts must all reflect this new goal; everything, both body and mind, must be redirected. As Yājñavalkya states in his conclusion, the knower of Brahman must become an ascetic, a silent sage, one whose thoughts are directed solely toward Brahman.

Asceticism and the Vedic Tradition

Rig Veda X.136 gives a striking description of long-haired ascetics called munis, men of extraordinary powers who went about naked or dressed in soiled yellow garments. In a manner similar to tribal shamans or witch doctors, munis in a state of ecstasy could transcend the limits of the physical body. They could "fly through the air, perceiving all forms," and could "know the thoughts" of others. Transformed by ecstasy, they could undergo godlike experiences beyond the ability of other men.

Asceticism, from this and other evidence, was clearly not a creation of Upanishadic thought. Early ascetics like the munis, however, were outside the Vedic mainstream. Soiled, naked, long-haired ascetics might have admittedly great powers, but there was no place for their wild ecstatic behavior in the tightly structured sacrificial ritual. As long as both worldly success and heavenly immortality were considered possible by means of the fire sacrifice, the temporary attainments of the muni met with the kind of ambivalent response found in *Aitareya Brāhmaṇa* 6.33, which praises the muni Aitaśa for discovering an important Vedic verse in a vision but reports also that one of his sons considered him insane.

As a way of life, asceticism had no place in the goals and values of the sacrificial priests and their wealthy patrons. Ascetic techniques, however, detached from asceticism as a life style and assimilated to Velic forms, could be used to increase the effectiveness of the sacrifice. Assimilation was carried out largely through the concept of *tapas,* especially as it related to ritual performance. Ascetic practices such as fasting, silent meditation, celibacy, and isolation were gradually adopted to "heat up" priests in preparation for ritual activity. Consecration for the Soma sacrifice, as we have seen, required the sacrificer to undergo a ritual heating involving silence, fasting, and confinement in a small hut. In the most extensive claim for the efficacy of such practices, Prajāpati himself was said to have created the universe after a prolonged period of toiling and practicing *tapas*—that is, after engaging in ascetic practices that built up the heat-power for his cosmic creative activity.

Vedic asceticism through the period of the Brāhmaṇas was nevertheless of limited duration, subordinated to the fire sacrifice and lasting only long enough to prepare a person for his ritual activities. The period of preparation might even last for several years, as in the requirement of celibacy and restraint for the Vedic student, but at the end of that period one resumed his normal way of life.

Full-scale asceticism within the Vedic framework came only gradually with the trend toward detached forest life reflected in the Āraṇyakas. This trend made ascetic life more acceptable and at the same time gave it a new rationale, as the concept of mental performance of sacrifices brought about an integration of the personal and ritual aspects of *tapas*. Ascetic life in the forest was no longer a *preparation* for ritual activity; it *was* ritual activity, the "heating up" of the individual who was himself the sacrifice and the source of truth.

The development of Vedic asceticism was completed by the Upanishadic doctrine of release from rebirth through knowledge of Brahman and the self. Yājñavalkya praises the man who seeks to know the self by means of *tapas* and fasting and who, knowing the self, becomes a muni or "silent one." The austere life of the forest dweller had become the principal form of practicing *tapas,* the search for knowledge its principal purpose. The *Chāndogya Upanishad* ranks asceticism of this sort as one of the three main duties of the dedicated Aryan, and we find extensive evidence in the early Upanishads of priests as well as others taking up an itinerant forest life.

A synthesis had been created that was to remain the basic framework of the orthodox Hindu tradition. Asceticism had been grafted onto the older pattern of Vedic study and ritual practice. *Tapas,* originally a strictly ritual concept, had been expanded to include—almost to be identified with—ascetic practices that had no established place in the earlier Vedic pattern. And, although sacrificial rituals remained a part of normal community life, it had come to be recognized that the knowledge that brought release from rebirth could only be finally secured by putting aside all worldly concerns and taking up life in the forest as an ascetic.

The Search for New Solutions

The concept of rebirth as a result of actions was not limited to the Upanishads, though the early Upanishads were the first to state the doctrine. By the sixth century B.C., transmigration and the "law of *karma*" had been generally accepted as basic facts of existence and were rarely challenged from that time on by any major Indian system of thought.

Acceptance of transmigration led to a view of human existence as a continual passage from one life to another. This was considered so characteristic of worldly life that the term *saṃsāra* ("passage") was applied to phenomenal existence in general to indicate its transient *karma*-produced nature. Existence conceived as *saṃsāra* obviously could not produce final security. Worldly gains, the gains of *saṃsāra,* always pass away, leaving only the effects of the actions that produced them. Whether worldly attainments are considered good or bad in themselves, they can never be considered permanent; they are at best irrelevant from the ultimate point of view.

The early Upanishadic solutions to the problem of *saṃsāra* did not involve a fundamental rejection of worldly goods. Even the final goal of asceticism, full knowledge, and final release from rebirth was seen more as a positive gain than as escape from a worldly life that was in itself undesirable. Ordinary life as a householder with family, wealth, and long life was devalued only by contrast to the ultimate identity with Brahman in which all things were obtained.

As transmigration became more widely accepted, however, a change in mood occurred. A new attitude of despair and rejection of the world developed, expressed in a statement in the *Kaṭha Upanishad* that worldly goods "wear out the vigor of the senses" (*Kaṭha Upanishad* 1.26). Mortal life is seen as brief and transient, mortal man decaying, and enjoyment of wealth as always dampened by the threat of death.

The transient rewards of the Vedic ritual were clearly no answer to this attitude, but neither was the early Upanishadic solution satisfactory. The Brahman-*ātman* identity was still debatable and was, moreover, based on Vedic knowledge inaccessible to the great numbers who now sought release from *saṃsāra*. The almost universal acceptance of transmigration therefore resulted not in greater reliance on Brahmanical guidance but in a desperate search for better solutions. Major social and political changes further complicated the problem, increasing popular anxiety and at the same time undermining priestly power.

By the end of the sixth century B.C., the Brahmanical tradition was on the defensive. After almost a thousand years, opposition to Vedic authority assumed effective form in rival religious groups. For the next several centuries, until a much altered Vedic tradition assumed control, these new groups, particularly the Buddhist and Jain movements, dominated the religious scene.

4. Challenges and Change

The sixth century B.C. began a period of great change in Indian life. The Persian Empire founded by Cyrus the Great (558–530 B.C.) established a province in western India in the latter part of the century, setting the stage for cultural influences from first Persia and then the Greeks. Political and economic developments in the Ganges-Jumna Valley brought forth an urban culture in North India. Increased trade and political expansion linked these two centers and carried their influences southward into areas outside the earlier Aryan orbit. New religious movements took root in the midst of these changes, challenging the Brahmanical tradition and introducing a host of new issues that further expanded the range of Indian religious concerns.

The Rise of Non-Vedic Movements

Long before the sixth century B.C., the central Ganges-Jumna Valley had become the true "land of the Aryans," Āryavarta, where the highest standards of Aryan culture and Vedic piety were maintained. It was there that Brahmanical ritualism flourished, supported in numerous small kingdoms by the wealth of Aryan rulers. This pattern was disrupted in the sixth century by a gradual absorption of small kingdoms and tribal groups into larger political units. By the end of the century, the Ganges-Jumna Valley was dominated by a few great kingdoms vying for power among themselves.

This development had widespread social and religious consequences. Established families and ruling classes fell from power as their kingdoms were conquered. Vedic ritualism, which had grown with the prosperity of these small kingdoms, no longer provided assurance of wealth and security. Belief in *samsāra,* now generally accepted as a fact of life, added to the sense of despair at the transience of worldly gain. What was achieved in the course of one's life in the world was easily lost; personal rebirth meant that this experience was to be endlessly repeated. The stronger this problem was felt, the less satisfactory traditional solutions appeared.

Brahmanical authority was further undermined by the rise to power of new monarchs from outside the former ruling classes. These new rulers, having gained power by their own abilities, were less bound by traditional loyalties and religious forms than earlier tribal and local rulers. Although they sought priestly support, they claimed highest authority for themselves. Free of traditional obligations, they provided new sources of support for a variety of religious groups, many of them explicitly non-Brahmanical and non-Vedic.

The combination of political change and religious unrest was greatest in the eastern Ganges Valley, the last area in North India to come under Aryan influence. The Vedic tradition had relatively shallow roots here, confidence in Brahmanical solutions was less firmly established, and pre-Aryan religious traditions were still alive. Widespread unrest brought these traditions to the surface and at the same time strengthened nonpriestly elements in the Aryan community. Popular religious traditions, long obscured by Brahmanical domination, emerged in a bewildering array of religious systems.

The new systems put forth as options during this period indicate the failure of Vedic religion to meet popular needs. Sacrificial rituals provided no release from *saṃsāra,* and the way of release taught in the Upanishads was not only unavailable to most people but still basically speculative in its results. The times required, in contrast, a means of salvation both more certain and, at least in principle, more accessible to all those who sought escape from worldly distress and endless rebirth.

These requirements were met by many of the systems proposed in the late sixth and early fifth centuries. Most of these were unencumbered by elaborate textual or doctrinal traditions. Their teachings put primary emphasis on personal training in a method or program of salvation available to anyone willing to learn it. They stressed personal effort and practice, not theoretical speculation; proof of their validity was found in personal experience, not textual authority or logical argument. Their doctrines and explanations centered on the experiences of founders and teachers who served as examples of what others could also do with proper effort. Such messages had great appeal in an anxious age when men asked what they must *do* to be saved.

Most of these systems died with the death of the founder or his immediate disciples, but three of them, the Jain, Ājīvaka, and Buddhist movements, had enough vitality to survive and permanently alter the Indian religious tradition. Both leadership and the conditions of the time were factors in their success. The founders were exceptional men: Gautama Siddhārtha, the Buddha (*ca.* 563–483 B.C.); Mahāvīra, founder of the Jain movement (*ca.* 540–468 B.C.); and Gośāla Maskarīputra, head of the Ājīvakas and a former disciple of Mahāvīra. It is striking that the three were contemporaries and that all three were active in and around the expanding kingdom of Magadha in the eastern Ganges Valley, locus of the greatest political and economic change in the sixth century.

The ferment of the sixth century broke through in concrete form in the movements founded by these three men. Each was in its own way a solution to the crisis of the times: the need for a way of life that would avoid the pains of endless rebirth. All were successful in terms of influence and popular support, the Ājīvakas for more than a thousand years and the Buddhists and Jains on into the present day. At least in the beginning much of this success was the result of their rejection of the sacrifice-oriented Vedic ritual system and their more direct personal solutions to the problems of human existence.

The Ājīvakas and Jains

The solution of Gośāla and the Ājīvakas was probably the oldest of the three in terms of antecedents and was at the same time the most radical. Its basic element was stark asceticism. Members of the Ājīvaka order went about naked, begged their food, followed strict dietary regulations, and often ended their lives by self-starvation.

The ultimate goal of the Ājīvakas was purity and liberation; but, in contrast to Buddhists and Jains, they held that this could not be gained by human effort. The course of transmigration and the eventual attainment of release were alike controlled by destiny, not by actions. While accepting transmigration and rebirth, the Ājīvakas rejected the doctrine of *karma.* Nothing a man did could, in their view, alter the course of his successive existences; like an unwinding ball of string, each course would stretch to its predetermined length and then stop. The Ājīvakas were ascetics not because they thought this would improve their future lives but because such a life was their present destiny.

The Buddhists attacked Gośāla more vigorously than any other opponent and considered the Ājīvaka doctrine of unchangeable destiny the most dangerous of all rival teachings. Buddhist concern is evidence of the Ājīvakas' influence, further documented by gifts from kings and donations of caves for use by Ājīvaka ascetics. Magical powers resulting from ascetic practices must have added to their appeal, but the underlying strength of the Ājīvakas was an asceticism so rigorous as to shut out all human sorrows and pleasures. It is a mark of the times that this uncompromising position could gain numerous followers and continuing support.

The Jain movement, though more broadly based, also had asceticism as its core. Its founder, Vardhamāna, was born the son of a clan chieftain. He took up asceticism at the age of thirty and led an increasingly austere life for twelve years. In the thirteenth year he achieved liberation from *karma* and acquired the title Mahāvīra, "Great Hero," placing himself in a long line of "ford-makers" (*tīrthaṅkaras*) who had followed the same path before him. The movement he led was called "the tradition of the *Jinas* ('conquerors')" or the Jain tradition, reflecting the heroic character of Mahāvīra's asceticism.

Mahāvīra's way had nothing to do with either ritualism or the gods and was explicitly non-Vedic. He and his successors developed their own unique doctrine of rebirth, *karma,* and release. According to this doctrine there is in each person a living entity or *jīva* ("soul" or, literally, "life"). These *jīvas* are present not only in animals and plants but also in objects such as rocks and stones that would not ordinarily be considered living. All the infinite number of *jīvas* have the same basic nature—bright, blissful, and intelligent—but differ in their circumstances and the course of their transmigration because of the *karma* that adheres to them.

Karma for the Jains is in the form of fine matter. Produced in different degrees by various kinds and qualities of actions, *karma* collects on the *jīva* and obscures its basic nature. Release of the *jīva* from this condition can come only when the acquisition of *karma* is stopped and accumulated *karma* is removed. Knowledge plays only a secondary part in this process, since the barrier to release is not merely ignorance but an actual material encumbrance on the *jīva*. It is necessary to know the cause of bondage and the means of release, but release itself can come only by living in such a way that *karma* is gradually destroyed.

Only a monk or ascetic could exercise the necessary rigor in fasting, study, mental control, and physical austerity to carry the destruction of *karma* to completion, though progress was possible even for laymen. Killing of living beings, the worst cause of *karma,* was forbidden to all Jains. Laymen as a result renounced agriculture with its slaughter of plants and animals and took up noninjurious occupations such as commerce and trade. But monks took vows to give up also all sexual activity and the possession of property, the latter including finally the renunciation of shelter and clothing.

The model Jain was an ascetic like Mahāvīra, naked and exposed to sun, wind, and cold, gradually cleansing from his *jīva* the impurities of innumerable lifetimes. In the final state of purification, the ascetic remained totally inactive to avoid the accretion of further *karma*. When finally restored to purity, the *jīva* remained eternally free and independent in a state of inactive omniscient bliss. This for Jains was the supreme attainment.

The Buddhist Rejection of the Vedic World View

The founder of the third major movement of the sixth century B.C. was called by his followers the Buddha, the "Enlightened" or "Awakened." Details of his early life are uncertain. According to later Buddhist accounts, his given name was Siddhārtha and his family or clan name Gautama; his father was a chief of the Śākyas, a small tribe of the Himalayan foothills north of Magadha; he led a sheltered and pampered existence for the first twenty-nine years of his life; and when he became aware for the first time of the suffering caused by sickness, old age, and death, he left his wife and infant son and set out to find a solution to this suffering.

Teachers and proposed solutions of every sort abounded in North India at that time. The Buddha tried two different systems of philosophy and meditation, and then spent several years as an ascetic punishing his body with fasting, trances, retention of breath, and exposure to the elements. None of these solutions was adequate, since none led to "aversion, absence of passion, cessation, tranquility, higher knowledge, and *nirvāṇa*."

He decided finally to try a system of his own that emphasized control of mental states instead of bodily punishment. He began to meditate under a tree that tradition has called the "Bodhi tree," the "tree of Enlightenment." Controlling his senses "without sensual desires, without evil ideas," he passed through progressively deeper stages of concentration. He reached a state of concentration in which his mind was completely undisturbed, and was then able to remember details of his own past lives and see the effects of actions on the passing away and rebirth of beings. Finally, directing his mind to the central problem of transmigration, he discovered the basic causes of bondage: sensual desire, desire for existence, and ignorance. These, he realized, can be understood in their true nature and eliminated; with their elimination comes cessation of the suffering, sorrow, and transiency that characterize the world.

The insight gained through meditation removed the causes of his continuing rebirth. Knowing his own past *karma,* seeing how it brought about and maintained the chain of his existence, and recognizing the essential ignorance that caused him to preserve—and desire the preservation of—that chain, he became at last enlightened and free. Knowledge and light replaced ignorance and darkness; no further cause remained to bring about attachment. From this point in his life Gautama Siddhārtha was the Buddha, the enlightened one.

The Buddha's experience set him against both the sacrificial Vedic tradition and the radical asceticism practiced by Jains and Ājīvakas. His was a Middle Way of discipline, meditation, and knowledge, leading to an awareness of the transience of all existence, including the existence of the so-called "self" of man.

Each individual was for the Buddha a combination of five "factors of grasping" (*skandhas*): matter, sensations or feelings, perceptions, mental formations and volitions, and consciousness. It is these factors, shaped into a particular "bundle" by past actions and desires, that constitute the individual and carry the effects of *karma.* What is called the "self" is *only* these five factors; no "self" or *ātman* exists as an independent entity apart from the bundle of factors.

The continuing existence of any particular bundle of factors—that is, of any particular person—is the result of ignorance and desire: ignorance of the impermanence of all existence, and desire for attachment and continuing individual existence. As fire is fed by fuel, so desire is fed by ignorant attachment to the impermanent world. Desire binds the bundle of factors together in an effort to gain satisfaction from what is inherently impermanent. This attempt must always end in disappointment, and as long as it continues, existence is characterized by *duḥkha* ("pain," "suffering," "sorrow," "despair").

Duḥkha can be ended only by enlightenment and *nirvāṇa,* the "blowing out" or "extinction" of desire, a condition of complete calm and detachment. When ignorance and attachment end, desire ends; when desire ends, the perpetuation of the individual ends. It is not that the self has been extinguished or eliminated, since there never was a real self; what has ended is the ignorant clinging to selfhood and personal identity. When the present life ends, there is no subsequent rebirth for the enlightened one.

Though there are certain similarities between the Buddhist analysis of the so-called self and Yājñavalkya's view of the subtle or transmigratory self, Buddhists denied that this personal self rests on an underlying permanent entity. The unchanging substantial entity called *ātman* underlying the individual person was unconfirmed by the meditative experience of the Buddha and his followers. What is discovered in the final stage of meditation is *nirvāṇa,* but *nirvāṇa* is not an entity or thing; it is a condition or state of calm and absence of desire. *Nirvāṇa* alone is uncreated and unchanging; *all* entities are transient, void of self-existence, dependent on other phenomena that are themselves in flux. This the Buddhists called "dependent origination," the origination of all phenomena from other transient phenomena and not from a single independent entity such as Brahman or *ātman.*

Buddhists thus rejected the entire metaphysical tradition of the Upanishads. All the constituents of existence are transitory and are *anatta* or *anātman,* "without a self." Metaphysical speculation will not solve the problem of individual rebirth, and Upanishadic speculation is, moreover, based on the false premise that there is a self that has independent existence.

The Buddhist solution was by contrast personal and pragmatic. Salvation is an individual problem. A person starts where he is and works toward enlightenment by his own efforts. All that he need know is that existence is in the last analysis always characterized by *duḥkha* because all phenomena are impermanent; that there is a way out of this through the elimination of desire; and that this way, the Buddha's noble eightfold path, will lead those who follow it to peace and *nirvāṇa.*

The Buddha's solution was not limited to an educated or trained elite, had no caste or class barriers, and presupposed nothing except a strong desire to be free of suffering and misery. Sacrificial ritual was rejected because of its world acceptance; metaphysical speculation was rejected as irrelevant to the conquest of desire. The rigorous total asceticism of the Jains and Ājīvakas was rejected as self-torture, along with the Jain emphasis on a permanent self and the Ājīvaka fatalism that made human effort useless in effecting salvation. In place of all of these was set the Middle Way of ethical action, self-discipline, and meditation leading to enlightenment and *nirvāṇa.*

The Mauryan Empire

Ājīvaka, Jain, and Buddhist activity from the sixth to the fourth centuries B.C. was confined largely to the Ganges-Jumna Valley. By the fourth century, this area was dominated by the kingdom of Magadha. Persia was still the center of a great empire in the West, but east of the Indus the center of power was Pāṭaliputra (modern Patna), the Magadhan capital city on the Ganges.

Then came the conquest of Persia by Alexander the Great and his invasion of western India in 326 B.C. Alexander's brief but victorious campaign stopped at the eastern tributaries of the Indus, but it sparked a revolution in the land beyond. The throne of Magadha was captured only a few years afterward by

Candragupta Maurya (*ca.* 322–298 B.C.), who began a campaign of conquest that carried the power of Magadha far beyond its previous limits.

The former Persian provinces in western India were recovered from the new Greek ruler of Persia, giving the growing Mauryan Empire control of northern India from Bengal to Afghanistan. Protected against external attack in the north, Candragupta and his son Bindusāra then extended Mauryan rule into central and south India. With the exception of Dravidian kingdoms in the far south, much of the Deccan, the central portion of the India peninsula, was for the first time open to extensive political and cultural influence from North India.

The political situation made it possible for the non-Vedic movements to expand into new areas. The Mauryans, who had no strong ties to the Vedic tradition, promoted this expansion by giving their support to non-Vedic as well as Vedic groups. Mauryan rulers donated caves to the Ājīvaka order, which reached its greatest strength during the Mauryan period. Jain tradition claims that at the end of his reign Candragupta himself became a Jain monk and went to live in South India. Whether or not this is so, a large number of Jain monks did follow the line of Mauryan conquests into South India and establish an important Jain community there.

Buddhists above all benefited from Mauryan rule, especially during the reign of Candragupta's grandson, Aśoka (*ca.* 269–232 B.C.). Aśoka followed the expansionist policies of his father and grandfather until, in his ninth year as emperor, he conquered the territory of Kalinga in eastern India at a terrible cost in human lives and destruction. Soon afterward, Aśoka began to set forth a new policy in edicts engraved on rocks and pillars throughout his realm. Addressing his people in unique confessionals, he expressed his distress at the misery caused by his warfare and dedicated himself thereafter to a "rule of righteousness (*dharma*)." He renounced further wars of conquest and substituted conquest by righteousness as defined by the Buddhists. For the rest of his reign, Aśoka used his powers as king to promote both the Buddhist movement and the welfare of his people.

Aśoka's edicts indicate little knowledge or concern for the fine points of Buddhist doctrine. His overriding interest was instead those Buddhist teachings that could be adopted and put into practice by all his subjects. He stressed the value of compassion, liberality, truth, and perhaps above all *ahiṃsā,* noninjury to living beings. His general concern for righteousness is indicated by his donations to Ājīvakas, who were bitter rivals of the Buddhists, and his praise of worthy Brāhmans as well as Buddhist monks. He encouraged his subjects to pay attention to *all* teachers of righteousness no matter what their label.

It was nevertheless the Buddhists who gained most from Aśoka's policies, both directly and indirectly. Aśoka promoted Buddhist missionary efforts and provided the means for expansion of the movement throughout the Mauryan Empire and beyond. The power and resources of the empire were committed to his new Buddhist-oriented "conquest of righteousness," which must have greatly increased Buddhist prestige and aided Buddhist missionary activity.

But without denying the personal contribution of Aśoka, it is clear that the Buddhist way could not have flourished unless it met the needs of the time. And, though Buddhists were given a decided boost by Aśoka, the greatest Buddhist achievements came not during his reign but in the centuries of chaos, warfare, and foreign invasion that followed the breakup of the Mauryan Empire less than fifty years after Aśoka's death. Asoka's policies in that sense failed. His goal had not been solely the advancement of Buddhism, but the integration of the Mauryan Empire. He had set a standard to be followed by all rulers of his time and afterward, and remained a model of what a good ruler should be. The disparate regions and peoples of India could not be held together by political policies, however, no matter how benevolent or wisely administered. Integration had been greatly advanced by Mauryan rule, but the structures were not yet available to sustain it.

Religion and Art in the Post-Mauryan Period

The Mauryan Empire disintegrated rapidly after Aśoka's death around 232 B.C. Regional kingdoms divided the old Mauryan territory in the south, Magadha declined into obscurity, and most of North India passed into the hands of invaders from the northwest. Greeks from the former Greco-Persian province of Bactria (northern Afghanistan) gained control of most of the Indus Valley and established Greek kingdoms throughout the area. By the middle of the first century B.C., the Greek kingdoms were supplanted by an invasion of Scythian or Śaka tribes from northern Iran and Central Asia. Śakas established their rule as far south as modern Gujarat and on into central India as far as the city of Ujjain, which became a major Śaka center.

Śaka rule in the far northwest was then replaced by Parthians or Pahlavas from Iran who captured Bactria and extended their conquest into the area known as Gandhāra in the upper Indus Valley. Parthia was an important link in trade between the Roman Empire and Asia, and Greek and Roman influence flowed along the trade routes into Gandhāra. Under the great Parthian king Gondophares in the early first century A.D., the city of Taxila in Gandhāra became a major center of Greek or Hellenistic culture in India.

Both Śakas and Parthians were replaced as rulers in northern India later in the first century A.D. by new invaders, the Kushāns. The Kushāns were a nomadic tribe from Central Asia like the earlier Śakas. Moving down from the north, they settled first in Bactria, where they absorbed Greek culture and adopted the Greek alphabet used in their inscriptions. They then moved into India, conquered Gandhāra, and established an empire that lasted until the third century A.D. North India as far east as Mathurā on the Jumna River came under Kushān control. Under the greatest Kushān king, Kanishka (*ca.* A.D. 100), the empire extended from Mathurā through northwest India to the Central Asian borders of the Han Empire of China.

These widespread political changes severely challenged the defenders of Brahmanical orthodoxy. The sacrificial tradition, already greatly weakened during the period of Mauryan rule, was even less suited to conditions created by the rise to power of foreign rulers. Though many foreign rulers were sympathetic to Indian traditions, they themselves were considered impure by orthodox Brāhmans and thus outside the Brahmanical scheme of things. Their personal involvement was thus largely with the more open and less orthodox sects, especially the Buddhists who received by far their greatest interest and support.

Without caste restrictions or Brahmanical standards of purity, resolutely anti-Vedic, and teaching an ethical way of life free in its essentials from traditional gods and rituals, Buddhists were less bound by their native culture than any other Indian religious group. The piety and powers of Buddhist monks inspired respect, and the subtle simplicity of Buddhist teachings made them readily accessible to foreigners. The Buddhist cause prospered during the period of foreign rule.

Other religious movements also benefited from foreign rule, though not to the extent of the Buddhists. Foremost among these were the popular theistic movements developing on the fringes of Brahmanical orthodoxy. As early as the second century B.C., an ambassador named Heliodorus from one of the new Greek kingdoms described himself as a Bhāgavata, a worshiper of the Indian deity Vāsudeva, and erected a commemorative column in honor of the deity at Besnagar in central India. Both the Parthian ruler Gondophanes and later Kushān rulers circulated coins bearing images of the Indian god later known as Śiva; and the Kushān ruler Kadphises II, in the second century A.D., circulated coins describing himself as a devotee of this popular deity. A stone carving from Mathurā around A.D. 150 shows two men wearing Kushān clothing worshipping a *lingam,* the later omnipresent symbol of Śiva. Clearly, distinct from both Brahmanical orthodoxy and the earlier non-Vedic movements, new religious patterns were emerging.

Religious changes during the Mauryan and post-Mauryan period were paralleled by developments in art. Here we have another clear contrast with the Vedic tradition, which was fundamentally aniconic. The overwhelming interest in the Vedas was in sound, not visual representation, and Brahmanical religion made no use of anthropomorphic images. We know from evidence in the Indus cities that certain art forms had been highly developed before the Aryan influx, and almost certainly popular or folk art had a place among both Aryan and non-Aryan people. But though some of this art may have had religious significance at the popular level, it was of no interest or value to the Vedic priesthood.

After the end of the Indus Civilization, we have no evidence of Indian art until the Mauryan period. Though sculpture in perishable materials must have been produced in the intervening millennium, the first examples of sculpture in India since the days of the Indus Civilization are on the capitals of pillars erected by Aśoka to honor the Buddha. Both the styles of the animals carved on the Aśokan pillars and the use of stone sculpture itself point to Persian or Hellenistic influences. These influences brought forth a flood of artistic activity, most evident in the widespread use of sculpted stone figures and engraved scenes from the life of the Buddha to decorate the gateways around Buddhist stupas or burial mounds.

In early sculpture of this sort dating from around the middle of the second century B.C., the Buddha was not represented in human form; since he had passed out of phenomenal existence, his presence in the scenes was indicated only by symbols such as an empty throne, the wheel of the law, or a Bodhi tree. This principle of older monastic Buddhism was gradually altered, however, by popular interest in veneration of the person of the Buddha. Around the end of the first century A.D., images of the Buddha himself were created for the first time.

Here again foreign influence was evident. Some of the earliest images came from Gandhāra in northwest India, an area of maximum foreign contact for several centuries. One of the first portrayals of the Buddha in human form is found on a coin issued by Kanishka, where Hellenistic influence is obvious not only in the appearance of the figure but in the accompanying Greek label: BODDO. Gandhāra sculptures of the Buddha in the round from the same period show the Buddha dressed in a Roman toga with the face and form of Apollo. Although later generations of Indian craftsmen modified the style along more indigenous lines, classical or Hellenistic elements were evident in many Buddha images for centuries afterward.

Foreign influence was not always so direct. In many instances only the use of stone as a medium was borrowed from foreign example, with little attempt to copy foreign style. As they did in early Buddhist gateway sculpture, Indian artists often transferred existing styles and subjects, though at first with some awkwardness, to the new nonperishable material. Affluence must also have been a factor, since work in stone was expensive and time-consuming and could be carried out on a large scale only with sustained support. At any rate the earliest and best examples of stone sculpture in indigenous styles are found either in major Buddhist or Jain cultic centers or in the cities that prospered under foreign rule.

One such city was Mathurā on the Jumna River, an important Jain center and a political capital under both Śakas and Kushāns. Greek writers state that a god whom they called Heracles—probably an early form of Vishnu—was popular in Mathurā, and they refer to an image of this god carried in front of Indian troops advancing against Alexander. Stone was probably not being used that early, but statues of gods were clearly well developed. By the late first century B.C., Jains in Mathurā were making stone plaques showing seated "ford-makers" in meditation. Buddhists, perhaps inspired by this example, began to carve images of the Buddha in stone.

The earliest of these Mathurā Buddha images probably predated the Buddha images of Gandhāra and were in any event stylistically independent. Their model was not the realistic Hellenistic style of the northwest but the more smoothly rounded, fleshy, and idealized style found on the early Buddhist gateways and on Jain decorative sculpture in Mathurā itself, a style that is certainly indigenous and may even date back over an undocumented gap of nearly two thousand years to the art of the Indus Civilization and its successive cultures.

The developments in Mathurā and Gandhāra were soon widely imitated. Not only was the development and propagation of Buddha images continued, but other religious groups, particularly the emerging Hindu theistic sects, also began to produce stone images and sculpture honoring their special deities. Standard features were developed for these figures to distinguish the various subjects one from another and to identify the special qualities of each. Some of the iconographic details were undoubtedly older than the use of stone images; others were added as the traditions themselves grew more complex and as images became increasingly more important in Indian religious life.

The development of Buddha images seems to have been typical of the general trend. These visual representations were primarily intended to aid meditation, to concentrate the devotee's attention on the special qualities and accomplishments of the Buddha. Emphasis was thus placed not only on the aesthetics of the sculpture but on the iconographic details that provided a catalog of the Buddha's powers and functions. Hellenistic influence somewhat obscured this purpose in early Gandhāran images, but the images from Mathurā show from the beginning a careful attention to the Buddha's *lakṣanas,* the characteristic marks or signs of the Enlightened One, and to the *mudrās,* the positions of the hands that designate the powers or functions represented by a given image.

Even the earliest images discovered show evidence of standardization of form, *lakṣanas* and *mudrās*. This again points to the likely production of earlier images in perishable materials and the gradual development of standard figures and symbols. Images of Śiva and of the various deities associated with Vishnu show the same pattern of standardization. Texts dated as early as the fourth century B.C. confirm this circumstantial evidence with references to images and image worship. The great grammarian Pāṇini (fourth century B.C.) refers specifically to images of Śiva and Skanda and to the worship of Vāsudeva, an early form of Vishnu. Texts from this period refer also to "houses of the gods," an indication that images were not only made and worshiped but that they were placed in special houses or shelters that prefigured the later Hindu temples.

All of this indicates the emergence from the time of the Mauryans onward of popular religious traditions quite different from the older Vedic systems and from the older Buddhist movement as well. The result within the Buddhist movement was the gradual development of the Mahāyāna, Buddhism of "the great vehicle," with its emphasis on the saving power of heavenly Buddhas and Bodhisattvas.

Both the Mahāyāna stress on divine compassion and human devotion and the sophisticated idealist philosophy worked out by Mahāyāna scholars had enormous influence on later Indian religious thought. The continuing strength of Mahāyāna, however, was outside India; and, like the older form of Buddhism, it had largely died out in its homeland by the eighth or ninth centuries A.D. The development of greatest long-term importance for India was the gradual emergence of a variety of popular gods and forms of worship which eventually merged with the older Brahmanical system to become what we call Hinduism.

Summary: The Challenge to Brahmanical Religion

The old base of priestly power, knowledge and control of the sacrifice, was seriously threatened by the developments of the Mauryan and post-Mauryan period. The threat is illustrated by Aśoka's assumption of a universal standard of righteousness applicable to all men regardless of religious sect or social class. Caught between the public power and prestige of kings and the high ethical standards of monks and ascetics, ritual priests found it hard to defend their claim to superiority. Brāhmans still received respect, but that respect increasingly had to be earned by proven worth. The effectiveness of the fire sacrifice remained largely unchallenged, but its ultimate value was questioned even within the Brahmanical system by the Upanishadic emphasis on knowledge and asceticism. As long as the Brahmanical tradition remained unaltered, rival systems continued to attract large numbers of followers.

The necessary Brahmanical alterations were not long in coming, though their effectiveness was obscured for centuries during the height of Buddhist and Jain popularity. The new Brahmanism had several overlapping emphases: development of techniques of meditation and means of release as practical and as experientially based as those of the Buddhists and Jains; accommodation to the great popular interest in anthropomorphic gods and images; and concern for the ongoing life of society, largely ignored by the Buddhists and ascetic groups. These emphases together undercut popular support for the non-Vedic movements and established the Brahmanical system once more at the center of the Indian religious life, but this time with much greater openness and flexibility and with much greater popular involvement. It is to the characteristics of this new Brahmanism, the Hindu tradition, that we now must turn our attention.

5.
The New Brahmanical Synthesis

The Brahmanical system had never been static. The Vedic texts reflect a dynamic process of growth and innovation from the early hymn collections through the Brāhmaṇas, Āraṇyakas, and Upanishads. Development of the fire sacrifice, accommodation to the doctrine of rebirth, and acceptance of asceticism all had involved major changes in the tradition. The new conditions of the Mauryan and post-Mauryan period stimulated further growth and adaptation, evidenced in the many basic Brahmanical works produced during this period. Obscured behind the more dramatic political events of this period and the more obvious successes of the non-Vedic movements, a revitalized Brahmanical tradition was developing.

Yoga in the Late Upanishads

Some of the first signs of the new Brahmanical tradition are found in the late Upanishads, those written after 500 B.C. There is no clear break between these and the earlier Upanishads, but the religious currents of the Mauryan and post-Mauryan period are reflected in several important new teachings that parallel developments outside the Vedic tradition. One of the most important of these teachings concerned yoga, "discipline," applied in the Upanishads specifically to techniques of mental discipline.

The practice of mental disciplines was much older than the Upanishadic descriptions of yoga. The Buddha's meditation involved systematic control of mental processes, and his practices in turn were based on even older techniques of mind control. Many of these practices, however, were associated with world views, such as the Buddha's denial of a permanent self, that were incompatible with the Upanishads. Brahmanical acceptance of meditation techniques required an interpretation that fit the Upanishadic view of the self and did not contradict basic Vedic principles.

An acceptable interpretation was provided probably for the first time in the *Kaṭha Upanishad,* where the human body is compared to a chariot driven by a charioteer (the intellect) using the mind as reins to control the senses. The self in this analogy (*Kaṭha Upanishad* I.3.3–9) is said to ride in the body as a passenger rides in a chariot, his journey determined by the charioteer's control. The analogy states several important principles. There is, first, a clear difference between the self and its vehicle, the body. Second, and of great importance for later developments, there is a hierarchy of controls within the body: the intellect (*buddhi*), by means of understanding, controls the mind; and the mind, acting as a rein, controls the senses. Third, and of equal importance, the self may serve as a stimulus to control but is not itself directly involved. Yoga, the discipline of the senses, mind, and intellect, involves only the body; yoga is the discipline that the higher powers of the body enforce upon the lower ones. The goal, as *Kaṭha* II.3.10–11 states, is to bring the whole body to a state of quiescence so that the self may be truly free, no longer distracted by the unrushing senses, mind, and intellect.

The statement in the *Kaṭha Upanishad* is relatively undeveloped. Later Upanishads developed the view of yoga further, elaborating both the analysis of the body and the techniques of discipline by which the body can be controlled. The *Śvetāśvatara Upanishad,* for example, not only refers to yoga and its effects but describes how it should be practiced:

> Holding the body steady with the three upper parts [head, neck, and chest] erect, causing the senses to enter into the heart by means of the mind,
> The wise man with the boat of Brahman should cross all the streams that bring fear.
>
> Suppressing the breaths here in the body, his movements controlled, he should breathe through his nostrils with diminished breath.
> As he would a chariot yoked to bad horses, so should a wise man vigilantly restrain his mind.
>
> (*Śvetāśvatara Upanishad* II.8–9)

Several of the basic characteristics of the later formal yoga are described in this passage: proper bodily stability in an erect seated position (*āsana,* "sitting"); withdrawal of the senses from external contact (*pratyāhāra,* "withdrawal"); and slow regular breathing through the nostrils, gradually lengthening the periods of exhaling and inhaling until breathing is almost totally suppressed (*prāṇāyāma,* "breath-restraint"). Another late Upanishad, the *Maitrī,* adds the further stages of meditation (*dhyāna*), concentration (*dhāraṇā*), and absorption (*samādhi*), and asserts that, in the final merger of thought into nonthought, the "subtle body" will be left with no support (*Maitrī Upanishad* VI.18–19).

It is evident from these passages that by the time of the late Upanishads there was an established procedure of mental control by which a state of heightened consciousness could be reached. The basic element in this procedure was controlled breathing leading to control of the *prāṇās,* the breaths or powers that activate the body. By perfecting breath control one could control the senses; by bringing the senses to rest one could gradually control the activity of the mind; and by controlling mental processes one could pass through a succession of stages in which the activities of the mind are more and more restricted—first to a limited area of concentration, then to uninterrupted contemplation of a single object of thought, and finally to a state in which the distinction between the mind and its object is eliminated and there is only pure undistracted consciousness devoid of all mental activity.

In the final stage of yoga, everything that is nonself is brought to rest. The self is finally freed from the "subtle body" consisting of psychomental processes with which the self is normally, but erroneously, identified. The self is left in a state which the *Maitrī Upanishad* variously describes as "release" (*mokṣa*) or "isolation" (*kevalatva*). In this totally unqualified state, the true blissful nature of the self becomes clear; there is no distinction between the self and Brahman, for the self no less than Brahman is pure, limitless, and unchanging.

The primary purpose of yoga is to attain this state of superconsciousness. From this perspective, however, there is knowledge not only of the self but of the nonself from which the self is freed. This knowledge, though irrelevant to the freed self, is important in the early stages of yoga as a guide or caution for those still caught up in the phenomenal world of nature. Since it is by control of natural processes that the body is finally brought to rest, discussions of yoga came to include also discussion of the world of nature and the human person.

The most complete explanation of the natural world and man is found in the *Śvetāśvatara Upanishad,* which attempts to relate the One, Brahman, to the multiplicity of the world. According to this view (in *Śvetāśvatara* I.8–16 and VI.1–18), Brahman is manifested in three modes: the Lord, the self, and Nature. Nature, Prakṛiti, the field of enjoyment or involvement of the self, is female; consisting of the three elements of fire, water, and earth, she continuously produces manifold offspring. The stimulus of this creation is the female power (*śakti*) of the Lord, the active self-power of the divine. This power is hidden in the world in the midst of the three qualities (*guṇas*) of the Lord: purity or goodness (*sattva*), passion (*rajas*), and darkness or inertia (*tamas*). The interaction of these qualities under the stimulus of *śakti* brings about a combination of the elements of Prakṛiti, producing the manifold world.

The self in ignorance becomes attached to the world of Prakṛiti as an "enjoyer," desiring the fruits of Prakṛiti. As an enjoyer, the self takes on the characteristics of the three qualities (*guṇas*) of *sattva, rajas,* and *tamas,* and by doing so becomes immersed in Nature and caught up in its processes. Fundamental to those processes is the perpetuation of karmic effects, a process in which the self becomes entangled through its attachment to the field of enjoyment.

> He who has qualities [*guṇas*] is a doer of deeds that bear fruit and an enjoyer of what he has done;
> Following the three paths (of the gods, the fathers, and men), characterized by the three *guṇas* and assuming all forms, he roams about [in successive rebirths] according to his actions.
> The embodied one [the self immersed in Nature] chooses forms—gross and subtle, and many in number—according to his qualities;
> Because of his union with these forms brought about by the qualities of his actions and of his embodied self, he is seen as something other than he is.
> He is released from all his bondage when he comes to know God, the one

embracer of all this universe, who in the midst of chaos is without beginning and end, who, having manifold form, is the creator of all this. (*Śvetāśvatara* V.7, 12–13)

Yoga, from this persepective, is the means by which the self can be extricated from Nature. It is the embodied self that passes through the endless cycle of rebirths, having taken on the qualities of Prakṛiti and the characteristics of an enjoyer. This is not the true self, but it is mistaken for the self until the qualities are stripped away and the true self is revealed.

Yoga achieves its goal by a controlled disengagement of the self from Prakṛiti, gradually eliminating the increasingly subtle influences and activities of the *guṇas*. This disengagement begins with withdrawal of the senses and proceeds to control of the mind, the storehouse of sense perceptions. It is not complete until even the most refined activities of the intellect are recognized as the products of Prakṛiti and the *guṇas,* and the consciousness is cleansed of these last most subtle attachments to the nonself.

What is the basic effort and goal of yoga? There is no single answer in the late Upanishads, and no formal unified system. The *Śvetāśvatara* at times advocates meditation on the form of God, at other times advocates yoga leading to knowledge of the pure unqualified Brahman or the undifferentiated self, at still other times affirms the knowledge of God free of all qualities as both the goal of yoga and the means by which God and the self are distinguished from Prakṛiti. The *Maitrī* offers further interpretations, interweaving its discussion of yoga with a reinterpretation of older Upanishadic and ritualistic principles that often seem inconsistent with its statements about yoga and Prakṛiti.

Consistency, however, is not the most important test of these texts. Like the equally inconsistent early Upanishads, their value lay in the new forms of thought and practice which they introduced into the Vedic system. Yoga was an important link to developments outside the older Brahmanical circles. Given Vedic sanction in the Upanishads, it provided a means of release that rivaled Buddhist meditation without compromising the concepts of Brahman and *ātman*. The openendedness of the Upanishadic acceptance of yoga, providing as it did a variety of viewpoints and points of departure, was a major factor in the success of the new Brahmanical synthesis.

The Yoga of Patañjali's Yoga Sūtras

Yoga was developed in a variety of ways in the post-Upanishadic period, both as an adjunct of other systems and as an independent means of release. It was given classical form as an independent system in the *Yoga Sūtras* of Patañjali, dating probably from the early centuries A.D. Patañjali's system reflects major refinements in theory and practice over the yoga of the late Upanishads. Further refined in commentaries and philosophical texts, it was the basis for one of the six recognized *darśanas* ("viewpoints," or philosophical systems) of later times.

Yoga is defined in Patañjali's system as *citta-vṛitti-nirodha,* "the suppression of the modifications of the mind (*citta*)." The goal is a state of pure consciousness in *samādhi,* undisturbed by psycho-mental processes or by any object of awareness. This is the purified consciousness of the self (the *puruṣa* in Patanjali's terminology), freed of the influence of the *guṇas* of Prakṛiti. It can be reached only by controlling and finally suppressing altogether the modifications of Prakṛiti that constitute mental activity.

The means to this goal is the "eightfold yoga" (*aṣṭāṅga yoga*) described in the *Yoga Sūtras.* The eight stages of this yoga represent a movement from external to internal control. External causes of mental distraction are eliminated in the first five stages, beginning with *yama* ("restraint") and *niyama* ("observance"). *Yama* (abstention from violence, falsehood, theft, incontinence and acquisitiveness) and *niyama* (purity, contentment, austerity, study, and dedication of actions to the Lord) lay the necessary moral foundation of yoga and remove the disturbances caused by uncontrollable emotions and desires. External discipline is completed by *āsana* ("sitting" or "posture") and *prāṇāyāma* ("breath control"), which remove disturbances caused by the physical body, and *pratyāhāra* ("withdrawal of the senses"), which detaches the mind from the sense-organs and leaves it isolated from the external world.

The goal of yoga is reached by internal control of the mind in the final three stages, referred to collectively as *saṃyama. Dhāraṇā* ("concentration"), the first stage of *saṃyama,* focuses the mind on a particular object of thought and confines it within a limited area. *Dhyāna* ("contemplation" or "meditation") then stabilizes the mind in an uninterrupted state of concentration on the object. In the first level of *samādhi* that follows, the awareness of a subject-object distinction is eliminated and there is consciousness only of the object of meditation. The mind is still fixed in a particular pattern by the object of consciousness, but all distractions and movements of the mind have been eliminated.

In the final level of *samādhi,* the object of consciousness is suppressed and all influence of Prakṛiti is removed. This is the state of *samādhi* "without seed," pure consciousness devoid of any object of consciousness, in which the self is isolated from even the most subtle mental forms of Prakṛiti. The self, freed to itself, exists in perfect self-consciousness.

Patañjali's yoga system, though similar in outline to the yoga of the late Upanishads, is distinguished by its acceptance of the dualistic *sāṃkhya* view of the world. There are, in this view, an infinite number of selves or *puruṣas,* each eternally distinct from the others and eternally distinct from Prakṛiti. Release of each *puruṣa* from Prakṛiti is brought about by the mental discipline of yoga alone, without the agency of a god, and the condition of *kevalatva* or "isolation" that results is permanent. Prakṛiti, also eternal, remains with its *guṇas* and modifications, but the *puruṣa* is free of its effects. In this condition, and this condition only, there is eternal bliss. The system in this respect differs from the Upanishadic ideal of union with Brahman, and differs as well from the goal of theism that also had its origin in the late Upanishads, though it shares with them a concern for release from the miseries and afflictions (called *kleśas* in the *Yoga Sūtras*) that characterize ignorant attachment to worldly existence.

Theism in the Late Upanishads

The goal of the early Upanishads was to become one with the highest Brahman, the Absolute beyond name and form. The highest knowledge was knowledge of the impersonal *nirguṇa* Brahman, Brahman "without qualities," and it was only this knowledge that brought release. The late Upanishads, however, reflecting the increased importance of popular gods, show much greater interest in the personal aspect of Brahman. This interest was expressed in the form of a new theism that merged the cosmic importance of the older Upanishadic Brahman-*ātman* with the appeal of personal gods.

Early Upanishadic thinkers viewed the gods of the Vedic ritual tradition as belonging to the phenomenal world; they were "the gods" in contrast to the cosmic reality of Brahman, "the many" in contrast to the One. Brahman was not a god or *deva* but the Absolute, the Real, knowledge of which freed men from attachment to the world and its gods. This point, once established, undercut the entire Vedic pantheon.

The Absolute did have a personal side, indicated by references to Brahman as "this Person" (*Aitareya Upanishad* I.3.13) or "the immortal Person" (*Bṛihadāraṇyaka Upanishad* II.5). Identified with the masculine personal *ātman,* the neuter Brahman was described as "the ruler of all" and "the king of all" (*Bṛihadāraṇyaka* IV.4.22); Brahman as the self was "the Inner Controller" (*Bṛihadāraṇyaka* III.7.3–23), the One "in the form of a person" (*Bṛihadāraṇyaka* I.4.1) from whom all this was created. These terms, however, defined only the personalized aspects of Brahman and not a *deva* in the older Vedic sense. The personal Brahman was always secondary, and never had the characteristics of a clearly defined personal god.

Development of Upanishadic theism occurred only when the personal aspects of Brahman where transferred to a god already well established in both priestly and popular religion. The initial choice was Rudra, who became in the *Śvetāśvatara Upanishad* a new kind of god, identified with Brahman, but having at the same time a distinct set of personal qualities derived from sources outside the Upanishads and, to some extent, from outside the Vedic tradition itself.

Rudra had long since grown beyond his relatively minor status as a malevolent deity in the *Rig Veda.* Already in the *Yajur Veda* he had been given the names Śaṃbhu ("Benign"), Śaṃkara ("Beneficent"), and Śiva ("Auspicious"). The *Śatapatha Brāhmaṇa* described how Rudra won a portion of the sacrificial offering previously denied him, and the *Kauśītaki Brāhmaṇa* explained how Rudra, born of the semen of the gods, was given the names Bhava ("the Existent"), Paśupati ("Lord of Creatures"), Mahādeva ("the Great God"), and

Īśāna ("the Ruler"). Special domestic rituals were directed to Rudra where he was given the additional name of Hara ("the Bearer" and/or "the Destroyer"), one of the more common later names of Rudra-Śiva.

By the time of the late Upanishads, Rudra had become one of the major gods of the Vedic tradition. He had also become the center of a growing synthesis of Brahmanical and popular religion. Many of the names given to Rudra in Vedic texts connected him with gods worshiped on the popular level, and much of his importance must have come from these associations. His popularity was, in any event, sufficient to single him out for even greater attention in the new Upanishadic theism.

The characteristics of Upanishadic theism in its formative stage can probably best be examined in the *Śvetāśvatara Upanishad,* where also are found some of the earliest statements on yoga. The *Śvetāśvatara* is concerned with release from *saṃsāra* as were the older Upanishads, but its approach to release is openly theistic: salvation comes not from knowledge of the impersonal Brahman, but from knowledge of the personal Lord identified as Rudra or Śiva. Rudra-Śiva is not just *a* god, one among many; he is *the* God, the personal manifestation of Brahman as ruler of the world and of the self.

A new metaphysical system and a new doctrine of salvation were developed around this theistic focus. There are, according to the *Śvetāśvatara,* three "unborn ones": the Lord, knowing and all-powerful; the individual *ātman,* unknowing and powerless; and Nature, Prakṛiti, made up of primary matter. In terms of relationships, this triad can be described as the Mover or Impeller (the Lord), the enjoyer (the individual self), and the object of enjoyment (Nature, or primary matter). Brahman, the infinite Self, encompasses these three aspects but is itself inactive.

Salvation for the individual self occurs by a change in the relationships within the triad. The self in his true nature is immortal and unchanging, but through ignorance he is attached to changeable matter. Not knowing the Lord, the self has become bound to Nature as an enjoyer—like a bird sitting in a tree eating its sweet fruit, like a male delighting in an ever-productive female (Prakṛiti). To become free, he must break his bondage; he must give up the fruit, leave the female with whom he has had enjoyment. This can happen only if he comes to know the Lord, the ruler of both the self and changeable Nature, all-powerful but uninvolved and content:

> The Lord (*Īśa*) supports all this which has been joined together—the changeable [Nature] and the unchangeable [the self], the manifest and the unmanifest; but the self, not being the Lord [or without the Lord] is bound because he is an enjoyer. Knowing God, he is freed from all fetters. (*Śvetāśvatara* I.8)

Knowledge of the Lord comes through meditation (*dhyāna*). Here the *Śvetāśvatara* makes a significant shift in the Upanishadic concept of knowledge. Saving knowledge is not knowledge of the impersonal Brahman but of the personal Lord, and it is gained by coming to know Him as resident within one's self. This is explained by means of an analogy: the form (*mūrti*) of fire is present in wood, even though it is not seen; it becomes visible when the friction of the drill used to make fire brings it forth. So meditation on the sound syllable *oṃ,* the seed mantra of the Lord, brings forth the vision of the Lord hidden in the self:

> By practicing the friction of meditation, making one's own body the lower friction-stick and the syllable *oṃ* the upper friction-stick, one may see God who is, as it were, hidden [within the body]. (*Śvetāśvatara* I.14)

Once the *mūrti* of the Lord is known within the self, the ignorance that kept the self in bondage is broken. No longer does he seek enjoyment of Nature out of weakness, for he knows that the Lord who rules Nature is present in his own self. Directing his thoughts and feelings to this all-powerful and unchanging Lord, uniting with Him through constant meditation, he loses attachment to the world.

The world deludes with its promise of satisfaction. It is really only a great magic show, produced by the magical creative power, the *māyā,* of the Lord. Nature (Prakṛiti), the product of the great Magician's power, has the characteristics of *māyā;* it beguiles and fascinates, but is ephemeral. Only in the Lord is there true permanence and peace, so the wise man turns away from the world to Him.

> Primary Matter is perishable, Hara [Rudra-Śiva, the Lord] is immortal and imperishable; the One God rules both the perishable and the self. By concentrating on Him through meditation and by coming more and more to His true essence, there is in the end cessation of all *māyā.*
> Knowing God, there is a falling off of all fetters; with afflictions destroyed, there is cessation of birth and death; from meditation on Him there is, thirdly, universal lordship at the time of separation from the body. Being absolute [alone, unconnected, *kevala*], the desire [of the self] is satisfied.
> That Eternal residing in the self should be known; truly there is nothing greater than it to be known. When one realizes the enjoyer, the object of enjoyment, and the Impeller (the Lord), everything has been explained; this is the threefold Brahman. (*Śvetāśvatara* I.10–12)

This is the core of the *Śvetāśvatara*'s position. It is important to note the many elements that have been brought together in its formulation: the Vedic Brahman and *ātman* and the Upanishadic goal of release by knowledge; a personal God who is not only the prime object of knowledge for men seeking release but also the creator and ruler of the world in which they are entangled; and a method (*dhyāna,* "meditation") by which individuals can know God and gain release from the world.

The synthesis of these elements in the *Śvetāśvatara* had great importance for later Hindu theism. Its value was obviously more immediate and direct for worshipers of Rudra-Śiva, since to the extent that God is identified he is given the names and qualities of Śiva. The theistic principle, however, could be—and was—applied to the worship of any personal god. What was essential was not the specific identity of the Lord but his accessibility through meditation. It was this that distinguished all later theism from the earlier worship of Vedic gods and greatly influenced the way in which popular gods were absorbed into the post-Vedic Brahmanical system.

Vedic sacrificial religion was aniconic. Visual representations of the gods had no place in Vedic rituals, and the physical appearance of the gods was seldom even a matter of interest. Attention was directed instead to the powers and functions of the gods. These, as we have seen, were eventually taken over by the fire sacrifice, where both the powers and the gods were represented by ritual mantras. Distinctions between both gods and powers were related to variations in the meters and sounds of mantras; the sound-form was all-important, since from it everything else could be produced.

The culmination of this trend came in the *Chāndogya Upanishad,* where *one* sound, the syllable *oṃ* or *auṃ,* is said to stand for *all* sounds and thus for the entire universe. As the three Vedas are the essence of the worlds, and the three syllables *bhūr, bhuvaḥ,* and *svar* are the essence of the Vedas, so *oṃ* is the essence of the syllables:

> As all leaves are held together by a stalk, so all speech is held together by *oṃ.* Verily, the syllable *oṃ* is all this [created universe], yea, it is all this. (*Chāndogya* II.23.3)

In sharp contrast to the Vedic pattern, popular religion was strongly iconic. There is no clear evidence to date the earliest use of images and other icons representing the gods of popular worship, but it is likely that image making, at least in perishable materials, was continuous from pre-Aryan times onward. The early stone images of Buddha and the Jain *tīrthaṅkaras* in Mathurā were already iconographically mature by the first century A.D., indicating a considerable prior development of images in other materials. Developed images of Śiva and of gods later associated with Vishnu are recorded from about the same time, along with images of a host of local and minor deities.

It was in this context that the *Śvetāśvatara*'s teaching on meditation assumed such significance. Meditation, the friction that brings forth the fire of the inner vision, involves concentration on the syllable *oṃ,* the essence of all Vedic mantras. What this produces, however, is something distinctly non-Vedic. Meditation enables one to see God's *mūrti,* His physical form, which is hidden within man's self. The procedure of meditation may involve Vedic mantras, but the goal is a mental image, the internal *mūrti* of God, whose characteristics could not have come from the aniconic Vedic tradition but only from popular religious traditions that made use of visual representations of the gods.

As the Āraṇyakas and early Upanishads had internalized the fire sacrifice by emphasizing its mental performance, so the late Upanishads now internalized images. What had, in both instances, been expressed by means of external physical symbols was now expressed by mental performance in meditation. The two were, moreover, brought together in the *Śvetāśvatara* by a conjunction of their most essential characteristics: meditation using the syllable *oṃ,* the sound essence of the Vedic sacrifice, led to the appearance of the *mūrti,* the visual essence of non-Vedic image worship. This synthesis, beautiful in its simplicity and completeness, remained in the tradition from this point onward as the primary form of Brahmanical theism.

Karma and Dharma in the Brahmanical Tradition

Development of yoga and theism within the Vedic tradition provided an important counterthrust to the intellectual and religious challenge of the non-Vedic movements and created a much broader base for the Brahmanical system. These teachings, however, still represented the traditional Upanishadic concern for knowledge leading to release. Most men were not prepared for final knowledge; their problem was how to live in society and work toward what was for them a desired but distant goal. The great strength of the new Brahmanical synthesis was its unique ability to deal with the practical concerns of this majority.

The Brahmanical synthesis as it applied to men in society was based not so much on *orthodoxy,* "right teaching," as on *orthopraxis,* "right practice" in accord with priestly social and ritual standards. The details of these standards had been gradually worked out from the time of the Brāhmaṇas onward, but in the period after 500 B.C. there was a great increase in the number of texts dealing with the duties of men in everyday life. The result was a large body of Brahmanical teachings on social as well as ritual responsibilities. These responsibilities were collectively called *dharma,* "that which is established," or in more specific terms, "what men ought to do."

In the early Vedas and Brāhmaṇas, "what men ought to do" was defined largely in terms of proper actions in the sacrificial ritual. The identities established in texts such as *Rig Veda* X.90, however, led to a much broader concept of ritual action. These identities affirmed in particular the parallelism between the ritual order, the cosmic order, and the order of society. The orders were integrally related in such a way that actions in one order were equivalent to actions in the others; actions in society, properly understood, are both ritual actions and cosmic actions. *Dharma,* what men ought to do, thus could not be confined to the circumscribed set of ritual actions in the fire sacrifice; it had to include all actions by which men express and define their place in the cosmos.

The Upanishadic doctrines of *karma* and rebirth were important in the development of this line of Brahmanical thought. For both Yājñavalkya and Uddālaka, *all* actions had continuing effects and *all* were important in determining the future conditions of the embodied self. Sacrificial actions in accordance with Vedic injunctions brought specific practical rewards, but the totality of men's actions determined the conditions of their rebirth and their progress toward release. If these conditions were to be controlled, men needed guides to what they ought to do in all the areas of their activity.

Guidance for this purpose was provided in a series of Brahmanical texts classified as *karma-kāṇḍa,* "having to do with actions," as distinguished from texts such as the Upanishads which were *jñāna-kāṇḍa,* "having to do with knowledge." The oldest *karma-kāṇḍa* texts were the Brāhmaṇas, but by the seventh century B.C. these had been supplemented by texts called Kalpa Sūtras, manuals containing concise rules or *sūtras* concerning *kalpa,* "what is fitting or proper."

The earliest Kalpa Sūtras dealt with the rites and ceremonies of the Vedic Saṃhitās and Brāhmaṇas, and were classified as Śrauta Sūtras: *sūtras* relating to the *Śrauta* ceremonies of the three fires in which Vedic mantras were used. A second class of Kalpa Sūtras, however, dealt with *smṛiti,* "tradition," the much broader range of domestic and social activities. These texts, called Smārta Sūtras (*sūtras* having to do with *smṛiti*), were further subdivided into Gṛihya Sūtras, which defined the rites and procedures for domestic (*gṛihya*) rituals, and Dharma Sūtras, which took as their subject matter the entire range of *dharma,* all those modes of life and codes of conduct that regulated a person's activities as an individual and as a member of society.

The Dharma Sūtras were one of the most important developments in the entire Brahmanical tradition. The domestic rituals in the Gṛihya Sūtras were important to every householder, but the principles and practices were, for the most part, well established. The Dharma Sūtras broke new ground in establishing Brahmanical rules for the social as well as ritual activities of every member of society. Consistent standards of *dharma* were assigned to all men, making explicit the relevance of Brahmanical goals and values for all aspects of life.

The development of a *dharma* for society was completed in a class of texts called Dharma Śāstras ("treatises on *dharma*"). Starting with the rules of the Dharma Sūtras, the Dharma Śāstras gave a more complete and systematic presentation of *dharma* that did not, as the Dharma Sūtras did, depend on the authority of particular Vedic schools. The most important early Dharma Śāstras, the *Mānava-dharma-Śāstra* ("The Laws of Manu") and the *Yājñavalkya Smṛiti,* were the starting point of an independent tradition that emphasized *dharma* itself and not its Vedic origins. The dates of this development are significant, since both *Manu* (completed some time between 200 B.C. and A.D. 100) and *Yājñavalkya* (between A.D. 100 and A.D. 300) were written during the period when the Brahmanical tradition was most seriously threatened by non-Vedic movements. There is little doubt that these texts and the view of society they represent were among the most effective Brahmanical responses to that threat.

The Varṇāśrama-Dharma System

The Dharma Śāstras agreed with the Upanishads that the final goal of life was release from *saṃsāra,* but beyond this common point the emphasis was quite different. The Upanishads and the later *jñāna* tradition put primary emphasis on knowledge of Brahman and the self. Ritual and social duties were recognized but given little attention, since the seeker after final knowledge had presumably gone beyond such worldly concerns. *Dharma* texts, on the other hand, noted only in a perfunctory way the final goal of Brahman knowledge. *Manu* says more about this than other texts, but even there only a few verses in the final chapter (XXI.118–125) state the goal explicitly.

The *dharma* texts concentrated instead on the particulars of social duty. The basic focus was not the goal beyond society but the arrangement of life within the social system. The basic principle of this arrangement was summarized in the term *varṇāśrama-dharma, dharma* in accordance with *varṇa* ("class") and *āśrama* ("stage of life"). *Dharma* for any given person should be appropriate to his place in society as determined by his *varṇa* (Brāhman, Kṣatriya, Vaiśya, or Śūdra) and his stage of life as a student, a householder, a hermit who has retired to the forest, or a *sannyāsin* (a "renounced" person) who has completely severed his ties to society. Each combination of *varṇa* and *āśrama* defined a specific set of duties and responsibilities, the *dharma* for a person in that particular situation.

Two dimensions of time were involved in the system of *varṇāśrama-dharma*. *Āśramas* marked the stages of a person's development within a given lifetime, while *varnas* were related to his development throughout many lives in the course of transmigration. It was assumed that a person belonged to that *varṇa* for which he was qualified by ability and temperament as a result of his actions in past lives. Birth into a family belonging to a given *varṇa* was *de facto* evidence of the quality of his past lives. The *dharma* of that birth was the proper recompense for past actions and defined the possibilities for future development. The wise man did not question his birth; he fulfilled his present *dharma,* knowing that it suited his current level of development and would advance him toward his ultimate goal.

The metaphysical aspects of reincarnation were only marginal concerns in the *dharma* texts. Their emphasis was on the practical situation: if a person *is* a Brāhman or a Kṣatriya, a householder or a hermit, what are his duties? Both general and specific answers were given to such questions. The general answers outlined the basic categories of *dharma* as they applied to the various classes and stages of life; the specific answers dealt with acceptable behavior in the wide range of situations encountered in daily life. The latter constitute the bulk of *dharma* teachings, but it is easier to understand the *dharma* texts if we start with their general categories.

A basic distinction was made between Śūdras and the three upper *varṇas*. Brāhmans, Kṣatriyas, and Vaiśyas were Aryans and were classified as *dvijas,* "twice-born," from their initiation ("birth") into study of the Vedas. Śūdras were excluded from Vedic study and from use of Vedic mantras, and hence could neither learn about nor practice Vedic ritual. Their *dharma* was only to serve the three upper *varṇas* on which they were both economically and ritually dependent. In the allocation of duties and privileges to each of the *varṇas,* Brāhmans alone were given control of Vedic rituals and the transmission of Vedic knowledge:

> Teaching [the Vedas], studying, sacrificing, assisting to sacrifice, giving, and acceptance of gifts are the six occupations of a firstborn one [a Brāhman, "firstborn" from Brahman or from the primeval Puruṣa].
> But of the six occupations, three are his means of livelihood: assisting to sacrifice, teaching, and accepting gifts from the pure.
> Three duties belong to the Brāhman only: teaching, assisting to sacrifice, and thirdly accepting gifts [i.e., these are forbidden to the Kṣatriya and Vaiśya]. (*Manu* X.75–77)

Kṣatriyas were assigned the duties of protecting the people, giving gifts, sacrificing, and studying the Veda; their means of livelihood was "bearing weapons for striking or throwing." Vaiśyas were assigned protection of cattle, giving gifts, sacrificing, studying the Veda, trade, lending at interest, and cultivation of land, with their livelihood to be earned from cattle, trade, and cultivation. In the event of economic distress, Brāhmans were allowed to adopt the means of livelihood of Kṣatriyas or even Vaiśyas as long as they were not involved in injury to living creatures, but no one who was not a Brāhman was allowed under any circumstances to earn a living by teaching the Vedas or performing Vedic rituals.

Society was preserved by the complementary activities of ritual, rule, and economic production directed by the *dvijas. Dvijas* were given the major benefits of the social system as well as its major responsibilities, and only they participated in the full scope of the *varṇāśrama-dharma* system. Progressive passage through the *āśramas* was closed to Śūdras, since they were excluded from Vedic study. *Dvijas* by contrast began life as Vedic students, and did not in fact become *dvijas* ("twice-born ones") until the initiation into studentship that formally set them apart from the rest of society.

Students and Householders

Entry into the *āśrama* of the student or *brahmacārin* was marked by one of the most important rituals in the life of an upper class male: the *upanāyana* ceremony in which a child was initiated into Vedic study. Since a young man usually left home to live with his special teacher, the ceremony marked also the end of childhood and the transition to a new life away from his family. The age at which this occurred was established as the eighth year after conception for a Brāhman boy and the eleventh and twelfth years for Kṣatriyas and Vaiśyas, respectively. No provision was made for girls, who by the time of the Dharma Śāstras were not admitted to Vedic study.

The boy's father performed the preliminary rituals of the *upanāyana,* and the new teacher completed it, symbolizing the nature of the occasion. The initiated student was given a special name by his teacher, was taught his first

Vedic mantra, and received a wooden staff to signify his new status. By the time of the later Dharma Śāstras he also was given a "sacred thread," a cord of twisted threads looped over his left shoulder and around the right side of his body as a permanent sign of Vedic initiation.

The stipulated duration of studentship was twelve years, the time required to learn—to memorize and understand—one of the mantra collections and its Brāhmaṇa, along with subsidiary works on grammar or other special studies. During this time the student was expected to remain ritually pure and celibate, and, in addition to study, was required to tend the teacher's fires, beg for his food, and in general act as his personal servant. Studentship was no casual period of leisurely academic study, but a time of rigorous discipline during which the student learned a way of life: rituals, values, duties, and patterns of behavior. He was well prepared when he left his teacher to perpetuate both the content and the style of the tradition.

A few students specially dedicated to asceticism or scholarly activities remained all their lives in the celibate condition of *brahmacārya*. Most, however, returned to their homes, married, and settled down as householders. This must have been true of almost all Kṣatriyas and Vaiśyas, most of whom probably did not complete even the twelve years of full-time study. Those with special needs, such as princes of ruling families, usually had private tutors who trained them not only in Vedic knowledge but also in politics and military skills. Studentship was in any event more important for Brāhmans who were to teach and perform Vedic ceremonies for their livelihood than for those who needed Vedic knowledge only for personal and domestic rituals. Thus, though *upanāyana* and at least some minimal Vedic study were required for all *dvijas,* completion of the first *āśrama* with thorough Vedic knowledge probably remained an ideal standard followed most often only by Brāhmans.

There was much more complete involvement in the second *āśrama,* that of the householder or *gṛihastha*. Householdership was the keystone of the Brahmanical system. Vedic study was important, but preservation of the entire society depended on householders. In their emphasis on this stage of life, the *dharma* texts contrast sharply with the various ascetic and monastic alternatives to the Brahmanical system. Though Brahmanical studentship and the final *āśramas* of hermit and wandering ascetic were characterized by celibacy and self restraint, lay life was not downgraded because of this. Householdership was instead highly valued as the base for all other activities, and the productive and fruitful householder was given great honor by the students, teachers, priests, and ascetics whom he supported.

The householder did more than just support others, however. Householdership in the Brahmanical system was not an alternative to a genuine religious life but an essential stage of personal spiritual development. Every Brāhman was said to be born with a triple indebtedness: to the sages, to the gods, and to his ancestors. He became free of these only when he had satisfied the sages with celibacy, the gods with sacrifices, and his ancestors with a son. The first of these debts was discharged by dwelling with a teacher as a *brahmacārin,* but the offering of sacrifices mainly and the raising of sons uniquely were the duties of householders.

The Dharma Śāstras made a similar point in their discussions of the four main goals of life: *dharma, artha, kāma,* and *mokṣa. Mokṣa,* "release" from rebirth, was the supreme goal, but only a few could attain it in their present lives; for most men it was a goal to be reached in future births. The attainable goals for the majority of men were *artha* (economic and political activity) and *kāma* ("desire," especially sexual desire) within the framework set by *dharma. Dharma* applied to all *āśramas,* but *artha* and *kāma* were appropriate only for householders. The *dharma* of householders was in fact largely the fulfillment of *artha* and *kāma,* since it was the householders' production and procreation that satisfied society's debts to the gods and ancestors and supported those who preserved the tradition. Through the discipline of his *dharma,* the householder purified the desires for wealth and sensual enjoyment carried over from his past lives and transformed them into spiritual benefits for himself, his family, and society.

The Importance of Marriage

Householdership began with marriage, the most important single ritual in a person's life. The marriage age for men depended upon their period of studentship and was subject to wide variation. Men who completed a full twelve years of Vedic study would have been at least twenty before they could marry, while those who did not finish Vedic study might be several years younger. There was no requirement of immediate marriage after studentship, but social and family obligations encouraged men to marry as soon as suitable arrangements could be made.

Women did not go through the period of studentship and were generally much younger than men at the time of marriage. In the Vedic period girls seem to have been married only after they reached puberty; but, by the time of the Dharma Śāstras, at least Brāhman girls were expected to marry before puberty. The father was responsible for arranging his daughter's marriage, and late *dharma* texts accused the father of destroying an embryo each time his unmarried daughter had a menstrual period. By around the sixth or seventh century A.D. marriage came to be considered the *upanāyana* for Brāhman girls and marriage between the eighth and tenth year became the norm, though the marriages were not consummated until the wife had reached puberty.

By the time of the Dharma Śāstras women did not engage in Vedic study themselves, but acquired religious merit from their husbands. Arranging a daughter's marriage was thus a serious responsibility, especially for a Brāhman family where the choice of husbands was limited by class restrictions. Women were expected to enter into what were called *anuloma* marriages, marriages "with the grain," in which the husband's *varṇa* was the same as his wife's or higher. Brāhman men, by this policy, could marry Brāhman, Kṣatriya, or Vaiśya women, but the freedom allowed upper-class men meant a reduction in the choices for upper-class women. Brāhman women in particular were allowed to marry only Brāhman men; any other marriage relationship would be *pratiloma,* "against the grain," and would bring disgrace on both the girl's family and her children.

Brāhman families, faced with the importance of marriage for their daughters and the limitations on eligible partners, understandably tried to arrange marriages as early as possible to ensure their daughters' future welfare. Neither marriage difficulties nor ritual concerns were as great for non-Brāhman girls, whose marriages tended to be later, but even there the Brāhman pattern set a standard for early marriage.

These developments throw important light on Brahmanical efforts to promote marriage and family life. In contrast to the Buddhist and Jain monastic emphasis, writers of the *dharma* texts sought to strengthen family ties and make householdership mandatory as a stage in every person's life. Their success can be measured by the pressure for early marriage, which ensured community involvement in locating marriage partners and made family support of marriage a major social duty.

Brahmanical support of family life had other important side effects. Members of the monastic orders were not only celibate themselves, but could not officiate in marriages and sanction what they considered mistaken entanglement in the world. Brāhmans, however, were both householders themselves and also household priests. As ritual specialists, they provided a variety of services to the entirę community, and it is likely that in most communities they performed marriage rituals for lay members of all religious groups. The Brāhmans' involvement in the life of the community undoubtedly increased their hold on society. Jains eventually formed a close-knit lay community of their own, but Buddhists seem never to have done so, a fact often noted as a cause of Buddhist decline outside the major monastic centers.

Astrology in the Brahmanical System

Further Brahmanical influence on householders of all sects came from the Brāhman's role as astrologer. Here perhaps more than anywhere else the traditional Vedic priestly role was expanded to include direct involvement in the full range of household concerns.

Priests as early as the *Rig Veda* calculated "auspicious times" for the performance of sacrifices based on the phases of the moon and the sun's passage around the ecliptic as designated by selected stars and constellations. Certain times defined by these observations were labeled auspicious and others inauspicious, and the results were used both for determining the proper times for rituals and for evaluating the lives of individuals born at those times.

Later, after contact with Babylonian astrology, increased emphasis was placed on the positions and influence of planets as well as the sun and moon, and a division of the ecliptic into twelve equal parts (the divisions of the Zodiac) was introduced. These developments were combined in the use of the horoscope, a system of calculating planetary influences and evaluating their effect on specific aspects of a person's life such as health, wealth, relations with relatives and friends, love, marriage, children, and death.

Astrology continued to be used to calculate proper ritual occasions, but predictions and life readings for individuals became more and more important. Priestly reaction to this trend was ambiguous. *Manu* and other *dharma* texts warned against undue attention to the portents of the stars and considered the prediction of future events for personal gain a low and degrading occupation. On the other hand, however, a knowledge of astrology, along with a knowledge of magical rituals to prevent calamities, was considered essential for the domestic priest who maintained himself by performing orthodox rituals. It is clear that the concern was to keep the knowledge and practice of astrology in the hands of those who carried out the ritual duties of the community, both to enhance priestly effectiveness and to prevent misuse of astrology by those who might sell predictions for profit.

Brāhmans in this way kept—or gained—primary control over astrology, adding yet another element to their involvement in society and the lives of householders. Priests not only performed domestic rituals, but on the basis of astrology gave advice on personal and domestic matters such as the proper times for building and occupying a house, starting on a journey, carrying out agricultural activities, conducting business, or engaging in various activities from love affairs and marriage to scholarly studies and artistic creation. Such involvement increased as astrology gradually acquired a consistent orthodox rationale and was integrated into the Brahmanical world view, making astrology an inseparable part of the new Brahmanical synthesis.

This development was not effectively completed until the writing of the classical texts of astrology from around A.D. 500 on. The greatest of these, Varāhamihira's *Bṛihaj-jātaka* ("The Great Jātaka"), makes clear how astrology was assimilated to the main Brahmanical assumptions. The text deals with *jātaka,* the branch of astrology in which birth times and horoscopes were used to interpret individual lives. Such interpretations are possible, Varāhamihira says, because of the effects of past *karma* on an individual's present life. Birth itself is an effect of *karma,* and a person is born (or reborn) with an accumulation of multiple karmic effects from past lives. The time of a person's birth is a product of these factors; it is the time at which cosmic forces, as represented by the positions and interrelationships of the stars and planets, are most closely attuned to the karmic condition of the transmigrating self.

The horoscope is a chart of the cosmic forces and thus of the karmic condition at birth. It is, according to Varāhamihira, a guide to the tendencies in a person's life arising from his past lives. The tendencies are not produced by the stars and planets, which only convey information about the individual's *karma,* nor are the effects of these tendencies inevitable. The purpose of the horoscope is not to record an unchangeable future but to indicate the karmic factors each person must deal with if he is to improve his life; it is a guide to personal strengths, weaknesses, dangers, and opportunities that call for the exercise of foresight and will.

Interpreted in this way, astrology was a valuable complement to the *varṇāśrama-dharma* system. Birth into a particular class, caste, or family brought with it a set of social and ritual duties that served as a lifetime guide. This *dharma* was nevertheless general: it applied equally to everyone in the same social category and assumed the same karmic needs for each. In a broad sense this was adequate, since similar social conditions could only result from similar karmic causes. Each individual nonetheless had a unique karmic history and thus special needs that a general system of *dharma* could not satisfy. Astrology provided a detailed assessment of these special needs. It could not change a person's karmic inheritance, but it could help him make the best of it, and priests by its use could recommend individualized solutions.

Astrology gave the layman a sense of his own individuality and unique life plan, and it brought priests into intimate involvement with the full range of lay activity. The mutual benefit of this development should be stressed. Priests increased their authority and their range of control, but laymen also gained both a greater sense of personal direction and a better chance to improve their karmic condition. And, what was by no means least important, astrology helped relieve the anxiety attached to the consequences of every action as all of life became increasingly ritualized.

Dharma texts in a general way and astrology in a very personal way provided the necessary guidance for each householder in accord with his place in society and his individual karmic needs. The purpose was twofold: to improve one's present life within the limits set by birth and ability (limits determined by one's previous karmic condition), and to improve one's karmic state and thus one's opportunities in the next rebirth. Brahmanical control, exercised through *dharma* regulations and through social and ritual sanctions, worked to coordinate all such individual efforts for the best interests of society as a whole.

Beyond Householdership: The Path to Release

For most people, householder life was the limit of their present existence: they married, raised a family, carried out their social duties, performed their prescribed rituals, and ended life as householders, hoping that they had prepared the way for a better future birth. This was not a cause for regret or for resignation, since householder life could be personally satisfying and, if properly lived, was preparation for future advancement.

A few, however, were ready to go further toward release from *saṃsāra* in their present life. For them two final *āśramas* were established, that of the "forest-dweller" (*vānaprastha*) and the "renounced" (*sannyāsa*). There were many early precedents for this development. The *Chāndogya Upanishad* recognized a way of life different from that of the student or the householder, a way characterized by *tapas,* the practice of austerities. Yājñavalkya in the *Bṛihadāraṇyaka Upanishad* left his wives and household state to wander forth as a seeker of Brahman knowledge. By the time of Buddha and Mahāvīra, numerous wandering ascetics were seeking power and/or release in a life separate from the rest of society. The "wanderer" (*parivrājaka*) and "mendicant" (*bhikṣu*) were a part of Indian life from this time on.

The Brahmanical synthesis systematized what already existed and brought it under Brahmanical control in establishing the two final *āśramas.* This was not done without a certain amount of confusion about the status of these *āśramas.* Some *dharma* texts such as the *Yājñavalkya Smṛiti* held that a man could become a wandering ascetic as soon as he completed his Vedic study and need not (though he might) marry and become a householder. Others rejected this, claiming that householdership was the only important *āśrama* and all others were inferior. Some even prohibited the wandering life of a mendicant in the present degenerate age.

The majority view, however, was the one advanced by *Manu:* that householder life is the most important of the *āśramas* because it alone leads to the production of offspring and the support of society, but that when this stage is completed those who are qualified should go on to seek release. To be qualified, one must first have lived a full and successful life as a householder, producing male offspring to the second generation and providing for the continuing support of one's family: "When a householder sees his skin wrinkled and his hair growing white and sees the sons of his sons, he may betake himself to the forest" (*Manu* VI.2). This option was limited to the three upper *varṇas;* Śūdras, excluded from Vedic study, were excluded also from all *āśramas* except that of householder.

The *vānaprastha* in effect retired from active household life to live as a hermit in the forest. His wife might accompany him to aid in performing rituals, but from this point on both were enjoined to celibacy. The forest-dweller took with him his three *Śrauta* fires or his household fire and for a time continued to perform sacrifices, but eventually he gave up external rituals and concentrated on internal sacrifices to the sacred fires in his own self. He had to live on plant foods from the forest or on a meager diet gained by begging; animal food was to be avoided. He practiced restraint of the senses and performed austerities, seeking constantly to achieve purity and self-control. The hope was that the disciplines and personal development achieved would bring about, if not final release from rebirth, at least a major step toward that goal. But for those who sought greater assurance and had the qualifications, there was an even higher way yet, that of the *sannyāsin,* whose life was aimed more distinctly at the attainment of *mokṣa* or release. Only those with the highest standards of purity and dedication were admitted to this final *āśrama.*

Unlike the *vānaprastha* stage, sannyāsinhood was entered by means of a formal ritual in which the initiate renounced all worldly ties including all relationships with wife and family: "No one belongs to me and I belong to no one." This was done with the performance of his last fire sacrifice in which he gave up finally his sacrificial vessels and his sacred fires, deposited the fires mentally within himself, and henceforth was bound no longer to home or household rituals. He affirmed vows of noninjury to any creature, truthfulness, unconcern for property or wealth, and total continence, declaring formally his renunciation of the world and entry into a state of *sannyāsa,* "abandonment."

The ceremony was concluded by offering to the gods his "sacred thread," the symbol of Vedic initiation and the beginning of "twice-born" life, and taking a new name to replace his old family identity. Wearing only sandals, loincloth, and an ochre-colored upper garment, and taking with him only a staff, a water jar, and a begging bowl, he should from this point on live alone and not seek the company of others. His life should be characterized by restraint of speech (observance of silence), restraint of action (noninjury to any creature), and restraint of mind (performance of breath control, meditation, and other yogic practices); by these he would gradually purify himself, attain desirelessness (*vairāgya*), and achieve knowledge of self and Brahman that would bring final release from the transitoriness of *saṃsāra.*

The formalization of the life of the *sannyāsin* as the last of the *āśramas* made the Brahmanical synthesis complete. It gave social and ritual sanction to what earlier had been an individual and largely independent effort to gain release. Vedic study, householder life, and final abandonment of the world were integrated in a sequential pattern that proved to have greater stability and appeal than the more one-dimensional Buddhist and Jain emphasis on monastic life.

Sannyāsinhood brought the Brahmanical way of life full circle from the pre-*dharma* stage of childhood through Vedic initiation and study, life as a householder, husband, and father, to gradual withdrawal into forest life and final renunciation of both worldly *dharma* and ritual knowledge. Having passed through life in the world and performed his duties to society, the *sannyāsin* was reinitiated into the celibate state of *brahmacārya,* became again like a child, and sought to regain the identity with Brahman that was his true permanent condition. Though the details of this procedure were centuries in the making, it was in its final form close to the ideal described by Yājñavalkya in *Bṛihadāraṇyaka Upanishad* III.5:

> The *Brāhmaṇas,* having known that self, having overcome the desire for sons, the desire for wealth, the desire for worlds, live the life of mendicants. That which is the desire for sons is the desire for wealth; that which is the desire for

wealth is the desire for worlds for both these are but desires. Therefore let a *Brāhmaṇa,* after he has done with learning, desire to live as a child. When he has done with the state of childhood and with learning, then he becomes a silent meditator. Having done with both the nonmeditative and the meditative states, then he becomes a knower of Brahman.

The Success of the Brahmanical System

The Dharma Śāstras set forth a model of how society *ought* to be organized, not a sociological description of existing society. The *varṇāśrama-dharma* system represented a Brahmanical religious ideal that was originally not shared by all members of the society. It was proposed in the early Dharma Śāstras at a time when the Brahmanical tradition was seriously threatened by non-Vedic movements, and gained general acceptance only as the Brahmanical synthesis eliminated or absorbed rival systems.

The eventual success of the Brahmanical synthesis was a product of many factors. New religious movements were vitally important to this success, as we shall see in the following chapters. The *varṇāśrama-dharma* system, however, provided an essential base for Brahmanical expansion. It offered a persuasive model for an integrated society in which great variety was allowed within the framework of a unified concept of *dharma.* Emphasis on *orthopraxis* made this model in the literal sense a practical one, capable of absorbing heterogeneous social and religious groups with a minimum of conflict.

An example of this absorptive capacity on the social level was the development of a complex pattern of castes within the Brahmanical system in the course of the first millennium A.D. The system of *varṇāśrama-dharma* was based explicitly on *Rig Veda* X.90, which assumed an original external division of society into four *varṇas.* Even by the time of *Manu,* however, there existed alongside or within the *varṇa* structure numerous smaller subdivisions identified mainly by their hereditary occupations. The origins of these groups were diverse: some came from a division of labor and the formation of specialized artisan or craft communities; others from an absorption of new tribes or regional groups into Brahmanical society; still others came from increasing regional and ritual diversity within the expanding Brahmanical system.

The existence of so many diverse groups threatened the assumption of four eternal *varṇas* and presented a practical problem of social and ritual organization. The threat to Brahmanical theory was dealt with in an explanation advanced by *Manu:* there were only four *varṇas* in the beginning, but marriage between partners from different *varṇas* had produced subgroups whose status differed from the *varṇa* of either parent. The practical problem of assigning social and ritual status to the various subgroups was solved by ranking a group in accord with its known or claimed origin, the occupations and degree of ritual purity of its members, and the extent to which it could gain recognition of its status from other groups. New categories were developed to differentiate the large number of groups in the lower level of society. A distinction was made between "pure" Śūdras who could associate with *dvijas* and "impure" Śūdras who could not, based on the customs of the group and the occupations of its members. Certain groups whose practices were especially abhorrent to *dvijas* were not granted even Śūdra status, but were classified as "untouchable," as being continually in such a state of ritual impurity that their touch would ritually defile a member of any of the *varṇas*.

The culmination of these developments came in the later centuries of the first millennium A.D. when social lines between the various groups became more rigid and the groups were crystallized into what we now call castes. Membership in caste groups was determined entirely by birth, as reflected in the term *jāti* ("birth") used by the *dharma* texts to distinguish them from the more functional *varṇas*. Though intermarriage even between members of different *varṇas* was relatively common in the earlier period, social exclusiveness now allowed only endogamous marriages between members of the same *jāti* or caste.

The diverse origins and activities of caste groups were reflected in different rituals and food regulations. These in turn raised problems of ritual pollution between groups, leading to restrictions on social and ritual relationships and elaborate rules governing intercaste exchange of food, water, and services. All these regulations were added to the duties assigned by *varṇa* and *āśrama,* with participation at every level determined by birth and enforced by marriage.

This situation might to an outsider seem ripe for social resentment or rebellion. From the inside, however, the response was just the opposite. Though hereditary caste identity made social mobility impossible within an individual's lifetime, the principles of *karma* and rebirth not only explained one's present condition but offered hope of future improvement. The means of this improvement was proper performance of *dharma,* which now meant the full range of duties assigned by both *varṇa* and caste. Only if one accepted his caste identity and performed his caste obligations faithfully would he have a chance for higher status and better opportunities in future lives. Caste values and duties were in this way internalized and reinforced, making present conformity not only bearable but desirable.

The development of the caste system is an excellent example of how the Brahmanical synthesis worked. Given the choice between eliminating caste differences and accepting them, the Brahmanical system accepted the differences by including a multiplicity of separate castes within the larger social order. The result was not social equality but social stability based on karmic principles of cosmic justice and progress by stages toward the ultimate goal of release.

The same approach was made to the variety of new religious patterns evident from the time of the late Upanishads on. Upanishadic yoga and theism were only the first signs of major religious change. New types of religious activity and new ways of salvation were proposed with increasing frequency in the following centuries, making the Hindu tradition by modern times probably the most varied and flexible religious system in the world. One is tempted to say, "despite the rigid social system," but it seems likely that the variety of religious patterns was made possible in large part because the stability—even the rigidity—of the social system allowed a greater acceptance of religious diversity.

6.
The Religion of the Epics and Purāṇas

Brahmanical learning centered on the Vedas dominated Indian intellectual and literary life until at least the time of the Buddha. The primary vehicle of thought was the Vedic textual tradition, supplemented by related works on phonetics, meter and prosody, etymology, grammar, and astronomy, and the texts dealing with ritual performances and *dharma*. The only evidence of secular stories, legends, and fables during this period is the inclusion of some materials of this sort in Vedic texts and the obvious antiquity of some of the contents of later collections.

The situation changed considerably during and after the Mauryan period. Buddhists and Jains, rejecting the Vedas and a thousand years of Brahmanical writings, were free to convey their teachings in new ways. One such way, particularly suited to mass communication, was the use of popular stories as teaching vechicles. Whether as a response to Buddhist and Jain challenges or as a part of a general trend, new forms of Brahmanical literature came into existence after the third century B.C. Among the earliest of these, and of greatest continuing importance, were two great epic poems, the *Mahābhārata* and the *Rāmāyana,* both originally secular poems passed down outside priestly circles by generations of bards.

Śiva and Vishnu in the Epics

The core of the older epic, the *Mahābhārata,* may well date back to pre-Buddhist times. Like the shorter and more unified core of the *Rāmāyana* (*ca.* first or second century B.C.), it is essentially a story of warriors and kings, of heroic exploits and martial struggles. Even before it passed into priestly hands, however, it had become much more than this. Material of all sorts, sometimes amounting to whole books, was inserted into the framework of the original story, changing the epic narrative into an encyclopedia of literature and legend. In its more or less final form, reached by around A.D. 200, the *Mahābhārata* contained nearly 100,000 verses, making it probably the world's longest poem, many times the length of the combined *Iliad* and *Odyssey* of Homer.

The contents, as its history indicates, are enormously varied in both quality and subject matter. This is as true of the religious material as of the epic as a whole. Much of it is orthodox Brahmanical teaching, a repetition of older

Vedic views and *dharma* regulations. Much of it also is new, however, and some is of great importance, for it is here that we see for the first time the developed character of the great popular gods Śiva and Vishnu.

Śiva does not appear as a clearly defined god in earlier Brahmanical writings, where the focus is instead on the Vedic god Rudra. Rudra-Śiva in the *Śvetāśvatara Upanishad,* though he is the divine Lord and ruler of the world, is an abstract god in terms of personal or anthropomorphic qualities. Śiva in the *Mahābhārata,* however, is not only a powerful god worshiped as the great unborn creator of the universe; he is also described in several stories as a personal god living in the Himalayan mountains with his wife Umā, or Pārvatī. These stories give us our first view of the Śiva of popular worship, a god complete with particulars of his residence and his divine consorts.

The most significant references to Śiva are those that refer to him in one of his standard later roles as the divine mountain-dwelling yogin, the performer of great austerities and supreme practitioner of yoga, who grants boons to those who propitiate him with their own rigorous practices. In this role also he is associated in two stories with his most important symbol, the phallus or *lingam.* Śiva in one account is described as the great creator who, deciding his creative powers are no longer needed, cuts off his generative organ, the *lingam;* the *lingam* sticks up in the ground, and Śiva goes away to practice austerities. In the other account, Śiva is said to be the god whose *lingam* is worshiped by men; he is the creator of all living beings and the only god whose creatures bear either his symbol (the *lingam*) or his wife's (her *yoni* or vulva).

Especially revealing in these stories is the association of Śiva's yoga powers with his *lingam,* and his *lingam* with his role as Lord of Creatures. It is this combination of elements that seems also to be associated with the "horned god" of the Indus Civilization, and it is possible that we have here the surfacing of a tradition carried on outside the Brahmanical tradition for nearly two thousand years. Whatever the origins, the Śiva tradition in the *Mahābhārata* is clearly centered on worship of divine power in the complementary polar forms of the erect creative *lingam* and the austere self-controlled yogin. It is these elements, combined with the already complex figure of Rudra and supplemented by Śiva's female cocreators, that distinguished the tradition of Śiva worship from this time on.

Despite this evidence of Śiva's importance in the *Mahābhārata,* his place in the epic as a whole is greatly overshadowed by that of Vishnu. The *Mahābhārata,* first a secular work, then a nonsectarian religious one, became in its final stages a vehicle predominantly for Vaishnavites, the worshipers of Vishnu. Here, as with Śiva, we get our first look at the complex tradition that had grown up around this now popular deity.

Vishnu, like Rudra, had grown in stature within the Brahmanical tradition since early Vedic times. In several Brāhmaṇas Vishnu was called "the highest of the gods" and was identified with the sacrifice itself, a significant honor in these ritually oriented texts. In perhaps the most important account of Vishnu in the Brāhmaṇas (*Śatapatha Brāhmaṇa* I.2.5.), he disguised himself as a dwarf to aid the gods against the demon Asuras; when the gods were allotted land for a sacrifice equal in size to a dwarf, Vishnu laid down to mark the space and then grew so large he covered the whole earth, winning the earth for the gods. Vishnu's great importance in the later tradition, however, came only with the merger of this Vedic Vishnu with the popular god Vāsudeva-Krishna and a second Brahmanical deity, Nārāyaṇa.

The first of these gods, Vāsudeva-Krishna, was the product of religious movements outside the Vedic or priestly tradition. At least as early as the second century B.C., a god named Vāsudeva was being worshiped by devotees who called themselves Bhāgavatas, worshipers of Bhagavān, "the Bountiful Lord." Krishna, who appears in the *Mahābhārata* both as a human hero and as the divine teacher of the *Bhagavad Gītā* ("The Song of Bhagavān"), is identified in the epic as Vāsudeva. A further element in this complex merger was a princely sage named Krishna Devakīputra ("son of Devakī") mentioned in *Chāndogya Upanishad* 3.17, from whom Krishna in the epic and later tradition got his identity as the son of Queen Devakī. In the later portions of the *Mahābhārata,* Vāsudeva-Krishna, son of Devakī, was identified with the Vedic god Vishnu to form one strand of Vishnu's developing character as a personal god.

The second major strand, Vishnu's identity with Nārāyaṇa, came from predominantly priestly sources. Nārāyaṇa can be traced back to the *Śatapatha Brāhmaṇa,* where a Puruṣa Nārāyaṇa is said to have performed a *Pañcarātra* ("five-day") sacrifice, and to the *Taittirīya Āraṇyaka* where Nārāyaṇa, called also by the name Hari, is referred to as the eternal supreme deity and lord. In the latter text and in Dharma Sūtras of the same period, Nārāyaṇa is identified with Vishnu; and in a late portion of the same *Taittirīya Āraṇyaka* (10.1.6), the Brahmanical deity Vishnu-Nārāyaṇa is further identified with the popular god Vāsudeva.

All these strands were merged in the later portions of the *Mahābhārata,* where the names Nārāyaṇa, Hari, Vishnu, Vāsudeva, and Krishna were used interchangeably with reference to the Lord, Bhagavān, worshiped by the devotees called Bhāgavatas. The merger combined both priestly and popular elements and vastly expanded the range of Vishnu's qualities. Vishnu gained the support of those who worshiped both Vāsudeva-Krishna and Nārāyaṇa; and, as the common link between these gods, he acquired their combined status. Vishnu from this point on was one of the great gods of the tradition, rivaled in importance only by Śiva.

Worshipers of Vishnu in his various identities inserted their teachings into the framework of the epic, further blending the various strands that merged in Vishnu and giving the Vaishnavites a doctrinal base not yet evident for Śiva worship. Some of these teachings were also important religious texts in their own right, none more so than the greatest scripture of the Bhāgavatas, the *Bhagavad Gītā,* inserted into the *Mahābhārata* at its most dramatic point.

The Bhagavad Gītā

The form of the *Bhagavad Gītā* is a dialogue between the god Krishna and the Kṣatriya prince Arjuna, third oldest of five brothers called the Pāṇḍavas. The setting is a battlefield where the Pāṇḍavas and their allies are arrayed for battle against an army led by their cousins, the Kauravas. The battle is for possession of the family kingdom claimed by both Pāṇḍavas and Kauravas. The main story line of the epic is the conflict between these rival cousins; the issue is now to be resolved in war.

The *Gītā* opens with Arjuna standing in the forefront of the Pāṇḍava forces surveying friends, relatives, and teachers in both armies. Krishna stands with him as his charioteer, known to Arjuna only as a prince who has volunteered to aid him in battle. Looking at the armies and hearing conch-trumpets sounding the call to battle, Arjuna is suddenly paralyzed by indecision. Should he go into battle and slay his own kinsmen, bringing the family to ruin? Would it not be better, he asks Krishna, to let himself be killed than to kill his kinsmen for the sake of a mere kingdom?

Krishna's reply is intentionally rude and simplistic, directed at the low level of Arjuna's argument. If Arjuna is so concerned about the preservation of the family and the standards of society, then as a Kṣatriya born to a family of warriors and kings he should not be so fainthearted in the face of battle. It is his impotence and misplaced pity that will bring disgrace on his family, not his actions as a warrior whose duty is to fight.

Arjuna then appeals to a somewhat different principle. Is not warfare itself wrong? It is not wrong to participate in a battle for worldly gain in which even the victor's spoils are soaked in blood? Would it not be better to withdraw from such a struggle, to retire to the life of a world-renouncing mendicant?

This argument, similar to that of the Buddhists and various ascetic schools, is not so easily answered, nor does Krishna pass it off as lightly as he did Arjuna's previous argument. It poses one of the main issues in the remainder of the *Gītā:* given the continuing effects of *karma,* how can one avoid the bad effects of actions required by inherited social duties?

The solution Arjuna proposes, withdrawing to become a mendicant, is an attempt to renounce actions and thus escape their bad effects. Krishna's response is to show Arjuna a new way of looking at the problem, a new perspective that makes Arjuna's renunciation of duty unnecessary and undesirable. First, however, Arjuna must be willing to listen and learn so he can understand the truth. He accepts Krishna as his teacher with the formal statement, "I am your pupil," but he is at first a poor pupil. Without waiting for Krishna's teaching, he immediately asserts, "I won't fight!" Arjuna has turned to Krishna in desperation; faith and understanding come only later, as Arjuna comes to recognize who Krishna is.

The *Gītā* is a very human document. Arjuna himself is realistically human in his confusion and doubt, and he poses a genuine problem—a problem for Arjuna in the narrative and a problem for the Hindu tradition as well. Buddhists and ascetics, defenders of Brahmanical ritualism and orthodox *dharma,* proponents of Upanishadic knowledge, and the new devotees of popular theism all had their views of religious duty. The work of the *Gītā* was to sort out these views, interpret them within a consistent framework, and develop a synthesis that preserved their strengths and reconciled their differences—all this while demonstrating throughout the importance of Krishna.

The greatness and continuing importance of the *Gītā* lie in its success in achieving such a complex and multipurpose synthesis. As a synthesis it represents a stage beyond that of its nearest Vedic equivalent, the *Śvetāśvatara Upanishad.* The *Śvetāśvatara* is still very much an Upanishad in structure and emphasis, and its teachings on theism and yoga are subsumed under Upanishadic modes of thought. The *Gītā* by comparison is more explicitly synthetic and, while it recognizes the Upanishadic way of knowledge as one approach to salvation, this and all other approaches are subordinated to its central concern for devotion to Krishna.

The way of *bhakti* or devotion is developed only gradually in the *Gītā* as Arjuna becomes aware of Krishna's divine status. Krishna begins his instruction by teaching Arjuna "the discipline of knowledge" (*jñāna-yoga*) and "the discipline of action" (*karma-yoga*) to correct Arjuna's initial confusion. The discipline of knowledge begins with "the discipline of discrimination" (*sāṃkhya-yoga*), recognition of the absolute distinction between the self and the permanence of the self alone. From this Krishna argues that there is no cause to grieve for one's own death or for the death of others; what dies is only the body, not the self which is free of all change: "He who thinks that the self is a slayer, and he who thinks it is slain, both are ignorant" (2.19). Arjuna's fears of the death resulting from battle are misplaced. The self can neither be injured nor killed; therefore, Krishna concludes, Arjuna should fight without fear or mourning.

This is Krishna's answer to Arjuna's initial despondency, and serves as an introduction to the second approach, the method of action (*karma-yoga*). Here the fundamental problem of *dharma* is faced directly. Krishna begins with an attack on those who perform Vedic rituals for the attainment of enjoyment or power, seeking merit and reward as the fruits of their action. These men are deluded, since all actions, Vedic ritual actions included, are carried out within the realm of Nature (Prakṛiti) consisting of the three qualities (*guṇas*) and characterized by the pairs of opposites such as hot and cold, pain and pleasure, misery and happiness. The fruits of actions can also only be within Nature, so pursuit of these fruits must lead to continuing rebirth.

The solution to the problem of *karma* and rebirth is *karma-yoga,* the discipline of action: performance of actions without regard to their fruits. "You have a right to action alone," Krishna says, "never to its fruits" (2.47). One need not—in fact, should not—abandon actions in order to escape the effects of *karma.* What is necessary is to abandon all desire for the outcome of your actions. It is not the actions themselves that cause rebirth, but attachment to the fruits of actions.

This is an argument against desires and attachments, and also an argument against inactivity, or attempted inactivity. One cannot stay alive without performing actions of some sort, since Nature and the *guṇas* are constantly forcing the body to act as long as there is life; but the wise man does what must be done without attachment to his body or senses, or to the consequences of his actions, knowing that all actions are performed by the *guṇas* of Prakṛiti.

As to what must be done, it is one's own *dharma,* the obligations set by the conditions of one's birth in the world. The actions prescribed by one's *dharma* should be performed as a sacrifice to the gods, a free gift to the gods who sustain the universe. To refuse one's duties is as much an act of selfishness as the performance of duties with the hope of reward, and both courses moreover lead others astray in the performance of their duties. The wise man, performing his own *dharma* with discipline and without concern for the fruits of his actions, makes all action attractive and helps to sustain order in the world.

These principles point out Arjuna's initial ignorance. He had sought initially to be inactive by refusing to fight; but, far from being disciplined, he was overwhelmed by his mind and senses and totally concerned with the consequences of his actions. His proposal to become a mendicant was equally foolish. He was not sufficiently disciplined to lead a life of detachment, and by choosing this in place of his own *dharma* he would lead both himself and others astray and bring about what he hoped to avoid: the collapse of order and the decay of morals.

Having taught Arjuna the basic principles of *jñāna-yoga* and *karma-yoga,* Krishna begins to reveal himself as God. His present life as a prince in the Yādava family, he explains, is only the latest of many lives he has passed through in the world. In reality he is apart from the world as the Lord of all beings, but whenever worldly righteousness declines he creates a form for himself out of Prakṛti by his mysterious power (*māyā*) and manifests himself among men:

> For the preservation of the righteous, the destruction of the wicked, And the establishment of *dharma,* I come into being from age to age. (*Bhagavad Gītā* 4.8)

This revelation is important not only for the narrative in the *Gītā* but for the entire later Vaishnavite tradition. It introduces the concept of God's entry into the world of Prakṛiti as a savior of righteousness, a concept on which the doctrine of divine *avatāras* ("descents") was later based. Applied to Vishnu, the *avatāra* doctrine linked Vishnu as Supreme Lord to the various forms or incarnations in which he entered the world to aid mankind. Here, the concept of divine births is used to reveal the divinity of Krishna as Lord of Beings.

From this point on in the narrative, Krishna begins to speak more openly about *bhakti* ("devotion") to Himself as a means of salvation.

The *Gītā* does not at first directly advocate *bhakti* as a replacement for more traditional religious forms. Its approach is instead more subtle, first giving the traditional teachings and then showing how the same goal can be reached by devotion. Typical of this is the treatment of renunciation and yoga.

The traditional example of renunciation in the Brahmanical system was the *sannyāsin,* the "renounced one," the man in his final stage of life who has given up all former attachments and duties. Krishna first praises the person who has renounced his actions by discipline and control of his senses, and then points out that renunciation of actions is nevertheless unnecessary: an even better result is obtained by performing actions without concern for their results. The true *sannyāsin* is not the person who has given up his duties, but one who has renounced all attachment to their fruits.

Such renunciation can be obtained only by yoga. Krishna then describes the traditional practice of yoga by which the senses and the mind are brought under control and the mind controlled by the intellect is fixed on the self alone. Although this is hard, the yogin who strives for perfection is said to be greater than the ascetic or even the wise man. But who is the greatest of yogins? It is "the one who, possessed of faith, worships Me with his mind absorbed in Me." (6.47).

Bhakti directed to Krishna thus becomes the highest form of yoga and the key to renunciation. It is the same with knowledge. Knowledge (*jñāna*) is highly praised in the *Gītā,* often in terms similar to those found in the Upanishads. *Jñāna-yoga* is, with *karma-yoga,* one of the two paths to salvation. But the *true* man of knowledge defined by Krishna is not the traditional possessor of Vedic wisdom; he is the constantly disciplined person characterized by single-minded devotion: "He, with disciplined self, takes refuge in Me alone as the highest goal" (7.18).

Even this is still within the framework of at least the late Upanishads. The boundary is finally broken when Krishna moves beyond his emphasis on yoga and declares his accessibility to all who worship him:

> Whoever offers Me a leaf, a flower, a fruit or water with devotion, that offering of devotion from the pure in heart I accept.
> Even if a very wicked person worships Me exclusively he should be considered righteous, for he has rightly resolved.
> Quickly he becomes righteous-minded and gains eternal peace; O Arjuna, know that my devotee never perishes.
> They who take refuge in Me, O Arjuna, even though of sinful birth—women, Vaiśyas, even Śūdras—they also reach the highest goal.
> Fix your mind on Me, be devoted to Me, sacrifice to Me and bow down to Me with reverence; having in this way disciplined the self and having Me as the supreme goal, you will come to Me alone.
> (*Bhagavad Gītā* 9.26, 30–32, 34)

There is nothing approaching this in the Vedic texts. In the Brahmanical writings on *dharma,* women and Śūdras in particular were denied access to Vedic knowledge and thus to salvation by Vedic means. Devotion to Krishna is something expressed here for the first time: a way of salvation open to all levels of society—women as well as men, Śūdras as well as *dvijas,* the wicked as well as the pure and righteous.

The *Gītā* reveals this teaching just before the full revelation of Krishna's cosmic form. Krishna in the tenth chapter of the *Gītā* is revealed as the supreme Brahman, the source of all, manifested throughout the universe as the best of each class of entities. And in the eleventh chapter he reveals to an awe-struck Arjuna his universal form as Vishnu, in the midst of whose radiance the whole world with all its beings can be seen: heaven, atmosphere, and earth filled with all the gods, and in the center the blazing Vishnu swallowing up the warriors of both the Pāṇḍavas and their enemies. Vishnu-Krishna is Time, the great destroyer, as well as the creator and sustainer of all, the eternal Puruṣa from whom all things come and to whom all things will return.

When Arjuna has recovered from this fearful vision, Krishna in his gracious form as Arjuna's friend and teacher explains the significance of what he has seen:

> Neither by the Vedas, nor by austerity, nor by gift or sacrifice can this form be seen as you have seen Me,
> But it can, by devotion to Me alone, be known and seen in its true essence and entered into.
> He who does My work, has Me as the supreme goal, is devoted to Me and is nonattached, he who is without malice for any creature—he comes to Me.
> (*Bhagavad Gītā* 11.53–55)

This is not the end of the *Gītā,* but it is the end of Arjuna's gradual enlightenment. Krishna has been revealed as the Supreme Lord, identified with the Vedic Brahman and Puruṣa and with the universal form of Vishnu. He is the culmination of all the religious forms of the Vedas, but these forms are subsumed under a new conception of God and a new way of salvation.

Krishna is the Lord of the Universe, but he is also the friend and teacher of Arjuna. He is God among men, born to restore righteousness in the world and make salvation more accessible. The impersonal Brahman of the Upanishads is not rejected, nor earlier ways of salvation, but alongside them the *Gītā* offers what is declared as a better way, easier and more open to all who will join in devotion to the Lord.

Some special aspects of this devotion should be noted. The *Gītā's* "discipline of devotion" (*bhakti-yoga*) is closely related to *karma-yoga* and renunciation of the fruits of actions. It is thus ideally suited to the needs of the lower classes and householders for whom the traditional ideal of a renounced life as an ascetic was at best a far-off hope. *Sannyāsa* ("renunciation") was not for the *Gītā* confined to *dvijas* or to the fourth *āśrama;* renunciation in the special sense of dedicating the fruits of one's actions to the Lord (5.10) and offering all actions to Him (18.57) is applicable to the *dharma* of all classes and all stages of life.

No inherited *dharma* is unacceptable to the Lord; what matters is the devotion with which it is performed. It is thus that the *Gītā* (3.35 and 18.47) advocates performance of one's *own dharma,* even though imperfect, rather than taking up duties unsuited to one's nature. This is, as it were, a kind of worldly asceticism, set over against an asceticism based on withdrawal from world activity. A life devoted to the Lord is the best asceticism and the best yoga; the circumstances of that life and the particular duties it involves are not important.

The Origins of Purāṇic Theism

The *Mahābhārata* and *Rāmāya* were essentially complete by about the third century A.D. The new theistic movements centering on Śiva and Vishnu were well developed by that time, as is evident from late Śaivite additions to both epics and the hundreds of chapters of Vaishnavite teachings added to the *Mahābhārata* subsequent to the *Gītā.* The epics, however, reflect only the beginnings of a great surge of theistic development. The most important record of this development is found in a class of writings called Purāṇas produced from the time of the late epics onward.

Writings called Purāṇas are referred to as early as the *Atharva Veda,* and both *dharma* texts and the epics contain quotations ascribed to Purāṇas. These writings, like the epics, were collections of material in verse form transmitted outside the Vedic schools. Their purpose was to tell of ancient times, as the name *purāṇa* ("ancient") implies, and traditionally they contained information on five topics: the creation of the universe, the re-creation of the universe after its periodic destruction and reabsorption, the genealogy of gods and sages, the ages of the world and their rulers, and the genealogies of kings.

These Purāṇas were taken over by theistic groups and were transformed even more than the epics by the addition of new material. Enough old material remains in some Purāṇas to give an outline of the original contents, but the great bulk of all the existing Purāṇas is the product of theistic developments during the first millennium A.D. As the primary repository of the new religious teachings, the Purāṇas became—and remain—the principal scriptures of theistic Hinduism. It is these texts, far more directly than the Vedas, that determine the majority of Hindu thought and practice up to the present day.

The earliest of the revised Purāṇas originated during the period when the new Brahmanical synthesis was emerging. Brāhmans were making a major effort to gain support for the principles of social and religious practice laid down in the Gṛihya Sūtras and other Brahmanical *smṛitis.* The more orthodox of these Smārtas ("followers of the *smṛitis*") attempted to reassert Brahmanical standards by the writing of Dharma Śāstras. Other Smārtas, however, though equally concerned to preserve the authority of the Vedas and the *varṇāśrama-dharma* system, had become worshipers of Vishnu and Śiva or other popular gods. These theistic Smārtas were the first to adopt the original epics and Purāṇas as vehicles for their teachings.

The purpose of their adoption was twofold: as worshipers of popular gods, they sought to give Brahmanical status to their theistic practices; and as Smārtas, they sought to regain support for Brahmanical authority by associating it with popular gods and the popular epics and Purāṇas. We have seen already how the *Gītā* served this dual purpose by promoting both devotion to Krishna and performance of one's own *dharma*. Other additions had the same intent. Stories of Vishnu and Śiva were presented side-by-side with blocks of *dharma* teachings, and popular gods were presented as teachers of Brahmanical doctrine. Special efforts were made to appeal to women, Śūdras, and the lower orders of the twice-born who were excluded from Vedic learning; and, as in the *Gītā,* salvation was offered to them for the first time in return for accepting Brahmanical standards.

Major religious innovations were made in these texts, but Smārta influence was dominant in both the epics and early Purāṇas. Popular religion was not adopted without Brahmanical revisions, and *dharma* teachings, though often influenced by devotional ideals, did not go beyond the topics covered in Brahmanical texts such as *Manu* and the *Yājñavalkya Smṛiti.* The result was early Purāṇic theism: much advanced over the theism of the late Upanishads in its wealth of myths and stories, but still largely Vedic or Brahmanical in theology and principles of *dharma.*

The earliest Purāṇic texts, written before A.D. 400, represent two patterns of development of Purāṇic theism: an eclectic or nonsectarian pattern, and a pattern of increasing sectarian emphasis on one god to the exclusion of all others. The late additions to the epics and the *Matsya* and *Mārkaṇḍeya Purāṇas* illustrate the former pattern, the *Vāyu* and *Vishnu Purāṇas,* the latter.

Both the *Mahābhārata* and *Rāmāyana* in their final form became theistic scriptures promoting the worship of Vishnu, but neither became purely sectarian documents. Despite their strong Vaishnavite learnings, both also contained important Śaivite material among their late as well as early additions. The same pattern of eclecticism is found in the *Matsya* and *Mārkaṇḍeya Purāṇas,* both of which contain mainly material from the old Purāṇas—stories of creation, genealogies, and the like—interwoven with Brahmanical or Smārta teachings on *dharma.* These texts as a result could be used as source books by a variety of theistic groups while preserving their essentially Brahmanical orientation.

The other early Purāṇas also deal with the five traditional Purāṇa topics and rules of *varṇāśrama-dharma,* but are less influenced by Smārta concerns. Each is a distinctively sectarian Purāṇa, and in each there is evidence of new sectarian developments: in the *Vishnu Purāṇa* and *Harivaṃśa,* Vaishnavite doctrines of creation and the *avatāras* of Vishnu, and major additions to the Krishna story; in the *Vāyu Purāṇa,* descriptions of the earliest major Śaivite sect, the Pāśupatas, and an important subsect, the Lakulīśas.

The Pāśupatas and Lakulīśas

The *Mahābhārata* mentions a religious system called Pāśupata, said to have been revealed by Śiva, and gives a brief description of its doctrines. The name Pāśupata is derived from Paśupati, "Lord of Creatures," one of the early names of Rudra-Śiva. Pāśupata theology, according to the epic, is summarized in the terms *pati* ("Lord"), *paśu* ("creature"), and *pāśa* ("bondage" or "fetter"): Śiva as Paśupati is the Lord, and man is his creature, bound to the world by the fetter of ignorant attachment; the goal of man is to be freed of his fetter by the Lord and gain release.

Pāśupata doctrine, on the basis of this description, is clearly related to the *Śvetāśvatara Upanishad:* "The self, not being the Lord, is bound because he is an enjoyer [of Prakṛiti]; knowing God, he is freed from all fetters" (*Śvetāśvatara* I.8). Pāśupatas seem from this to be Brahmanical theists following the teaching of the late Upanishad. In the *Vāyu Purāṇa,* however, we get a description of actual Pāśupata practices and a somewhat altered view of these first Śaivite sectarians.

The dedicated Pāśupata is described as one who follows the discipline of Pāśupata Yoga defined in the *Vāyu Purāṇa* and in the *Atharvaśiras,* a related sectarian Upanishad. He takes a vow (*vrata*) to give up anger and greed and adopts an attitude of forgiveness. He takes up the life of an ascetic, smearing his body with ashes as a symbol of the worthlessness of the world. By such renunciation, and by yogic meditation on the mantra *oṃ,* he frees himself from worldly attachment.

The ideal Pāśupata yogin, the *Vāyu Purāṇa* says, is *tapasvin,* "characterized by the practice of *tapas* or austerities," and *ūrdhva-retas,* "one who keeps his semen above [i.e., withholds his semen and stores it up]." Such a yogin, following the disciplines of Pāśupata Yoga, is superior to a thousand students or householders or a hundred forest hermits. There is clearly no concession here to the importance of householder life and social duties emphasized in the Dharma Śāstras and the *Gītā.* Life as a *sannyāsin* who has totally renounced the world is the highest standard and only acceptable ideal for religious life.

This attitude is strikingly emphasized in a subsect of the Pāśupatas, the Lakulīśas, mentioned in another section of the *Vāyu Puraṇa.* There it is foretold that at a time when Krishna shall be incarnated as Vāsudeva, Śiva by means of his yogic powers will enter a dead body left untended in a burning ground where corpses are cremated. Taking on this body as his own, Śiva will appear as an ascetic named Lakulī. He will have four disciples and they will practice Pāśupata Yoga, smearing their bodies with ashes and dust. Inscriptions and other records refer to such a Pāśupata teacher who was considered an incarnation of Śiva, and it seems certain that the *Vāyu*'s reference is to this historical person.

Lakulī must have lived some time before the third century A.D. In later times he was worshiped as a form of Śiva and his image appeared in numerous temples. The images are unique, since he appears in human form with only two arms in contrast to the four or more arms of most images, he is naked, carries a short club in one hand, and has an erect penis. His followers formed a subsect of the Pāśupatas, called after their founder-god the Lakulīśa-Pāśupatas. Later evidence indicates that they followed the ascetic practices ascribed to their founder: nakedness, matted hair, begging for food, smearing themselves with ashes, sleeping on dirt or ashes, and living in cemeteries. They advocated asceticism or *sannyāsa* without regard for completion of prior *āśramas,* and initiated both women and Śūdras into their ranks as ascetics.

Pāśupatas claimed to be followers of the Vedas, but the validity of this claim depends largely on their use of doctrinal principles derived from the *Śvetāśvatara Upanishad.* In terms of practice, Pāśupata Yoga contains many sexual and sectarian elements that set it apart from the Brahmanical tradition and from Upanishadic theism and yoga. The contrast is best illustrated by the Lakulīśa system, which brings together a number of distinctive Pāśupata characteristics.

Lakulīśa is the ideal Pāśupata yogin, the incarnation of Śiva in a corpse. The body is dead; only the penis is alive and erect as the *lingam,* the symbol of Śiva and of Śiva's power. The erect penis is not a sign of sexual excitement but of sexual restraint; it is the visible symbol of the *tapas* or energy stored up by the withholding of semen. Pāśupata ascetics demonstrated the death of the body and of sexual desires by smearing their bodies with ashes and living in cemeteries and cremation grounds. Their yoga practices, including the recitation of mantras (a practice called *japa,* "muttering"), were directed toward further withdrawal from the world and building up inner power that would bring them enlightenment and eternal association with Śiva.

The combination of religious elements in the Pāśupata system is uniquely Śaivite. Śiva is the divine Yogin and the eternal creative *lingam;* Pāśupata Yoga is the practical expression of these religious principles. The theology of the system can be described in Brahmanical terms, but its origins must go back to ascetic worshipers of Śiva who rejected both the eclectic religious approach and the householder and ritual concerns of the Brahmanical Smārtas. The Pāśupata system nevertheless gave these ascetics a place in Brahmanical society as *sannyāsins,* much as the munis of earlier times were accepted into the Vedic system. From the early centuries A.D. on, ascetic yogins of the Pāśupata type were an important element in the Hindu religious pattern.

Vaishnavite Sectarianism and the Vishnu Purāṇa

The Pāśupatas and Pāśupata-Lakulīśas represent the first important Śaivite sectarians, as distinguished from Smārtas who worshiped Śiva within the framework of the Brahmanical *varṇāśrama-dharma* system. Vaishnavite sectarian development had begun earlier, as is evident from the many advanced Vaishnavite sectarian writings added to the *Mahābhārata.* The *Bhagavad Gītā,* the major scripture of the Bhāgavata sect, was only the first of these additions. Later additions carried sectarian development even further and prepared the way for the writing of the first Vaishnavite Purāṇa, the *Vishnu Purāṇa.*

The *Vishnu Purāṇa* was the product of a Vaishnavite sect called the Pāñcarātras, represented earlier in the *Mahābhārata* by a long section called the *Nārāyaṇīya* added to the epic some time after the date of the *Gītā.* The Pāñcarātras continued the development of Vaishnavite doctrine begun in the *Gītā,* and by Purāṇic times were the most important Vaishnavite sect.

A continuity of theological effort is evident in the development of Vaishnavite sectarianism from the early Bhāgavatas through the Pāñcarātra sect. Far more than the early Śaivites, the Vaishnavites attempted to relate their theism in a systematic way to the full range of Brahmanical concerns while retaining a primary focus on the worship of their chosen deity. This effort is evident in both the *Gītā* and the *Nārāyaṇīya,* and reached a new stage of development in the *Vishnu Purāṇa.*

The *Vishnu* preserves better than any other Purāṇa the five traditional topics of the old Purāṇas. Of its six books, the first four and the last contain classical Purāṇic material. This material, however, is given a consistent Vaishnavite interpretation and is interwoven throughout with accounts of Vishnu's incarnations and stories of great devotees of Vishnu. As the *Gītā* and *Nārāyaṇīya* had earlier established devotion to Vāsudeva-Krishna and Hari-Nārāyaṇa as the fulfillment of traditional Brahmanical religion, so the *Vishnu Purāṇa* now encompassed all the traditional Purāṇic concerns within the framework of Vishnu worship.

As is true of many Vaishnavite texts both before and after, the approach is conservative with regard to the Brahmanical tradition and ardently sectarian with regard to the focus of religious interest on Vishnu. The theology of the *Vishnu Purāṇa* is largely a Vaishnavite interpretation of Upanishadic theism, and its social teachings are compatible with Brahmanical *dharma.* The scope of Vishnu worship is greatly expanded, however, and two major additions are made to the growing Vaishnavite system: a Vaishnavite doctrine of creation, and the story of the cowherd Krishna, Krishna Gopāla.

Creation and the Yugas

The *Vishnu Purāṇa* begins with an account of the creation of the universe by Vishnu. Vishnu in this account is Brahman, of one essence but containing in his own nature the entire universe. He exists in the forms of Spirit (Puruṣa), Primary Matter (Prakṛiti), and eternal Time (Kāla) which brings about the connection and separation of Puruṣa and Prakṛiti. With these forms Vishnu engages in creation as his "sport" (*līlā*).

Creation occurs by a progressive devolution from Prakṛiti, following the general lines of what is designated in the *Gītā* and in later philosophical systems as the *sāṃkhya* theory of creation.

Prakṛiti is endowed with the three *guṇas* ("qualities") of *sattva* ("purity" or "goodness"), *rajas* ("energy" or "passion"), and *tamas* ("inertia" or "dullness"). In the unevolved state of Primary Matter the *guṇas* are in equilibrium. When the time for creation arrives, Vishnu stimulates the immutable Purusa and the mutable Prakṛiti; the *guṇas* are stirred into activity, and the first evolved principle is brought forth. This principle, called Mahat ("the Great") or Buddhi ("Intellect"), consists of the active but unseparated *guṇas;* it is the creative intellect prior to the differentiation of the created world.

Mahat-Buddhi is enveloped by Prakṛiti and becomes threefold, differentiating itself as *sāttvika, rājasa,* and *tāmasa* Mahat in accord with the relative influence of the three *guṇas*. From the threefold Mahat then comes forth the threefold Ahaṃkāra, the "I-faculty," the principle of individuation that relates perceptions and thoughts to the concept of "I": "I think," "I feel," and so on.

The threefold Ahaṃkāra is enveloped by Mahat-Buddhi, and from it come forth the final elements of primary creation. Ahaṃkāra under the predominant influence of *tamas* brings forth the five subtle elements (sound, touch, sight, taste, and smell) and the corresponding five gross elements (ether, wind, fire, water, and earth). Ahaṃkāra under the predominant influence of *rajas* brings forth the five sense organs (ear, skin, eye, tongue, and nose) and the five organs of action (voice, hands, feet, and the organs of procreation and excretion). From Ahaṃkāra under the predominant influence of *sattva* comes forth mind (*manas*), the coordinator of all sense impressions and the producer of perceptions and thoughts.

The gross elements come together to form one mass surrounded, as if by shells, by water, fire, air, ether, Ahaṃkāra, Mahat-Buddhi, and Prakṛiti. This whole complex forms a vast egg resting on the cosmic waters. Vishnu enters into this egg as the creator god Brahmā, creates from the evolved elements the three worlds of earth, atmosphere, and heaven, and populates them with gods, sages, and all other living things. He becomes Vishnu the Preserver, and sustains the world through successive ages until the world is exhausted. Then he becomes Rudra the Destroyer, destroys the world with flames, and brings down rains until the whole of the three worlds is one great ocean.

Vishnu then sleeps upon the ocean on the coiled body of his great snake Śeṣa ("Remainder") or Ananta ("Unending"), covered by the canopy of Śeṣa's thousand overarching heads. This setting, Vishnu reclining on the coils of Śeṣa, is one of the great Vaishnavite images, often referred to in Vaishnavite stories and portrayed in Vaishnavite art. It is from this position of rest that Vishnu observes the cycles of the world as it passes through successive creation and destruction.

The period from the beginning of Brahmā's creation to the destruction of the worlds is called a day of Brahmā or a *Kalpa.* Within this period the world goes through cycles called *Mahā Yugas* ("Great Yugas"), each of them lasting 12,000 years of the gods or 4,320,000 human years (one human year is one day of the gods, 360 human years is one year of the gods).

Each *Mahā Yuga* of 12,000 years of the gods is divided into four lesser *Yugas* of declining length: the *Kṛita Yuga* lasting 4,800 years, the *Treta* lasting 3,600, the *Dvāpara* lasting 2,400, and the final *Kali Yuga* lasting only 1,800 years of the gods. During this period *dharma* steadily declines from its initial perfection in the *Kṛita Yuga.* In the *Kali Yuga* unrighteousness is rampant, men are weak and unable to follow their proper duties, rulers plunder their subjects, students disobey parents and teachers, pursuit of wealth is men's only concern, and the world in general is a place of suffering and strife. Renewal then takes place, a new cycle starts with an again perfect *Kṛita Yuga,* and decline once more begins.

A thousand such cycles of *Mahā Yugas* make up a *Kalpa,* which ends in the destruction or dissolution of the world by Vishnu as Rudra. This period, a day of Brahmā, lasts 4,320,000 human years, followed by an equally long night of Brahmā during which Vishnu sleeps. At the end of this night, Vishnu as Brahmā again recreates the world and a new day of Brahmā begins.

This process continues throughout a lifetime of Brahmā, 100 years of 360 days and nights of Brahmā each. At the end of that lifetime, the entire process of evolution is reversed until Vishnu remains alone with Time, Prakṛiti and Puruṣa absorbed into his pure infinite Supreme Self. When Vishnu again decides to play, the process begins anew.

This account of creation indicates the perspective on time and the universe that marked the Purāṇic world view. All the Purāṇas adopted essentially the same concept of creation out of Prakṛiti, though Śaivites and others changed the originating deity to fit their own sectarian positions. What is more important, all the Purāṇas agreed on the pattern of *Kalpas, Maha Yugas,* and *Yugas,* and all agreed that we now live in a *Kali Yuga,* immersed in the worse stage of one of the thousands of *Mahā Yugas* through which our selves must struggle for salvation.

The *Vishnu Purāṇa's* view is a remarkable integration of Upanishadic monism and Vaishnavite theism. Vishnu as Brahman is both Puruṣa and Prakṛiti, both the creator and the material of creation. In the evolved universe, Vishnu in his cosmic form reclines on Śeṣa and manifests himself as Brahmā to create the three worlds at the beginning of each *Kalpa.* As Vishnu the Preserver, he oversees the cycles of *Mahā Yugas* and *Yugas* through which the three worlds pass. And, as the *Vishnu Purāṇa* goes on to state, Vishnu in the form of his *avatāras* actively intervenes in the world in the midst of the *Yugas* for the welfare of created beings.

Both Krishna and Rāma, the princely hero of the *Rāmāyana,* were already considered *avatāras* of Vishnu in the late *Mahābhārata.* The *Nārāyaṇīya* portion of the epic identified several other important incarnations: Vishnu was the Boar (*Varāha*) who killed the demon Hiraṇyākṣa and raised up the earth on his tusk to save it from the depths of the cosmic ocean; he was the Man-Lion (*Narasiṃha*) who killed the demon Hiraṇyakaśipu for persecuting his son, Prahlāda, a pious devotee of Vishnu; and he was the Dwarf (*Vāmana*) who asked the demon Bali for as much land as he could cover in three strides and then, becoming a giant, destroyed the power of the demon with three strides that spanned the three worlds.

The *Vishnu Purāṇa* took these *avatāras* and placed them in the context of the present *Mahā-Yuga* as Vishnu's benevolent descents in this age. The most important contribution of the *Vishnu Purāṇa* and the slightly later *Harivaṃśa,* however, was not their perpetuation of the earlier stories of Vishnu's *avatāras* but the addition and elaboration of a major new story: the story of Krishna's childhood as Krishna Gopāla, friend and companion of cowherds and lover of cowherd maidens.

Vishnu as Krishna Gopāla

Krishna is known throughout the *Mahābhārata* only as an adult. He appears as the son of Vasudeva and Devakī; as a prince of the Yādava tribe; as a friend of the Pāṇḍavas who is Arjuna's charioteer during the great Pāṇḍava-Kaurava war; as the teacher of the *Bhagavad Gītā;* and as Vāsudeva-Krishna, a god eventually identified with Vishnu. His home is consistently referred to as Dvārakā (modern Gujarat), where he lived with his brother Balarāma. A rival king, Śiśupāla, refers to Krishna once as a "cowherd" whose childhood feats are not to be thought remarkable, but nowhere in the epic is this late reference to Krishna as a "cowherd" explained and nowhere is his childhood described.

The situation is startlingly different in the *Vishnu Purāṇa.* Book V of this work is devoted entirely to the story of Krishna's childhood as a cowherd boy, the defeat of the evil king Kaṃsa by Krishna and his brother Balarāma, and the subsequent history of Krishna and Balarāma in Dvārakā. The *Vishnu Purāṇa*'s history of Krishna does not, however, contain the story of his participation in the great war described in the epic or his teaching of the *Bhagavad Gītā.* We have here a separate tradition celebrating a new and different aspect of Krishna: Krishna Gopāla, the divine cowherd.

Krishna is not born as a cowherd in the *Vishnu Purāṇa.* He is still Vāsudeva-Krishna, prince of the Yādavas, son of King Vasudeva and his wife Devakī. But instead of Dvārakā, the new stories place his birth and childhood in the region of Mathurā on the Jumna River. There a demon has taken form as King Kaṃsa, ruler of Mathurā, and his power has grown so great that he threatens even the gods. The gods have appealed to Vishnu, and Vishnu has agreed to help them by being born into the world as the eighth child of Devakī.

Kaṃsa, learning of this threat in a prophecy, has imprisoned Vasudeva and Devakī in Mathurā so he can kill their offspring. Thus the story begins.

The first six children of Devakī are put to death, but her seventh conception is an incarnation of Vishnu in the form of Balarāma. Balarāma, before his birth, is transferred to the womb of Vasudeva's second wife Rohinī, and is born in the nearby cowherd settlement of Gokula. When Krishna is born as Devakī's eighth child, he also is taken to Gokula and exchanged for the newborn child of a cowherd woman named Yaśodā. Kaṃsa, bewildered by Vishnu's power of illusion, has missed his chance to save his life. Krishna has escaped, and he and his brother Balarāma are now both raised in the cowherd settlement by Yaśodā and her husband Nanda, chief of the cowherds of Gokula.

The story thus far has as its purpose the connection of Krishna and Balarāma with both Vasudeva and Devakī, the traditional parents of the epic god Vāsudeva-Krishna, and with the setting of the new Krishna stories. The need for this connection is created by developments prior to the writing of the *Vishnu Purāṇa* that have brought these two parts of the Krishna story together. These we can trace only dimly from other records.

The earliest known Vaishnavite worship center or sanctuary was a stone-walled enclosure dedicated to the worship of Vāsudeva and Saṃkarṣaṇa, dated around the second century B.C. and located in the area between Mathurā on the Jumna River and Dvārakā in Gujarat. The column of Heliodorus dedicated to Vāsudeva was located at Besnagar south of Mathurā and dated around the same time. We can assume from these sites that worship of Vāsudeva and Saṃkaraṣaṇa was well established in this region by the first or second century A.D., the time of the late *Mahābhārata*.

Worship of Vāsudeva and Saṃkarṣaṇa is described also in the *Nārāyaṇīya* portion of the *Mahābhārata*. The devotees of these gods are there called Sātvatas, a group known from other evidence as a subgroup of the Yādava tribe. By the time of the late epic, Vāsudeva and Saṃkarṣaṇa had been given the names Krishna and Balarāma, and Vāsudeva-Krishna and Saṃkarṣaṇa-Balarāma were known both as Yādava princes and as gods worshiped by the Yādavas. Krishna and Balarāma themselves were associated only with the Yādava kingdom in Dvārakā, but Yādava tribes were settled throughout the area from Dvārakā to Mathurā. These tribes must have been involved in the worship of Vāsudeva and Saṃkarṣaṇa noted in this area. There is no evidence this early, however, for the worship of a *cowherd* Krishna. This addition came only after Yādava contacts with a separate cowherd tradition near the end of the epic period.

There are references in Indian texts from the second century B.C. onward of a forest-dwelling tribe of cowherds called Ābhīras. First noted east of the Indus River, they gradually migrated southward and eastward into the area from Mathurā to Dvārakā. In the critical period of the late *Mahābhārata* and early Purāṇas, they occupied the same territory as the earlier Yādava tribes. The details of their contacts with the Yādavas during this period are not known, but one consequence of the interaction seems clear: from the older residents they acquired the worship of Vāsudeva-Krishna and Saṃkarṣaṇa-Balarāma, and to the new religion they added something of their own, the story of a cowherd god whose life was modeled on their own life as cowherds on the outskirts of Mathurā.

By the time this story first appears in the *Vishnu Purāṇa,* it has been thoroughly blended into the Vaishnavite tradition. The cowherd god is Vāsudeva-Krishna, born as an incarnation of Vishnu into the Yādava family of Vasudeva and Devakī. The difference in origins is obvious, however, when Vāsudeva-Krishna and Balarāma are turned over to their foster parents Nanda and Yaśodā and the *Vishnu Purāṇa's* account focuses on their life in the cowherd settlement.

Krishna, though only a baby, soon gave evidence of his divine powers. A demoness named Pūtanā came to Krishna at night and gave him her poisoned breast to suck, but Krishna sucked with such violence that Pūtanā's life was drained away and she fell dead by his side. Krishna on another occasion was put to sleep beneath a wagon; waking up hungry, he cried and kicked his feet and the loaded wagon was overturned. When Krishna and Balarāma began to crawl, Yaśodā tied Krishna to a heavy wooden mortar by a cord around his waist to keep him out of trouble; Krishna, crawling away, dragged the mortar behind him between two trees and uprooted them.

The cowherds took these events as evil omens and moved their families, wagons, and cattle to a new site called Vṛindāvana near the banks of the Jumna River. There Krishna and Balarāma grew up with the cowherd boys, wandering through the forest decorated with garlands of flowers, playing their flutes and singing and winning the hearts of all with their charm. There also they continued their wondrous feats, defeating many demons and carrying out their divine role as protectors of the world.

Once Krishna found a great serpent, Kalīya, dominating the river. He leaped in and challenged the serpent-king; and, while all the people of Vṛindāvana watched in fear, he subdued Kalīya, danced on his hooded heads, and sent him away to the sea. On another occasion, Krishna persuaded the cowherds to stop their worship of Indra. Indra in anger sent down a storm of wind and rain that threatened to wash away both cowherds and cattle, but Krishna plucked up the mountain Govardhana and held it aloft with one hand in sport, sheltering all Vṛindāvana through seven days and nights of Indra's torrent. The cowherds, recognizing Krishna's powers and suspecting that he might be Hari (Vishnu) himself, did not know how they should act toward him and could only recite with awe the succession of feats so inconsistent with the Krishna they knew as a cowherd boy.

The stories up to this point in the *Vishnu Purāṇa's* account establish Krishna's human appeal as a baby and a young cowherd boy, and his divine power as an incarnation of Vishnu. These stories were told and retold in later Vaishnavite texts and devotional songs, and were the basis for most of the early sculptural representations of Krishna. The most important story for later theological developments, however, is Krishna's dance with the cowherd girls of Vṛindāvana at the time of the autumn moon, the climax of Krishna's life as a cowherd.

When the lotus was in full bloom at autumn time, Krishna, observing the perfumed air and the clear moonlit nights, decided to join in dance with the cowherd girls, the *gopīs*. He and Balarāma began to sing, calling the *gopīs* to leave their homes. Some came bashfully, while others, more bold, clung to his side; still others, afraid of their elders, remained at home and meditated on Krishna with devotion. Then, when the *gopīs* had gathered around him in the moonlit forest, Krishna suddenly disappeared.

Left alone, the *gopīs* whiled away their sorrow by imitating Krishna's songs and sports. Finding Krishna's footprints leading through the forest with the marks of a girl's feet beside him, they began to trace the footprints and imagine the two together. The footprints suggested that the girl had staggered, drunk with passion; then she had stopped while Krishna picked flowers for her, and the two sat on the ground while he covered her with garlands; then Krishna left because of her arrogance, and her footprints show her running to catch him; then, having caught his hand, she was again abandoned and wandered aimlessly; here Krishna has come running back; but here the footsteps lead into the darkness of the thick forest and can no longer be followed.

Envious of Krishna's companion, and giving up hope of seeing him again, the *gopīs* went to the banks of the Jumna to sing his songs. Soon Krishna joined them, soothed their feelings, and started to dance. He took each of the *gopīs* by the hand in turn, deprived them of perception, and joined their hands together in a circle so that each thought she danced with Krishna beside her. Then, while Krishna sang, the *gopīs* danced the dance called *rāsa-līlā,* following the steps of Krishna and pervaded by his essence. So they danced that night and other nights, defying the prohibitions of fathers, brothers, and husbands.

Krishna's stay in Vṛindāvana ended soon after this when he and Balarāma were called to Mathurā to destroy the evil king Kaṃsa and release Vasudeva and Devakī. Krishna carried out this task with Balarāma's aid, established a Yādava ruler on the throne, and then after further trials led the Yādavas to a new capital at Dvārakā. There the *Vishnu Purāṇa*'s story ends with the collapse of the Yādavas and Krishna's death from an arrow in his foot shot by a careless hunter.

Krishna's history after Vṛindāvana had little religious value for the *Vishnu Purāṇa.* The *Gītā* belonged to this later stage of his life as prince of Dvārakā in the epic, but it is not a part of the *Vishnu Purāṇa*'s account. Even the later *Bhāgavata Purāṇa,* which combined the epic and Purāṇic accounts of Krishna's life, took little notice of the *Gītā.* For the tradition that followed the *Vishnu Purāṇa,* the meaning of Krishna's incarnation was found in Vṛindāvana with the *gopīs,* not with Arjuna on the battlefield of Kurukṣetra at the time of the Bhārata war.

Krishna never returned to Vṛindāvana after he left for Mathurā to take up his life as a Yādava prince. His departure had great meaning for the Purāṇas and later devotees, since Krishna left behind in Vṛindāvana the cowherds and *gopīs* who loved him. The *gopīs* felt his desertion most, and wept bitterly at his absence; they feared he would shift his affection to others, raged at his desertion, and, fondly remembering his graces, were consumed by the fires of separation. The significance of these emotions was that they could be used religiously, since Krishna is God and love of God is a means of salvation.

Much of the power of the Krishna Gopāla story is the contrasts it presents. Vishnu, the Supreme Lord of the universe, is the baby held in the arms of a cowherd's wife; the creator and ruler of the cosmos is the mischievous child who steals butterballs from the neighbors and upsets his mother's churn; the giver of all *dharma* and the object of all austerities is the carefree flute-playing youth who wanders flower-bedecked in the forest with his friends and wins the love of the *gopīs* from their families and husbands. It was the work of the tradition from the *Vishnu Purāṇa* onward to develop the potential of the story in all its aspects.

Nanda, Yaśodā, the cowherds, and the *gopīs* related to Krishna with different emotions as father to son, mother to child, friend to friend, lover to beloved. But since Krishna was at the same time divine, these various relationships and their emotions could be seen as various forms of devotion to God. Human feelings were thus transformed into devotional moods suitable for devotees with different religious inclinations. Reverence, service, parental affection, friendship, or passionate love—all could be expressed in terms of different relations to Krishna as God. Though these relationships were not systematized until later, already in the *Vishnu Purāṇa* the possibilities were recognized. This is most evident in the story of the *gopīs*.

Krishna left the *gopīs* in Vṛindāvana with emotions they could not satisfy directly, just as he had left them at the time of the *rāsa-līlā*. But there they had spent their time in his absence imitating his actions and imagining his presence; though their beloved was gone, he was constantly present in their minds and was the sole object of their thoughts and feelings. In this way, the *Vishnu Purāṇa* points out, even those who had to remain at home were purified by their regret at not beholding Krishna.

Krishna's later absence from Vṛindāvana was permanent, but the *gopīs'* earlier solution was no less fitting; though physically absent, Krishna could be kept alive in their minds by constant remembrance fed by the fires of longing. Such devotion fits in fact the condition of every person in the absence of the Lord, for Krishna, though no longer incarnate, can be present in the consciousness of anyone who directs his feelings and thoughts to him as the *gopīs* did.

The *Harivaṃśa* added further details of Krishna's incarnation as Gopāla, especially in its suggestion of sexual relations between Krishna and the *gopīs* at the time of *rāsa-līlā*. The emotions are then even stronger, for what longing can be more intense than the longing for him who has satisfied all one's desires and has then gone on to other women? Krishna has since returned to his form as Vishnu, with his consort Śrī or Lakṣmī always at his side to satisfy every need. What hope then for abandoned earthly *gopīs?* Or, as the *gopīs* state their case in the later *Bhāgavata Purāṇa,* "What can the Lord of Śrī want from us who are only *gopīs* living in the forest?"

The answer given by the *Bhāgavata Purāṇa* is *bhakti,* devotion from *gopīs* no less than any other beings in his creation. As they have given him their bodies before and been satisfied, let them now give him their minds and hearts in longing devotion and gain release, not the temporary release of sexual enjoyment but the permanent release of salvation. Such intense emotion as the *gopīs* felt for Krishna, emotion that removes all other thoughts and desires, satisfies the *Gītā*'s definition of *bhakti-yoga;* it, no less than quiet meditation, results in single-minded concentration on the Lord. It has the further advantage of accessibility to everyone, for salvation cannot be confined to those of high birth if the human emotions of longing and devotion are the only qualifications. Krishna Gopāla has introduced a new attitude that, in later Purāṇas and devotional movements, became a major source of religious inspiration.

7. Late Purāṇic Religion: The Full Tradition

The Purāṇas written before the fifth century A.D. reflect only the first sages in the growth of Hindu theism. Temples, scarcely mentioned in these Purāṇas, became a major focus of interest in later Purāṇic writings. New forms of worship were developed that further widened the gap between Smārta and sectarian religious practice. Differences between Śaivite and Vaishnavite sects became more pronounced, reflected to some extent in the late Purāṇas but even more in the increasing production of sectarian texts that began in the early centuries A.D. Worship of female deities, long practiced at the popular or village level, entered the mainstream through the increased attention given to wives and consorts of Vishnu and Śiva and through the formation of semiautonomous cults of Devī ("the Goddess").

These developments, moreover, occurred at several social and intellectual levels and had quite different patterns in the various regions of India. The complex religious system that resulted defies simple description. In what follows we can single out only a few of the more important developments in this final stage of the Hindu tradition, recognizing that a variety of patterns and mixtures occurred in different areas and among different groups.

Theism under the Guptas and Their Successors

The early development of theism took place during the politically unstable post-Mauryan period, a time of foreign rulers and small rival Indian kingdoms. This period ended in A.D. 320 when a new line of kings, the Guptas, began to reunite northern India. Starting from the old Mauryan capital of Pāṭaliputra, the Guptas carved out a new empire north of the Deccan that lasted until the late fifth century, reaching its height under Candra Gupta II (A.D. 380–413).

The imperial Guptas for the first time gave strong and continuing dynastic support to the new theistic gods, especially Vishnu. Gupta rulers referred to themselves as *parama-bhāgavatas,* "supreme Bhāgavatas" or chief of the devotees of Bhagavān (Vāsudeva-Krishna). Though this did not indicate exclusive devotion to Krishna, it did indicate a new status for this popular *avatāra.* Other *avatāras* of Vishnu also were given special recognition, notably Vishnu's incarnation as the Boar to save the earth from destruction. This role fit the

Gupta self-image as representatives of Vishnu's preservation and protection of the world, and from this the *Varāha* or Boar incarnation became a common symbol of royal power. An image of Viṣṇu-Nārāyaṇa as the Boar was worshiped even by one of the invading Hun kings who succeeded the Guptas around A.D. 500, and the Boar *avatāra* was adopted about the same time as the dynastic emblem of the South Indian Calukya kings.

This illustrates a process of great importance throughout the Purāṇic period. The Guptas raised theism from the popular level to the level of a state religion, paralleling in the political sphere what was being done theologically under Brahmanical auspices in the epics and early Purāṇas. Their support gave theism a new legitimacy, and the fact that it was supported by prestigious rulers made it attractive to those who sought to emulate their power. Once the Guptas expressed themselves as worshipers of Vishnu and his *avatāras,* other rulers could borrow from their prestige by similar expressions of piety.

This pattern of imitation greatly increased the support available to theistic groups. Kings had long since demonstrated their piety and power by elaborate sacrifices; now they sought to rival each other in support of the new Purāṇic theism. Theistic groups were added to the list of Brāhmans, ascetics, Buddhists, and Jains to whom royal patronage was given. From the time of Candra Gupta II onward, there are records of donations to various theistic sects by kings, devotees, and wealthy patrons. Many of these donations were to build and maintain temples and provide them with images of the sectarian gods, and it is from this time that we begin to get temples made of stone.

Buddhists since around 100 B.C. had built stone stupas (burial mounds commemorating the Buddha) and had carved elaborate caves out of living rock for use as assembly halls and monastic cells. Hindu temples or "houses of the gods" were also in existence that early, but until Gupta times they were built of perishable materials. The first transition to stone was the creation of rock-hewn cave temples. Then, in late Gupta times, free standing stone temples were built by placing heavy stone slabs together in the form of a rectangular cell to house the image of the deity. From the early sixth century onward, the building of stone temples became an increasingly important focus of wealth and artistic effort. More elaborate temple forms developed, stone sculpture was further perfected, and temples became major works of art.

We can see in these developments a pattern similar to the rise of Buddhist art in the post-Mauryan period. Public support for theistic worship made available the means to create permanent temples and develop theistic art in stone. The necessary skills in stone carving had already been perfected during the centuries of work on Buddhist monuments, images, and caves. This craftsmanship now needed only to be redirected under new auspices to bring forth a vital new art.

The new political situation provided the support for this further stage of theistic development. The new theistic movements provided the rationale and the content. Most of the new art was based on the stories and gods set forth in the epics and Purāṇas, and the meaning of the art and of the temples themselves was provided by the new Purāṇic theology. Most fundamental of all was the basic purpose of the temples, for they represented a pattern of religious practice that has characterized Hindu theism down to the present day: the performance of *pūjā* ("worship") to images of the gods.

Pūjā

The major change in religious practice from Vedic to late Purāṇic and modern times was the gradual replacement of *yajña* ("sacrifice") by *pūjā* as the principal form of worship. An inscription dated around the second century B.C. referring to the performance of *pūjā* to Vāsudeva and Saṃkarṣaṇa is perhaps the earliest use of the term in the sense of worship, and gives some indication of when the practice began. It was slow to receive Brahmanical sanction, however, and it was not until around the beginning of the sixth century A.D. that sections dealing with *pūjā* were included in the Purāṇas. From that point on, *pūjā* increasingly dominated religious practice. Though some Vedic sacrifices contined to be performed, *pūjā* in temples and homes became the norm even for Brahmanical worship.

The rise of *pūjā* is a good example of the pattern of change in religious practices. The term itself as well as many of the later practices can be found as early as the Gṛihya Sūtras, but *pūjā* there refers to the honoring of Brāhmans invited to family ceremonies. Regular procedures were laid down in the Gṛihya Sūtras for welcoming and serving these honored guests, and these procedures were simply transferred to the honored gods when image worship was introduced into family rituals.

Pūjā performed to images in both homes and temples has largely preserved its characteristics as a hospitality ritual. The ritual from start to finish is a sequence of acts of service or respect. Though the specific acts vary with the circumstances of the ritual or the ritual tradition being followed, the usual complete sequence includes invocation of the deity, offering him a seat, offering water for washing his feet, water for washing his hands, and water for sipping, bathing the image, offering a fresh garment, offering a sacred thread, anointing the image with unguents or sandalwood paste, offering flowers, offering incense, offering a lighted lamp, offering food or a gift, making obeisance to the deity, *pradakṣiṇa* ("clockwise circumambulation of the deity"), verses of praise, and bidding the deity farewell.

Other elements might be added, such as offering a honey mixture to drink, offering ornaments, offering a fan, a looking glass, or an umbrella, or offering betel leaf after presentation of food. Bathing the image might be done with plain water or it might be done first with *pañcāmṛita* (the "five ambrosial things:" milk, curds, clarified butter, honey, and sugar) followed by a bath with water. If a person cannot afford ornaments, new garments, and the like in the home ritual, he may offer only sandalwood paste, flowers, incense, a lamp, and food, or in an even simpler ritual he may offer only flowers or flowers and incense. Whatever the acts performed, they are always accompanied by the recitation of mantras—either Vedic mantras or sectarian mantras such as *Śivāya namaḥ* ("adoration to Śiva") or *Vishnave namaḥ* ("adoration to Vishnu").

The water used in bathing the image is collected for further ritual use. This water, called *tīrtha,* has been purified by contact with the deity and is considered specially sacred. At the end of the ceremony it is distributed to the officiant in the ritual and to his family and friends or, in a temple ceremony, to the priests and assembled worshipers, small ladles-full of water being poured into the right hand of the recipients who then sip it, drink it, or sprinkle it over their heads. The flowers offered to the deity are also often distributed to the worshipers, as is the food which has been offered. The latter, considered the remnants of the deity's meal, is called *prasāda* ("free gift" or "graciousness") in recognition of the deity's benevolence in sharing his food with his worshipers. Worshipers at a temple will often bring offerings of flowers and food to the deity in order to take the remnants home for those who could not attend the *pūjā* in person.

In a home, the deity is an honored guest to be treated with the highest degree of hospitality possible. In a temple, which is the deity's home, he is treated more in the manner of a king or holy person presenting himself to his worshipers. There, as with a king or holy man, the deity's graciousness is expressed not only in his *prasāda* but also in his presentation of himself for *darśana,* "seeing" or "viewing" by his worshipers. This is particularly true in temples that are the focus of pilgrimages. On special holy days and festivals, for the benefit of those who cannot get into the temple for *pūjā,* the deity (often in the form of a replica of the main image of the temple) is taken outside the temple for a tour in a palanquin or in a special cart so the maximum number of people can see him ("receive *darśana*"). Such occasions may be the high point of the ritual year, as at Purī in Orissa where the deity, a form of Krishna as Lord Jagannātha, "Lord of the World," is pulled through the streets by his worshipers in a gigantic cart that has given us the name "juggernaut." Similar activities are carried out at other temples either annually or on periodic occasions related to the life of the deity: he may go on trips at special times, visit other deities, hold special assemblies, or may simply travel around for "sport" (*līlā*) or recreation.

Worship of a deity in the form of an image by means of *pūjā* is a direct expression of popular theistic religion. At its most basic level its meaning is summed up in Krishna's statement to Arjuna in the *Gītā:* "He who offers me with devotion a leaf, a flower, a fruit or water, that devout offering of a pure-minded one I accept" (9.26). The *pūjā* ritual for honoring invited Brāhmans in the Gṛihya Sūtras provided a structure for such devout offerings, but did not change the human, personal relation of the worshiper to his god. The image in *pūjā* is treated as one would treat the god himself in person, for the image *is* the god in person: it is his *mūrti,* his "form" made manifest for his worshipers. This sense of the deity as a person and the image as his representative personal form is fundamental to the meaning of *pūjā* and is always preserved in *pūjā* rituals.

Sectarian Āgamas and Tantra

It was not until the early sixth century A.D. that the Purāṇas began discussing topics such as *pūjā,* vows, and pilgrimages, and until the end of the eighth century their rules for these practices reflected Smārta efforts to maintain Vedic and Brahmanical standards. As early as the fifth century, however, the Vaishnava Pāñcarātra sect and probably also some Śaivite groups had begun to produce ritual texts called Āgamas separate from the Purāṇas and much less influenced by Smārta ritual concerns. Here we get a great expansion of sectarian rituals and for the first time a thoroughgoing acceptance of the principles and practices called Tantra.

Tantra is an elusive term to define, and has been given a wide range of meanings. The term sometimes refers to any non-Vedic practice. At other times it is restricted to a particular set of teachings that emphasize the cosmic male-female polarity, or to practices that use this polarity ritually to bring about the experience of release. The general definition of Tantra we will use falls somewhere between these two. "Tantra" here will refer to those non-Vedic beliefs and practices that emphasized the existence in man of divine powers that could be activated and experienced by means of special ritual procedures.

The sexual elements so important in later Tantra are not much in evidence in the early Āgamas. The powers within man are not defined in terms of a male-female polarity or as manifestations of the female Śakti power. One aspect of later Tantra is equally important here, however: emphasis on the physical body as the locus of these powers and thus the focus of ritual practice.

Man in the various Tantric systems is considered a microcosm of the universe, containing within himself the full range of cosmic realities. The ordinary person, however, is unaware of his true nature. His inner powers lie dormat, unactivated, and hence useless in his quest for salvation. Only by actually experiencing the realities within can he free himself from his condition of ignorance and bondage and realize his identity with the absolute. This cannot be done theoretically, but can only be achieved by practice, *sādhana.* As the Brahmanical tradition had earlier sought to tune the sacrifice to the macrocosmic universe, so man must tune himself—his body no less than his mind—to the cosmic realities within. The means to be used for this tuning are mantras, yogic meditation, and the ritual use of visual images.

The heart of Tantra is practice, *sādhana,* the actual procedure by which the inner powers are activated and experienced. Before we can examine Tantric *sādhana* in the Āgamas, however, we must look at developments in the concept of images that paralleled the rise of Tantra. These developments, essential to Tantric practice, constitute one of the major topics of the early sectarian Āgamas.

The Standardization of Images

An image, as we have seen, is divine power made manifest in form. The emphasis in popular worship and in *pūjā* is on the worshiper's personal relation to the god who is present in or revealed in his image. Tantra, however, emphasizes the formal characteristics of the image itself, the particular set of attributes of the god revealed in the symbols of the image. An important part of Tantric *sādhana* is identification with the deity in the form of an image, and this is only effective if the image is true. The characteristics of an image may not be arbitrary; they must accurately state the qualities and powers of the god as revealed to those with insight.

This requirement led rapidly to the standardization of iconography for those images used in Tantric rituals. The importance of an image for these rituals was its use as an iconographic device. An image, if it accurately stated the truth about a god, gave access to the god and to his power. It was an expression of the truth in visual symbols, as a mantra was an expression of the truth in sound. As early as the first Pāñcarātra Āgamas, these visual symbols were codified to ensure their accurate reproduction.

The codification of images was precisely detailed with respect to allowable poses, dimensional proportions, and the special characteristics of each god. The iconographic device of multiple arms was used to indicate manifold divine powers, each arm representing a characteristic quality or activity and the combination indicating the special form of the god. The symbols appropriate to a given god were standardized for the variety of possible forms, and each form and set of attributes was identified.

The standardization of forms and symbols was remarkably uniform across sectarian lines, regardless of which god was identified as the Supreme Lord. The actual physical images in wood, stone, or metal were made by craftsmen who produced *mūrtis* for all sects on the basis of standard iconographic descriptions. Special texts called Śilpa Śāstras were gradually developed for the use of these craftsmen, and these in time tended further to eliminate variations in representation. As a result, though sectarian texts concentrate on images of their principal deities and give them special theological significance, the representations themselves are not uniquely sectarian.

As examples of standard representations we may take the images of Vishnu and Śiva. Vishnu is usually represented with four arms (two "natural" arms in front and another pair behind them), with his hands holding two or more of his standard symbols: mace, discus, conch, and lotus. One or both of the front hands (usually the lower hands), instead of holding symbols, may be placed in positions called *mudrās,* positions of arm and hand expressing an attitude or action of the deity. The most common *mudrās* are the *abhaya-mudrā* (hand turned to the front with fingers pointing upward) expressing tranquility or assurance of protection to the worshiper, and the *varada-mudrā* (hand turned to the front with fingers pointing downward) expressing bestowal of a boon or benediction.

The usual images of Vishnu show him seated or standing with a combination of symbols and *mudrās* indicating one of his particular aspects or attitudes. Vishnu's various incarnations may be indicated either by special combinations of the mace, discus, conch, and lotus symbols or by separate images of the *avatāras*. The most common *avatāra* images are the Boar (Vishnu as a boar-headed giant raising the earth on his tusk), the Man-Lion (Vishnu as part man, part lion, ripping the entrails from the demon king who threatened his devotee Prahlāda), or Krishna (the cowherd boy as a crawling baby carrying a stolen ball of butter, as a youth dancing on the head of the defeated serpent Kalīya, or playing his flute as the divine lover of the *gopīs*).

Reclining images of Vishnu are almost always of Vishnu on the serpent-couch formed by the coiled body of Śeṣa, or Ananta, resting on the cosmic waters during the "night of Brahmā," an indication of the influence of Purāṇic mythology on the form of images. This image, however, is usually reserved for the main image in temples; it is a cosmic image, the Vaishnavite equivalent of the *lingam* of Śiva as an expression of cosmic creative power in its potential form, the iconographic equivalent of the creative cosmic sound syllable *oṃ*.

Śiva's standard image is the stylized cylindrical *lingam,* often set in a key-hole-shaped base representing the *yoni* (the "womb" or "vulva," the female aspect of Śiva's creative power); by far the greatest number of Śiva images in both homes and temples are of this type. Śiva also is represented anthropomorphically, however, usually seated as the Lord of Yoga or standing either as an ascetic or as the Destroyer in his Rudra aspect. In these images Śiva has matted hair and a third eye in the middle of his forehead, symbolic of his yogic insight. Around his neck is coiled a snake, and his hands hold various symbols such as a trident (his main identifying symbol), a battle-ax, bow, club, spear, or noose, an hourglass-shaped drum, or a garland of skulls. Other images show Śiva in a more benevolent or protective aspect dressed in his royal finery and accompanied usually by his wife Pārvatī, or in his active creative aspect as the Lord of Dance holding his trident that represents the three *guṇas* and beginning the activation of Prakṛiti.

These images have continued down to the present day and have been accepted by all Hindus, but their standardization was most important to the sectarian theists who followed Tantric practices. Any representation of the appropriate god could be used in devotion and *pūjā,* where both the image and the god were external to the worshiper and emphasis was on the devotee's attitudes and acts of service. Tantra, however, added a new understanding and use of images. Where *pūjā* was directed outward, Tantra emphasized internalization of the image and identification of the worshiper with the divine powers represented by the image and its symbols. This was accomplished by new practices first described in the sectarian Āgamas.

Tantric Practices in the Sectarian Āgamas

There are few sectarian differences between Vaishnavite and Śaivite Tantric practices in the Āgamas. Much more evident is the common Tantric emphasis on internalization of images, identification with the deity and divine powers, the use of Tantric mantras, and reliance on sectarian or Tantric teachers rather than orthodox Brāhmans for religious instruction.

Internalization begins with meditation on the image of a deity in order to learn its form and understand its symbolism. This requires standardized iconography, since the initial process of visualization cannot be accomplished in the abstract and individual variation is not allowed. It is the specific iconographic details of the image that express the powers and qualities of the god. If these are to be assimilated within the worshiper, they first must be represented with precision and consistency so they can be clearly visualized.

Next, they must be appropriated. Yogic methods of concentration are used to absorb both the outward form of the image and its inner truth. The image then is visualized internally and the external image is transferred to a purely mental plane, constructed and established mentally within the individual. Here again details are essential, since the powers of the god can be assimilated only if the iconographic symbols of these powers are accurately reproduced internally.

The final step is identification with the god represented by the image. This is possible because in Tantra, as we have seen, man is considered a microcosm of the universe. All divine powers are present within him already, but in a quiescent or latent state. Internalization of the divine image is the means by which these powers can be activated and the god and his powers established within. Worship of the god is in this way transformed from external worship to *mānasa-yāga,* "mental worship."

Mānasa-yāga is clearly more technical than *pūjā,* which requires only devotion and an external discipline. The stages of "mental worship" are the final three stages of yoga—meditation, concentration, and absorption—which can only be perfected by rigorous training with the help of a guru or preceptor. Similar technical guidance is required for related practices called *nyāsas* and *mudrās* advocated for the first time in the Āgamas.

Nyāsa, "placing" or "projecting," is a system of "ritual projection" using mantras to establish gods or divine powers in various parts of the body. The worshiper meditates on the god or power he wishes to appropriate and then, while reciting the appropriate mantra, touches his body to establish them at the desired points. *Mudrās* or hand poses are used to identify with certain divine qualities or achieve certain states of consiciousness. A variety of *mudrās* are employed, all of them symbolic positions of the hands and fingers which, like the *mudrās* of images, express specific emotions or powers. Appropriation is achieved by mental concentration that activates the corresponding emotions or powers in the worshiper.

Mental worship, *nyāsas,* and *mudrās* were only a few of the new Tantric elements introduced in the Āgamas. More basic than these specific practices was the widespread use of mantras for almost every ritual purpose. What was new here was not the use of mantras per se but the emphasis and the type of mantra used.

Smārta texts from as early as the Gṛihya Sūtras and *Manu* had advocated the practice of *japa,* the repetition of Vedic mantras such as the *Gāyatrī* (*Rig Veda* III.62.10) or the *Puruṣa Sūkta* hymn (*Rig Veda* X.90). *Manu* even claimed that daily repetition of the *Gāyatrī* and the Vedic syllables *bhūḥ bhuvaḥ svar* at sunrise and sunset would bring the merit of reciting all the Vedas and would purify a man from guilt, and that repetition of the syllable *oṃ* constantly for three years would bring union with Brahman at the time of death. *Japa* thus was not a Tantric innovation, nor was the ritual use of mantras, which went back to Vedic times. The Āgamas, however, substituted Tantric mantras for Vedic mantras in what had formerly been Brahmanical rituals, and considered that these mantras had power in themselves to purify and bring spiritual rewards apart from any Brahmanical qualifications.

In the earliest Āgamas of the Pāñcarātra sect, Tantric mantras were specified as necessary for initiation, consecration of images, ceremonies to the ancestors, and all daily rituals. Certain Vedic mantras, especially *oṃ,* were used in Pāñcarātra rituals, but they were rivaled in importance by Tantric mantras such as *phaṭ* (the "weapon-mantra") or *oṃ āḥ hūṃ* (the "root-mantra"). *Japa* of Tantric mantras was substituted for many older penances and rites of purification. Vedic austerities of specified duration were replaced by a specified number of *japas* counted off on a rosary of 108 beads. The special sectarian mantra *namo Nārāyaṇāya* ("homage to Nārāyaṇa") was granted the power to remove sins and even to confer salvation on those who recited it regularly with devotion.

Śaivite Āgamas show the same pattern of development among the worshipers of Śiva. Like the Pāñcarātra Āgamas, these texts contained instructions on temple building, image making, and religious practice with emphasis on the use of mantras and other Tantric features. The Śaivite mantra *nama Śivāya* ("homage to Śiva") replaced the Vaishnavite sectarian mantra, and emphasis was on Śiva rather than Vishnu, but the concerns of the Āgamas were otherwise similar and reflected the same pattern of Tantric influence.

Such sectarian developments had important social implications. Vedic mantras could be taught only by Brāhmans and were restricted in their use to twice-born men who had undergone Vedic initiation and study of the Vedas; the claims for their effectiveness in *Manu* and other Smārta texts were similarly restricted. Tantric mantras, however, could be taught by any preceptor or guru who knew their meaning and use, and could be taught to women, children, and Śūdras who were excluded from Vedic rituals. The only qualification was initiation, and this was offered to anyone who sought refuge in the Lord.

Religious authority was in this way shifted from orthodox Brāhmans who knew the Vedas to those whose qualities of devotion and knowledge set them apart as preceptors within the sectarian community, regardless of their status outside that community in terms of the traditional *varṇāśrama-dharma* system. This was reflected in instructions in the Āgamas for offering gifts at religious ceremonies not to the traditional invited Brāhmans but to the gurus who initiated and taught the members of the sect. Emphasis was no longer on Vedic knowledge and Brahmanical status, but on development in the use of Tantric practices and the sectarian Tantric mantras.

The New Devotionalism

The Āgamas and Purāṇas of the fifth to seventh centuries A.D. emphasize the value of the new sectarian means of salvation in the *Kali Yuga*. This last of the four *Yuga* cycles in which we now are living is described as a time of general deterioration of standards. In the past, it is said, men were purer and capable of greater learning and performance of religious duties. Men in the *Kali Yuga* are not able to learn all the Vedas and engage in extended practice of austerities. If the standards of the seers of the past were required, everyone in the *Kali Yuga* would fall short of salvation and be condemned to endless misery. For this reason, an easier way has been given: devotion to the Lord and the use of mantras for purification. These are accessible to all who earnestly seek them, and can be used by even the lowly and unlearned to gain salvation. All one need do now is seek refuge in Vishnu or Śiva, worship them and call on their name in devotion, and they will give relief.

This attitude found a dramatic expression in the Tamil-speaking area of South India with a succession of great Śaivite and Vaishnavite poet-saints beginning around the sixth century A.D. Both the Śaivite saints (called collectively Nāyanārs, "leaders") and the Vaishnavite saints (the Āḷvārs, "divers" into the divine) included among their number women and members of the lower classes of society as well as Brāhmans and scholars. Though their individual messages differed in detail and emphasis, their common theme was intense devotion to God. Their teachings moreover were not in Sanskrit, the language of the Vedas, Purāṇas, and Āgamas, but in Tamil, the language of the people—poetic Tamil that could be recited and sung by everyone.

The poetry of the Nāyanārs and Āḷvārs was strongly influenced by the stories of the gods in the epics and Purāṇas. They brought these to the popular level in their hymns and songs, transforming them by the quality of their devotion into a message of divine love. The message was highly emotional and intensely personal; it was their own relationship to God that they expressed, conveyed in terms of human feelings—love, friendship, despair, and joy. The language of devotion was for them the language of the emotions, human and personal, and at times so intense that it was painful. The goal they sought was salvation, but it was salvation in very personal terms: not union with the impersonal Brahman or even merger with the Lord, but an eternal relationship of blissful devotion in which the distinction between the devotee and the Lord would be preserved. The spirit of their devotion was well expressed by the later Indian saint Śrī Rāmakrishna when he declared that he wanted "to taste sugar, not become sugar."

The hymns of the Nāyanārs were preserved in several collections that were finally combined in the tenth century to make up *The Twelve Tirumuṛai* ("Holy Books"), the major canonical scripture for Tamil Śaivites. Taken as a whole, the hymns in the *Tirumuṛai* brought together the epic and Purāṇic accounts of Śiva, local legends and stories, the saints' own experiences at the temples and shrines of the Tamil area, and the teachings of the Śaivite Āgamas —all infused with a spirit of emotional devotion. The hymns remained the favorite expression of popular devotion among Tamil Śaivites, and along with the Śaiva Āgamas they were the base for the most important Tamil Śaivite sect, the Śaiva-siddhānta. Developed in the thirteenth century, the Śaiva-siddhānta gave theological and ritual expression to the Nāyanārs' devotion in its emphasis on divine grace and the eternal distinction between God and the self.

A similar development occurred in Tamil Vaishnavism as a result of the Āḷvārs. A major factor in this instance was the popular cult of Krishna Gopāla, apparently brought into the Tamil region by a southern branch of the Ābhīras. The Tamil epic *Śilappadikāram,* written sometime before A.D. 600, has numerous references to stories of the cowherd boy Krishna and a detailed description of cowherdesses performing Krishna's dance with the *gopīs* outside the South Indian capital of Madurai.

The Krishna Gopāla theme more than any other inspired the poetry of the Āḷvārs. The *gopīs'* relation to Krishna was for them the prototype of the devotee's relation to God. In their effort to express their relation to the Lord, they often adopted the *gopīs'* role of abandoned lovers longing for their beloved, filling their songs with the passion, despair, and joy of love for the fickle but desirable Krishna.

The songs of the Āḷvārs were brought together in the early eleventh century into a collection called the *Nālāyira Divyaprabandham* ("The Four Thousand Sacred Hymns"). This work is credited to Nāthamuni (A.D. 824–924), the first of a line of Tamil Vaishnava *ācāryas* ("teachers") who sought to bring together Tamil devotion and the Sanskritic Pāñcarātra Āgamas introduced from North India. Nāthamuni and his successors established regular singing of the Āḷvārs' hymns in Vaishnavite temples and gave the *Divyaprabandham* canonical status in the Śrī-Vaishnava sect which they founded. Their efforts were thus similar to those of the later Śaiva-siddhānta; but, unlike the Tamil Śaivites, the Śrī-Vaishnavas produced major works of Sanskrit scholarship which give them influence far outside the Tamil area.

The Major Lines of Hindu Development

The new emotional devotion of the Nāyanārs and Āḷvārs and the founding of the Śrī-Vaishnava sect brought into existence the last of the major elements in the Hindu synthesis. From around A.D. 1000 onward, the Hindu tradition presented a spectrum of religious options ranging from Brahmanical orthodoxy to popular devotion and Tantra. Important developments occurred later within this spectrum, but the main lines of development were by now established.

The late Hindu tradition can perhaps be understood best if we examine representative lines of development in the form of a typology of options, focusing on the basic characteristics of each option. Four typical options seem most important to examine in detail: the continuation of Brahmanical orthodoxy in its intellectual and practical forms, the synthesis of devotion and Vedic authority in a major theistic sect, popular devotionalism in the tradition of poet-saints, and Tantric systems centered around the worship of the Goddess Devī in her many forms.

Brahmanical Orthodoxy: Śankara and the Smārta Tradition

Brahmanical orthodoxy from early times had two major emphases: Vedic knowledge (*jñāna*) and proper action (*karma*). These two emphases, one philosophical and the other practical, were preserved in the later Hindu tradition in the systems of Vedānta philosophy based on the Upanishads and in the Smārta concern for Brahmanical *dharma*.

The most important exponent of the *jñāna* tradition in later times was the great Vedānta philosopher Śankara (A.D. 788–820). Śankara's philosophy was set forth in commentaries on the major Upanishads, the *Bhagavad Gītā,* and the *Brahma Sūtras* of Bādarāyana, the latter a compendium of brief aphorisms that summarized Upanishadic teachings. In all his commentaries, and especially in his major work on the *Brahma Sūtras,* he maintained a strict *advaita* ("nondualistic") philosophy.

Śankara argued that the entire Vedānta, in which he included the *Gītā* as well as the Upanishads and the *Brahma Sūtras,* taught the sole reality of the impersonal Brahman devoid of all qualities (*nirguṇa*). The assumption of qualities and of name and form is a result of ignorance (*avidyā*) resulting from *māyā* ("illusion," as Śankara interprets it). The entire phenomenal world is thus ultimately illusory, since its existence results from the false imposition of qualities on Brahman. It is not unreal in a practical sense, but in comparison with *nirguṇa* Brahman it has no real existence.

Śankara's position had two basic religious implications. If all distinctions and qualities are illusory, then there can be no permanent individual selves; what is taken to be the individual self is the result of ignorance, the erroneous imposition of particularity on the one true Self which is Brahman. And if individual selves are ultimately unreal, then bondage and rebirth are ultimately unreal; so-called bondage is the result of ignorance, the false assumption of an individual self. Release is thus also ultimately unreal, since there is no individual self to be released. What is called release is merely knowledge that there is nothing other than Brahman and thus nothing to be released.

The second implication follows from the first. As there is no means of release other than knowledge of the pure unqualified Brahman, then knowledge of a Lord with qualities cannot bring release. A personal god is the result of falsely imposing qualities on the impersonal unqualified Brahman. As long as Brahman is the object of ignorance there is the assumption of such categories as devotee, object of devotion, and the like, but these are as unreal as the individual self. Devotion assumes distinctions between the Lord and his devotee and assigns different qualities and attributes to the Lord as the object of devotion. Devotion is a valid religious practice, and may eventually lead to true knowledge of Brahman as the devotee is led beyond the qualified Lord to the underlying real unqualified Brahman, but devotion itself without true knowledge is insufficient.

Śankara recognized the relative truth of the discipline of actions (*karma-yoga*) in the *varṇāśrama-dharma* system, as he recognized the relative truth of the discipline of devotion (*bhakti-yoga*), but both were only preparations for *jñāna-yoga,* the discipline of knowledge. He had little interest in householder life, since the way of *jñāna* can ultimately be followed only by one who has renounced the world as a *sannyāsin*. Śankara was credited with founding ten orders of *sannyāsins* based on his *advaita* or monistic doctrine of salvation by knowledge alone. Consistent with his emphasis on *jñāna-yoga,* the *sannyāsins* in his orders gave up their sacred threads and all religious duties to devote themselves completely to the saving knowledge of Brahman.

The practical side of Brahmanical orthodoxy has been preserved largely by Smārtas, whose central concern from the time of *Manu* onward has been with householder life within the framework of *varṇāśrama-dharma*. The Smārta tradition that has survived is the Purāṇic Smārta tradition, a blend of Vedic and Brahmanical standards of *karma-yoga* with the worship of popular gods by means of *pūjā*. Those who tried to preserve a strict Vedic ritual pattern gradually lost ground as popular devotion, Purāṇic influence, and the rise of theistic sects made image worship almost universal.

Theistic Smārtas, as we have seen in examining the epics and early Purāṇas, were characterized by an eclectic theism and an emphasis on Brahmanical rules of *dharma*. Smārtas continued to resist sectarian involvement and rejected the Tantric elements that were adopted by both Vaishnavite and Śaivite sects. Their positions was thus Brahmanical rather than Tantric, theistic rather than sectarian, Purāṇic rather than Āgamic.

The characteristic Smārta religious form is *pañcāyatana-pūjā* (*"pūjā of* the five shrines"), developed some time after the beginning of the seventh century as a compromise between early Smārta practices and the new Purāṇic theism. The Smārta ritual involves the worship of not one but five representative deities: Vishnu, Śiva, Sūrya, Gaṇeśa, and Durgā. The first two are the main sectarian gods; Sūrya is the Vedic sun god to whom Smārtas offered regular morning worship; Gaṇeśa is the popular elephant-headed god associated with Śiva, worshiped as the remover of obstacles and patron of scholars; and Durgā is the consort of Śiva and a powerful deity in her own right, raised to prominence with the growth of cults to the Goddess. The group of five is truly eclectic, though slightly weighted toward Śiva as the Smārta tradition itself has been since Purāṇic times.

All five deities are worshiped in *pañcāyatana-pūjā,* though the worshiper usually singles out one of the five for special attention as his *iṣṭa-devatā* or "chosen deity." The five allow a wide range of choice, since Vishnu may be worshiped in any of his aspects or incarnations and both Śiva and Durgā have many separate identities. A Smārta family usually has a traditional choice of one of the five for the central place in household *pūjā,* but each individual family member may have his own *iṣṭa-devatā.* Smārta temples give one god, usually Śiva, the place of prominence at the head of the temple, with the others represented in separate shrines, but here also *pūjā* may be offered to any of the five.

Aside from the eclectic nature of the five gods, Smārta worship differs from sectarian worship on two basic points: the ritual and the mantras used are Vedic (that is, based on Smārta and not Tantric texts), and the purpose of the worship is not desire for divine salvation, but performance of a ritual duty. For Smārtas, ritual purity and adherence to Smārta duties are more important than the god being worshiped and are important whether a god is worshiped at all. The system of thought called Karma-mīmāṃsā, the philosophy of ritual duties accepted by all Smārtas, is not concerned even with the existence of God; as often as not Karma-mīmāṃsā philosophers denied God's existence or considered it irrelevant. The only concern is the proper performance of duties established by the Vedas to eliminate the painful effects of *karma.* This was the central purpose of the Smārta system, whatever philosophy might be adopted to explain the ultimate goal of release.

Final release is not a concern of the Smārta system as such, but historically the Smārta tradition has been closely associated with Śankara's philosophy of release by knowledge alone. Śankara's *advaita* philosophy was widely adopted by Smārtas from the ninth century on as an ideal complement to the Smārta position, since for Śankara also worship of a deity endowed with qualities was a duty and not a means of salvation. In South India in particular, where the majority of Smārta Brāhmans and Smārta temples are found in later times, being a Smārta includes acceptance of Śankara's *advaita* Vedānta system of thought.

Sectarian Theism: Rāmānuja and the Śrī-Vaishnava Sect

Theistic devotion was for Śankara only a preliminary to final release by means of *jñāna-yoga;* for Smārtas, theistic worship is a part of the ritual duties of *karma-yoga*. For theistic sects, however, worship of the sectarian god and devotion to him are the central and ultimate concerns. *Karma-yoga* and *jñāna-yoga* must be subsidiary to *bhakti-yoga,* for release can come only by means of devotion and the reciprocal grace of God.

One of the earliest and best examples of this position is the Śrī-Vaishnava sect. Founded by Nāthamuni on the basis of the devotional hymns of the Āḷvārs and the Tantric-influenced Pāñcarātra Āgamas, the Śrī-Vaishnavas were clearly sectarian from the start. The establishment of Śrī-Vaishnavism as a major sectarian system, however, was largely the work of Rāmānuja, the fifth in the line of *ācāryas* after Nāthamuni and the leader of the sect in the eleventh and early twelfth centuries. Brahmanical opponents had challenged the sect on the grounds of its non-Vedic devotional practices and its use of the Pāñcarātra Āgamas. Rāmānuja took on himself the task of proving the orthodoxy of Vaishnava devotion and, what is more important, proving the validity of devotion as a way of salvation.

Rāmānuja argues most directly against the position of Śankara, whose *advaita* Vedānta commentaries were classics of Brahmanical orthodoxy by Rāmānuja's time. Śankara had asserted that both the individual self and the phenomenal world are the product of ignorance and illusion, so the apparent bondage of the self can only be removed by knowledge. Against this position, Rāmānuja argued in his own commentaries on the *Brahma Sūtras* and *Gītā* that the phenomenal world is real, being the product of the Lord's creative power of *māyā*. *Māyā* is not illusion, nor is the world in any sense illusory. The world is created as a result of Brahman's intention to become manifold; it is the body of Brahman, existing periodically in subtle and gross form. Individual selves also are real and eternal, related to Brahman as parts to a whole or as light is to the fire from which it issues; their true nature is an "I," of which they are permanently conscious in the state of release.

Embodied selves are engrossed in ignorance as a result of *karma* and do not recognize their essential nature. They can be released from ignorance and bondage only by knowledge of Brahman endowed with all auspicious qualities, knowledge which is of the nature of meditation. But since bondage is real it cannot be put an end to by knowledge alone; the cessation of bondage can come only through the grace of the Highest Self pleased by the devout meditation of the worshiper. The resulting relationship of the worshiper to the Highest Self is real and permanent. It is eternal blissful devotion, not to be superseded by knowledge of an unqualified Brahman.

Rāmānuja's entire argument was for the purpose of defending theistic devotion as philosophically and scripturally valid and effective for salvation. Strategically, he did not defend the orthodoxy of the Āḷvārs' emotional devotion to Krishna Gopāla. Instead, he directed his apologetics toward a defense of the older and more acceptable *bhakti* of the *Bhagavad Gītā* and the early Pāñcarātra tradition of the epic, drawing his evidence from the Upanishads instead of less authoritative or less respectable sources such as the sectarian Purāṇas and Āgamas.

What Rāmānuja defended was *bhakti-yoga* as a blissful knowledge of the Lord gained by devout meditation. Only the twice-born man could, in his view, practice this. True *bhakti-yoga* required a preliminary study of the Vedas and Upanishads and a knowledge of the philosophy of ritualism; both *karma-yoga* (proper performance of *dharma*) and *jñāna-yoga* (proper knowledge) were necessary for effective devotion. Emotional devotion characterized by self-surrender as taught by the Āḷvārs was not ignored by Rāmānuja, but this was for Śūdras and others who were not qualified for Vedic study or who lacked the ability to learn from the scriptures and pursue the more arduous method of *bhakti-yoga*.

Consistent with this limitation of *bhakti-yoga* to those qualified on orthodox grounds was Rāmānuja's general support of the *varṇāśrama-dharma* system and the performance of religious duties. A contrast with Śankara can be seen again here. *Sannyāsins* in Śankara's orders gave up all religious duties in pursuit of the saving knowledge of Brahman. Śrī-Vaishnava *sannyāsins* who followed Rāmānuja's principles, however, kept their sacred threads and maintained their ritual duties even after renouncing the world, since for Rāmānuja devotion should always be supported by *karma-yoga* and was an outgrowth of proper ritual performance.

Rāmānuja's defense of the Śrī-Vaishnava system had many similarities to the technique of the *Gītā*. Salvation was offered to all through some form of devotion, but emphasis was at the same time placed on performance of duties according to *varṇāśrama-dharma*. The devotional fervor and religious inclusiveness of the Āḷvārs were preserved, but their charisma was fit into the framework of the Brahmanical social system. By accommodating his teachings as far as possible to the Smārta position without losing the central emphasis on devotion, Rāmānuja achieved a stable synthesis between popular and Brahmanical religion.

The Śrī-Vaishnavas have continued down to modern times as a model of sectarian theism, establishing a pattern followed by many other sectarian groups. The system in general is, like Rāmānuja's theology, a synthesis of popular and Brahmanical elements. Socially it is a part of the Brahmanical synthesis, accepting the basic pattern of *varṇāśrama-dharma,* but Smārta regulations are replaced by sectarian rules based on the Āgamas. It derives the authority for its theology from the Vedas and Upanishads, but its religious practices reflect the influence of the Purāṇas, Tantric practices, and popular devotion, and center around *pūjā* performed according to the Āgama traditions. Ultimately, it is sectarian, deriving its strength not from Brahmanical authority but from its own institutions and its devotional religious life centered on Vishnu alone.

The stability and continuity of Śrī-Vaishnavism, as of all theistic sects, is in its homes and temples, in the local traditions and practices that have developed around them, and in the *maṭhas* or teaching centers where the tradition is passed on to new generations of sectarian scholars. Binding all these together, and giving the sect its meaning, is the common worship of the same god with the same rituals by the entire community.

Emotional Devotion: The Bhāgavata Purāṇa and Popular Poet-Saints

The Śrī-Vaishnavas represent a structuring of popular devotion within clearly defined sectarian institutions and practices. The vitality of Hindu devotion, however, cannot be easily captured within sectarian limits. The religion of the people is much closer to the devotional enthusiasm of the Āḷvārs than to the refined theology and *bhakti-yoga* of Rāmānuja. Typical of this popular devotion are the *Bhāgavata Purāṇa* and the succession of popular poet-saints and religious movements that have followed it.

The *Bhāgavata Purāṇa* is the latest of the major Purāṇas, most likely produced in South India in the ninth century following the impact of the Āḷvārs' devotional activity. Its central focus is worship of Vishnu through devotion to Krishna, with emphasis on the cowherd Krishna of Vṛindāvana. The tenth book of the *Bhāgavata* tells in great detail the story of Krishna Gopāla, expanding significantly the account of Krishna's sports with the *gopīs* found in the earlier *Vishnu Purāṇa* and *Harivaṃśa*. In full agreement with the Āḷvārs' songs and actions, the love relationship of the *gopīs* to Krishna is taken as the ideal example of man's relationship to the Lord.

Devotion to Krishna sets the emotional tone for the whole Purāṇa. Other *avatāras* are described and more traditional types of worship are set forth, but these are of little interest compared to Krishna and his devotees' emotional attachment to him. Teachings on *varṇāśrama-dharma* and rituals have a relatively minor place compared to earlier Purāṇas. Love of Krishna and service to him is for the *Bhāgavata* the principal *dharma* for a devotee, and the principal ritual is surrender to the Lord in devotion—calling on his name, reciting praises of him, and keeping him always in one's mind.

The devotional emphasis carries over also into the *Bhāgavata*'s social attitudes. Great compassion is shown for the poor and lowly, caste distinctions are declared irrelevant for the devotees of Krishna, and there is great praise for devotees who are Śūdras or members of lowly castes. The appeal throughout is to the simple followers of Lord Krishna who claim no qualifications except devotion and no purity except purity of heart in love.

This message had great power when it was first set forth by the Āḷvārs, and its power remained as it was transmitted through the *Bhāgavata Purāṇa*. Later Vaishnava devotional movements almost all had the *Bhāgavata* as a base, and almost all were characterized in their initial stages by intense devotional fervor. The Krishna-centered movement started by Madhva in Mysore in the thirteenth century was directly influenced by the *Bhāgavata,* and its influence on the great Maharashtrian saint Jñāneśvara later in the same century is evident in his devotional writings. From this time on a succession of Vaishnava devotional movements swept through Maharashtra and North India, not all Krishna-centered but all distinguished by ardent devotion and appeal to a popular following. The movement founded by Caitanya in Bengal in the early sixteenth century brought the development to a fitting close both in its intensity and its direct reliance on the *Bhāgavata* as a manual of devotion.

A distinctive feature of the movements from Jñāneśvara through Caitanya was the vast quantity of vernacular devotional literature they produced, much of it in the form of poetry and song. After Jñāneśvara in Maharashtra came a series of great poets: Nāmdev in the fourteenth century, Eknāth in the sixteenth, and Tukārām in the seventeenth, all producing songs sung today by peasants and scholars alike. Kabīr in the fifteenth and Tulsī Dās in the sixteenth centuries wrote devotional poetry to Rāma in Hindi. Caitanya in Bengal followed two great fifteenth-century vernacular poets, Caṇḍī-dās and Vidyāpati, who wrote about the love of Krishna and his favorite *gopī* Rādhā, developing further the devotional and erotic themes of the great Sanskrit poem *Gītāgovinda* written by Jayadeva in the late twelfth century.

The devotional poets from the Āḻvārs through Caitanya produced literally thousands of poems in the regional languages of the people, reflecting local culture and expressing the personal religious search of men who were saints and yet human. We have seen the impact of this combination on the Nāyanārs and Āḻvārs in the Tamil area, and it was no less when carried into Maharashtra and the North. No formal institution could contain the power of this flow of devotion, though institutions could, as did the Śrī-Vaishnavas, use it for their purposes.

Devotion of this kind, like the poetry that expressed it, belongs to the people. When pilgrims from all levels of society come together at Pandharpur in Maharashtra to worship at the temple of Viṭhṭhal (Viṭhobā), a form of Krishna, they sing about the great saints who have been there before them and sing the songs of Tukārām, the greatest poet among their saints. When devotees of Caitanya come together they sing songs about Rādhā and Krishna and their love, and dance as the *gopīs* danced; they tell the stories of Krishna and of Caitanya who was Krishna born among them, and they chant the names of the Lord: *Hare Krishna.* Wherever the songs are heard and sung and the stories are told, the tradition is alive.

The modern Indian scholar V. Raghavan has called the saint-singers "the great integrators," and it is this role of integration that has made them so important. They have carried the stories of the Sanskritic epics and Purāṇas to the people in their own language; they have carried religious movements from region to region; they have absorbed the teachings of Smārtas and sectarians and have passed them on enhanced by their own religious experience; they have sung their songs at the pilgrimage places and festivals of all sects, and have themselves established holy places that draw pilgrims from all sects and regions. The poet-saints have been Śaivite as well as Vaishnavite, or they have sung in praise of many gods. Their popular appeal has reached across sectarian and social lines, challenging fixed ways of thinking and creating new alignments. Though many have been outcastes and Śūdras, they have helped make the Brahmanical synthesis work by constantly revitalizing Hindu religious life and making its highest products available to all.

Devī, the Śāktas, and Tantra

We come finally to the worship of the Goddess Devī and the fully developed Tantric tradition. This too is the religion of the people, at least in origin and on one level. Worship of local goddesses is probably as old as the people of India, and village worship to goddesses has always gone on independent of the Vedas or other high traditions. The names and modes of worship of such figures are legion, as many perhaps as the places where they reside, and on the local level represent a myriad of separate popular traditions.

It was not until fairly late in the tradition that certain specific names and personalities of the Goddess began to emerge. The *Mahābhārata* celebrates a goddess Durgā, a virgin goddess who upholds heaven by her chastity but who delights also in wine, meat, and animal sacrifices. She is the sister of Krishna and wears like him a crest of peacock feathers. In what is probably a later passage in the epic she is still associated with Krishna but is now the wife of Śiva and is called Umā. In both passages she is praised for slaying Mahiṣa, a buffalo demon, and in the latter passage the now no longer virgin goddess delights in drinking the demon's blood.

The same goddess is again celebrated in the *Harivaṃśa* and in a section added to the *Mārkaṇḍeya Purāṇa* called the *Devī-* or *Caṇḍī-Mahātmya.* In the latter hymn she is said to have been formed from the fierce radiance of Śiva, Vishnu and Brahmā in order to slay the buffalo demon; she is described as having come forth from the body of Śiva's wife Pārvatī while she was bathing, and from her forehead came a female named Kālī, "the Dark One," wearing a garland of skulls, a tiger skin, and a terrible weapon. As Kālī she kills two other demons and is given the name Cāmuṇḍā, and she is called also the *śakti* or "power" of Śiva.

At this stage of development the Goddess is a powerful deity. She is *Mahiṣāsura-mardinī,* "the slayer of the buffalo demon," known also as Durgā, Caṇḍī, Cāmuṇḍā, or simply as Devī, "Goddess," described and shown in sculpture as riding on a lion and killing the demon in buffalo form with her trident; or she is the Dark One, Kālī, wearing her garland of skulls. In either of these forms, or as Śiva's wife Pārvatī or Umā, she is the object of worship in temples dedicated to the worship of the Devī.

But Durgā is more than that. She is Śakti, the female power formed of the fiery cloud that came from the mouths of the male gods. She is the consort of Śiva, the active female energy that complements Śiva's pure passive intelligence. She is the creative power that activates Prakṛiti, Primal Matter, from which comes forth the universe made up of the three *guṇas*. She is *māyā,* the magical power of creation and illusion. She is the female manifestation of Brahman, the Divine Mother who has brought forth the world of *saṃsāra* and who will, as Kālī, destroy it in the end. She has created the universe in which men live and is thus the divine power nearest and most important to men. Those who worship her are Śāktas, devotees of the divine creative Śakti present in all things.

It is at this point that Tantra entered into the cult of the Goddess, creating alongside the popular cult of Devī worship a new system of thought and practice. The new system drew on two earlier Vedic concepts: mantra and yoga. We have seen earlier how mantras in the Vedic sacrificial system were held to have creative power; they were the sound forms of reality, the proper expression of which would bring forth and establish the realities they represent. From this arose the concept of the *bījā-mantra,* the "seed mantra," the minimal sound form of a given entity. *Oṃ* was the primal seed mantra, the sound form of Brahman and of the Vedas, from which all things came forth as developments from a seed. All things must in the same way have seed mantras to bring them forth, knowing which one could bring forth all things.

According to Tantric teachings, the place to discover these powers is the body, within which are contained all realities. Yoga and careful meditation can activate and locate the seed mantras in the body, gradually building up a complete picture of man as a locus of forces in the form of the mantras resident within. Since these mantras have cosmic referents, the body is—like the fire sacrifice earlier—a microcosmic model of the universe; it is the body of Brahman as the universe is the body of Brahman, the resident place of all the manifested powers of Brahman-Śiva brought forth by Śakti.

The model developed in Tantric yoga locates the *bījā-mantras* in six primary centers called *cakras* or "circles" situated from the base of the spinal column upward to the center of the forehead. Each of these has the form of a lotus with a certain number of petals, and each is the locus of certain mantras, colors, shapes, symbols and gods. The *cakras* are connected by a conduit or artery called the *Suṣumnā* running from the base *cakra* to the top of the head and passing through each *cakra* in turn. Coiled around the *Suṣumnā* at the base is the "Serpent Power," Kuṇḍalinī, energy or power in the form of a serpent, whose head blocks the entrance to the *Suṣumnā.*

This scheme, it should be emphasized, describes a "subtle body" discovered by yogic meditation, not a physical structure that might be seen by a surgeon. The *cakras, Suṣumnā,* and so on are nonetheless real, more real in fact than the gross physical body because they represent the existence within the body of real cosmic forces in latent form. The purpose of Tantric practice is to activate these forces, to make the human body a cosmic body. We have seen how this was done by yogic concentration and absorption using images in "mental worship," and on a point-by-point basis using mantras in the practice of *nyāsa,* but more advanced Tantric practice utilized the Kuṇḍalinī.

In the normal condition of the body, bodily energy circulates through channels called *nāḍīs,* the most important of which are the *Suṣumnā* and the *iḍā* and *piṅgalā* on the left and right sides of the *Suṣumnā.* The *Suṣumnā,* however, is blocked by the Kuṇḍalinī and the energies cannot reach the *cakras.* To activate the *cakras* one must first activate the Kuṇḍalinī. This is done by yogic breath control which stops the energies from circulating through the *iḍā* and *piṅgalā* and concentrates them on the Kuṇḍalinī, "wakening" the sleeping power and sending it up the *Suṣumnā* to activate the *cakras* in turn. As the Kuṇḍalinī, blazing hot, rises up the *Suṣumnā,* it draws energy and life upward with it, leaving the body behind it cold and lifeless. The final goal is to pass through all the *cakras* to the thousand-petaled lotus at the end of the *Suṣumnā,* where Kuṇḍalinī is united with Śiva. Having activated the *cakras* and made the body a cosmic body, the body and the cosmos are at this point, and for this moment, resolved into the primal oneness.

What does all this mean? In the Tantric view, Śiva is passive, pure intelligence, while Śakti is the active female power of Śiva who brings about the creation of the phenomenal world. Śakti is the Tantric equivalent of the female Vāc, "Speech," of the Vedic system, the creative agent in the process by which Brahman is manifested as name and form. Tantra makes the Brahmanical cosmology tangible, identifying the human body with the cosmos so that the body can be used as an instrument to restore the original oneness. The *cakras* are the depository of all the names, forms, and gods brought forth in creation. The Kuṇḍalinī is Śakti, the creative energy or power of Śiva, resting at the opposite end of creation from Śiva. The Tantric yogin rouses Śakti and brings her back into union with Śiva, bringing back with her all that has been created. The *cakras* are heated by the passage of Śakti on her return and are left cold and lifeless as Śakti reabsorbs the created entities into the unformed state, gathers the seeds of creation, as it were, and brings them back to their primal place of rest. The final union of Śakti with Śiva is, for the person who experiences it, an actual resolution of the duality that constitutes the phenomenal world.

The union of Śakti and Śiva by means of the *Kuṇḍalinī yoga* just described is the most advanced form of Tantric *sādhana* or practice, suitable only for those with the most refined character. Such persons, in whom the quality of *sattva* ("purity") predominates, are classified as *divya,* "divine" or "godlike." Other classes of men, the *vīra* ("heroic") and *paśu* ("animal") classes, must rely on other *sādhanas.*

The *vīra,* the "heroic" man, is characterized by a predominance of *rajas.* The *sādhana* suitable for him is the most distinctive Tantric ritual: *cakra-pūjā,* "circle-worship," using "the five elements." The elements chosen are all things that activate the animal senses of man and are normally forbidden to those seeking purification: *madya* ("wine"), *māṃsa* ("meat"), *matsya* ("fish"), *mudrā* (normally a ritual hand position, but here "parched grain," considered an aphrodisiac), and *maithuna* ("sexual intercourse"). The use of these elements, sometimes called *pañca-makāra* ("the five m's"), is uniquely Tantric, and points out the basic Tantric approach to *sādhana* as a means of purification and union.

The Brahmanical approach to purification is prohibition: "the five m's" are dangerous, so they are forbidden. This is the approach also in the orthodox yoga of Patañjali, which begins with vows of continence, purity, and austerity and goes on to a withdrawal of the senses and elimination of sense-contact with the world. Tantra, however, is the religion for the *Kali Yuga* when men's self-discipline is weak. It advocates not the denial or suppression of natural qualities, including sexual impulses, but their use as ritual means. This is the *sahaja-yāna,* the "natural way," suitable to the *Kali Yuga.* Annihilation of sexual impulses in particular is considered by Tantrics as unnatural and impossible; the wise approach, the easy way, is to transform them by ritual means and use them to gain release.

In *Kuṇḍalinī yoga,* the *sādhana* of the godlike man, the body is the manifestation of Śakti and the Kuṇḍalinī is the most powerful manifestation of Śakti's sexual force. This sexual force is not denied; it is used to activate the *cakras* and bring about union. The *vīra,* however, the hero or hero-to-be, is not capable of the discipline needed to use *Kuṇḍalinī yoga* and obtain internal union of Śakti and Śiva. He must first conquer his *rajas* tendency, his inclination to passion and sensual gratification. This is accomplished in the *sādhana* of *cakra-pūja* by using the five elements, the five most dangerous things, in such a way that they aid his spiritual progress.

Śakti is present in all things, in the forbidden food and drink and especially in sexual intercourse. Śakti is the Goddess, the eternal female partner. The danger is that men fail to recognize their human partner as the Goddess and use her to gratify their senses. They should instead worship her, or the Goddess in her, and turn their senses from gratification of selfish desires to an expression of devotion. This cannot be done by the *rajas*-dominated person under normal circumstances, but it can be done by means of a disciplined ritual.

Cakra-pūjā is anything but an orgy. It is a difficult religious ritual requiring long training, and has as its purpose not the free gratification of desires but their redirection into worship. The worshipers sit in a circle, men and women alternately, with each man's female partner seated on his left (the position of goddesses in relation to gods). The leader of the ritual sits in the center with his female partner, his Śakti. The wine and food are consumed first, with recitation of mantras to establish the Śakti nature of the elements consumed. The elements viewed ignorantly as wine, meat, and so on are dangerous, but the elements as Śakti are pure. So too with the female partner in sexual intercourse, the final stage in the ritual. Mantras are recited to establish the female partner as Devī. This process, called *āropa,* "attributing," is crucial to the ritual, for if the partner is not recognized totally as Devī the male is performing an impure act. Once the identity is established, the male worships the female as Devī, performing *pūjā* to her as he would to the Goddess present in an image. Sexual intercourse with his partner is then the culminating act of devotion, the union of the worshiper with the divine Power.

Cakra-pūjā, if properly performed under the guidance of a Tantric guru, removes the danger of the forbidden elements. Both male and female worship the Goddess in the wine and food, and then act out and identify with the union of Śiva and Śakti. Sense gratification is replaced by worship and sensual desires are conquered by transforming them into emotions of worship. This is the path to becoming a hero, and will lead eventually to the purification of the godlike man and the stage of internal *sādhana* using *Kuṇḍalinī yoga.*

There is yet another class of man, however, for whom the *cakra-pūjā* of the *vīra* is too dangerous and unsuitable. This is the *paśu,* the person of animal nature characterized by a predominance of *tamas,* "darkness" or "inertia." The *paśu* is ignorant and unable to recognize the unity of all things as Śakti. "The five m's" would be poison to him, for he could not see them as anything but forbidden and would think he was sinning if he participated in the ritual. He must first purify himself by the normal means of abstention, self-discipline, and devotion to the Goddess in her image form. In performing ordinary *pūjā* he can view the Goddess as other than himself without the great risks that this attitude would entail in *cakra-pūjā.* By worshiping her, and by following the practices of *nyāsa* and *mudrā* prescribed in the Āgamas, he can gradually achieve an awareness of the presence of the Goddess within himself and in all things. Purified, and his dualistic view of the world corrected, he will then be prepared for further progress.

The context of the *divya*'s ritual is his own body, and the context of the *vīra*'s ritual is the circle of worshipers. The context of the *paśu*'s worship is the temple, which presents in tangible form the truths which he seeks. The temple is the body of God in the world, and thus a model of Śakti's manifestation. The Lord Śiva in his image form rests in the inner room of the temple, the *garbha-gṛiha* or "womb-house" around which the temple is constructed. He is the *lingam* at the heart of creation, from which the temple expands as a visual manifestation of Śakti. The temple is itself an image of his universe with all its names and forms, a display of all the manifold expressions of Śakti.

The world-bound worshiper in the temple honors the Lord who has also entered the world as Śakti to make himself known to his creatures. If he cannot resolve his own universe like the Tantric adept, he can at least take solace in the knowledge that the Lord will in the end resolve the entire universe back into himself. As far as he is able, the worshiper prepares himself for that time by identifying with the Lord and his powers by less demanding Tantric practices and by *pūjā.* In this *Kali Yuga* that is all that the *paśu* can do—but perhaps, given the Lord's grace and infinite time, it is enough.

8.
The Continuing Tradition

The Hindu tradition has never ceased to grow and develop new forms to meet new circumstances. This is as true in the modern period as it was in the past, though it is harder to see clearly the directions of growth or the shape of the emerging forms. Some patterns and developments are established, others are as yet tentative; the lines of development we have traced are even more complex than before. The tradition is nonetheless alive not only in India but, increasingly in recent years, beyond India in Europe and America.

Muslims and the West

India was relatively undisturbed from outside for centuries after the Gupta Empire. During these centuries the entire country was brought into the Brahmanical synthesis and a comprehensive cultural integration was achieved. Sectarians, Smārtas, and Tantrics, all levels of society and all regions, were woven together in a complex but stable system.

The movement of people and influences during this period was outward. Buddhists carried their teachings northward to China and eastward to Southeast Asia. Hindu and Buddhist kingdoms were established in Cambodia and Indonesia, bringing a high culture to these areas for the first time. Externally, it was a time of expansion, as internally it was a time when the fabric of society was woven more tightly and the network of religious systems strengthened and matured.

Political integration did not, however, follow social and cultural integration. The breakup of the Gupta Empire left North India divided between small regional kingdoms; South India, beyond the reach of the Guptas, continued its pattern of rivalry and shifting alliances between a succession of aggressive dynasties. When India was finally united politically, it was not Indians who did it; it was Afghan and Mughul Muslims in North India and then the British throughout the subcontinent.

Arab expansion after Muhammad's death in A.D. 632 touched India only briefly, but in the aftermath Muslim kingdoms were established in Afghanistan. Muslims from these kingdoms entered India from around A.D. 1000 onward, first as raiders and then, from the early thirteenth century, as rulers. Most of North India was under at least sporadic Muslim rule after 1236, and a century later independent Muslim kingdoms were established in the Deccan. Then, starting with the conquests of Akbar (1556–1605), most of India was brought under the control of the Mughul Empire. At the greatest expanse of Mughul territorial control under Aurangzeb (1658–1707), only the far south remained under Hindu rule.

The Mughul Empire rapidly declined after Aurangzeb, but by then Western powers were vying for Indian trade and acquiring land bases in India. The Portuguese had settlements at Goa and other ports on the western coast as early as 1510. The British set up trading centers in India in the early seventeenth century, followed later in the same century by the French. New land was gradually acquired by the British, partly by peaceful annexation and partly by warfare with their French rivals and with local Indian rulers. By the middle of the eighteenth century the British were the dominant Indian power, and from the early nineteenth century onward they effectively ruled all of India.

For seven hundred years, from the thirteenth century until Indian independence in 1947, major portions of India were under rule by non-Hindus and often non-Indians. Muslim rulers introduced new principles of law and administration, new art and literature, and a new religion. Many Hindus in the Muslim states of north and central India converted to Islam, giving India by the early twentieth century the world's largest Muslim population.

Muslim rule and contact with Muslims had little direct effect, however, on Hindu religious patterns. Islam did not in general offer a system of thought or a religious philosophy that could be appropriated by Hindus; it offered instead a radical alternative to Hinduism: submission to Allah as the one true God. This alternative was chosen by many Indians, but those who remained Hindus within the framework of the *varṇāśrama-dharma* system were little changed by Muslim teachings and practices. Significant interaction and appropriation occurred only at the popular level and, as we shall see, in the teachings of certain poet-saints.

British influence, though shorter in duration, was largely secular and more easily appropriated by Hindus. Education in English was introduced in the first half of the nineteenth century, and employment preference for all government and public service jobs was given to those who knew English. A coordinated system of mass education through the university level was established in the second half of the century, and the first universities on the British model were founded. These measures affected only a small percentage of the population, but those who were affected gained access to English education and through it access to the English intellectual tradition. Muslims at first refused English education, so most of this English-trained minority were Hindus.

English literature, history, and law reflected the mood of social criticism and social reform that characterized nineteenth-century England. Concern for social improvement was conveyed also by liberal British administrators who applied Western social and moral standards to Indian society and found it wanting. Partly on the initiative of these administrators, partly as a result of pressure by English-educated Indians, several important reform measures were passed during the nineteenth century to correct abuses that had grown up in Indian society such as early marriage for girls, denial of widow remarriage even for child brides, and the practice of *satī* (burning a widow on the funeral pyre of her husband).

The legal system imposed by the British exposed Indians to social principles and standards of justice that challenged the old Brahmanical system. The privileges of Brāhmans, the restrictions imposed on outcastes and untouchables, and the caste system itself all were questioned from the new perspective. Some of the English-educated Indians questioned whether the Hindu religion could be true if it led to such abuses. Others sought to correct the abuses, or eliminate from Hindu religion what British humanism and Christian teachings led them to believe were the causes: image worship, polytheism, excessive supernaturalism, and the like. Though these were the attitudes of a minority, this minority had great influence in British India. Out of such new attitudes came most of the modern Hindu reform movements, led by the new Indian elite.

The Movements of Hindu Reform

Hindus had responded to Muslim rule and the expansion of Islam in a variety of ways. Some Hindus, as we have seen, converted to the new religion; others, the majority, retained their old traditions or withdrew into a defense of the Brahmanical system. A few, however, rejecting both Muslim dogmatism and Hindu rigidity, sought to reform their own tradition by accepting what they felt was the best in Islam. The outstanding examples of this response were the poet-saints Kabīr (1380–1460) and Nānāk (1469–1538).

Kabīr, a weaver from Banaras on the Ganges River, was an heir to the long tradition of devotional singers stretching back to the Āḷvārs. He was the disciple of Rāmānanda, a great devotee of Rāma and the founder of an important order of ascetics who worship Rāma alone as God. Kabīr, though also devoted to Rāma, combined his Hindu *advaita* theology with the strict monotheism of Islam and called himself a child of both Rāma and Allah. He taught that the names of the one God are only names; there is no distinction between them. He condemned Muslim and Hindu dogmatism and separatism, identified with the holy men of both traditions, and rejected the ritualism of Hindus and Muslims alike. Image worship, temples, and mosques were all to him a wrong attempt to locate God, who makes Himself known to his devotee in worship without the need for stones or buildings.

Kabīr's teaching was carried even further by Nānāk, who broke with both Hinduism and Islam to found a new religion that would join Hindus and Muslim in worship of the True One, the True Name, the one omnipotent God. This new religious community, called the Sikhs ("Disciples"), was Hindu in world view and thought forms but Muslim in its strict monotheism and rejection of image worship. Sikh worship centers around devotional hymns brought together after Nānāk's death in a collection called the *Granth*. Sikhs later formed themselves into a community of warriors to resist Muslim persecution, but remained in their religious life faithful to Nānāk's reformed theology and the teachings of the *Granth.*

These early movements of Hindu reform or revision during the Muslim period grew out of the religious experiences and devotion of poet-saints. Reform movements under the British tended to draw more on European or Christian humanistic concerns. This can be seen in the first great English-educated reformer, Rammohan Roy (1774–1833).

A gifted intellectual and social critic, Rammohan was trained in Persian, Arabic, and Sanskrit and became as fluent in English as in his native Bengali. Exposed in his studies to a variety of doctrines and fields of thought, he was liberal in his social and political views and a freethinker in religious matters. He was publicly active as an advocate of social reforms and the establishment of Western scientific education in India. Having published in 1815–1819 the first Bengali and English translations of the Upanishads, he became also an advocate of religious reform based on what he considered the Upanishadic doctrine of monotheism or Unitarianism. In 1828, he founded a religious organization for Hindus who believed in the unity of God as taught in the Upanishads and were prepared to abandon all image worship and ritual.

This was the beginning of the Brāhmo Samāj, the first of the modern Hindu reform movements. The next important leader of the movement, Devendranath Tagore (1817–1905), responded to the rationalist attitudes of younger members of the society by moving away from the early doctrine of Vedic infallibility to a principle of natural and universal theism. The Brāhmo Samāj began actively urging social reform and received a steady influx of idealistic young educated Hindus who joined to work for the improvement of India's social conditions. One of these new members, Keshab Chandra Sen (1838–1884), carried the message of the Brāhmo Samāj throughout India and promoted its popularization. He eventually broke with the parent group in 1868 to start the Brāhmo Samāj of India, a more progressive organization that moved even further away from the original monistic Hindu religious position of Rammohan Roy.

Keshab Chandra Ṡen exemplified many of the conflicts of the educated Hindu in the mid-nineteenth century. He was strongly influenced by Western ideals of social reform and by Christian religious teachings. He considered himself a disciple of Jesus, yet was also drawn to the Goddess Kālī, the Divine Mother of Bengal popular religion. He totally rejected image worship and gave a rationalist or allegorical interpretation to Hindu deities, yet introduced into Brāhmo Samāj services the practice of *saṃkīrtana,* the group devotional singing popularized in Bengal by Caitanya and the Krishna devotees who followed him. In the end he, too, like Devendranath Tagore, was judged to be too tied to the old social and religious traditions, and in 1878 a new and yet more rationalist and progressive branch of the Brāhmo Samāj was founded.

Only three years earlier, another reform movement had been founded on quite different principles. The Brāhmo Samāj acknowledged in many ways the superiority of Western values and Western science. The new Ārya Samāj founded by Swami Dayānanda (1824–1883) granted none of this. The Vedas were to Swami Dayānanda literally true and the ultimate source of religious authority. The Vedas taught monotheism and morality, not worship of images or caste discrimination. India did not need Western learning as a basis for reforming society; it needed only the Vedas. If Indians wanted to improve society, let them go back to the Vedas and strip away all the wrongs that had accumulated over the years. Hindus should be proud of their past, not ashamed of it.

The Ārya Samāj, with this message, began an active campaign to unify India around belief in God and faith in the Vedas. The society was active in social reform no less than the Brāhmo Samāj, but made a more direct appeal to the masses. The Ārya Samāj's approach was dogmatic and forceful, and the movement was an important factor in revitalizing the Hindu community and giving it greater self-confidence. Especially important was the model it provided for education and reform at the mass level where the Brāhmo Samāj, with its Westernized leadership and humanistic teachings, was weakest.

But even the Ārya Samāj lacked the depth of tradition that was the strength of popular and Brahmanical Hinduism. Though less obviously than the Brāhmo Samāj, the Ārya Samāj was also greatly influenced by Western and Muslim values. Both reflect Hindu self-criticism and self-doubt in precisely those areas most condemned by non-Hindus: image worship and the caste system. Though reforms in Indian society and religious institutions were certainly needed, it is not obvious in retrospect that the solution to India's ills lay in abandoning fifteen hundred years of cultural and religious development centered around the Purāṇas, theistic sects, popular devotional movements, and Tantra. It is indicative of the mood of the time that both the Brāhmo Samāj and Ārya Samāj worked hard for such abandonment.

The reform movements, however, brought about few direct changes in Hindu religious life outside their own relatively small groups of followers. The vague monotheism of both the Brāhmo Samāj and the Ārya Samāj had little religious appeal to most Hindus in comparison with the richness of the established traditions. The attitudes of the reform movements, however, had much wider effect than their specific proposals. The Brāhmo Samāj represented a new spirit of accommodation with Western learning and Western values, and the Ārya Samāj fostered a new pride in the Hindu past. To some extent these attitudes were contradictory, but in the area of Hindu social reform they strongly reinforced each other. Here the reform movements brought about major changes.

New laws were passed as a result of reformist efforts to abolish social injustices. What is more important, a new attitude toward social practices was developed. The reformers for the first time made a distinction between Hindu religious life and the social practices that had developed within the Hindu system. Caste regulations in particular were for them an unnecessary and undesirable accretion that could be treated separately from religious thought and practice. Removal of social injustices was not an infringement on religious freedom but the removal of cancerous growths that poisoned religious life. Some of the spirit of Kabīr can be seen in this separation of human institutions from the essence of religion, and much support could be found in the lives of poet-saints of all ages. One of the major contributions of the reformers was to open the way for a new understanding of these saints and prepare the way for saints in the future.

The Vitality of the Tradition

Calcutta in Bengal was the principal seat of British power in India in the early nineteenth century and the major center of British influence. In 1836, eight years after Rammohan Roy founded the Brāhmo Samāj, a Brāhman boy named Gadadhar was born in a small village in southern Bengal, not far from Calcutta in miles but utterly removed from it in culture. There Gadadhar lived for sixteen years, his main contact with the outside world the holy men and pilgrims passing through on their way south to the great Jagannātha Temple at Purī in Orissa.

Gadadhar at sixteen went to live in Calcutta with his older brother and became a family priest for several Calcutta households. His brother, in 1855, became priest of a Kālī temple at Dakṣineśvar on the Ganges north of Calcutta. Gadadhar was appointed priest of an adjacent smaller temple to Krishna; and when his brother died a year later Gadadhar, now known as Rāmakrishna, became priest of the main Kālī temple.

He had little interest in temple ritual. Most of his time was spent in meditation on the Goddess and singing devotional songs to her as the Mother. He soon had his first of many visions of Kālī, and from that time on would often pass into a trancelike state of total absorption or *samādhi* in which he would commune directly with the Mother. Many considered him ill or insane. He was replaced as priest in the Kālī temple and returned to his home village where his family, hoping to restore him to a more normal life, married him to a young girl five years old from a neighboring village. His wife, as was the custom, returned to her family after the wedding. Although she later lived with him after reaching puberty, the marriage was never consummated.

Rāmakrishna returned soon after his marriage to the grounds of the Kālī temple at Dakṣineśvar, where he lived for the next twenty-five years until his death in 1886. He began intense meditation and experienced numerous visions, trances, and moods of ecstasy that marked his intense rapture of love for Kālī. Rāmakrishna was passing through the madness of divine love described in Vaishnavite scriptures as the love of Rādhā and the *gopīs* for Krishna, the madness that had characterized the earlier Bengal saint Caitanya. He acquired a guru in the person of a female Tantric adept who trained him in Tantric *sādhanas.* He learned to discipline what had before been uncontrollable states of emotion, and achieved *samādhi* through the rising of the Kuṇḍalinī and the awakening of his *cakras.* He learned also Vaishnavite disciplines of devotion, taking on the role of Rādhā and acting out her passion for Krishna. From a new guru, an ascetic follower of Śankara's *advaita* doctrines, he was taught to experience identity with Brahman in pure monistic *samādhi.* He studied Muslim and Christian teachings and experienced what he interpreted as visions of Muhammad and Jesus. The focus of his religious life remained, however, the Goddess Kālī, the Mother of infinite variety and forms.

Rāmakrishna began to acquire householder devotees and a group of monastic disciples who had renounced the world. In 1875 he met Keshab Candra Sen, then the leader of the Brāhmo Samāj, and formed a close friendship with him. Keshab introduced Rāmakrishna to the intellectual and activist world of the Brāhmo Samāj, and he and his disciples were in turn regular visitors to Rāmakrishna. Keshab learned the depth of Rāmakrishna's Hindu devotion from his teachings and his frequent passage into *samādhi,* and in his later years moved away from his early Christian leanings to a more Hindu devotional position. He also began to spread news about Rāmakrishna to others, bringing in new devotees in increasing members.

Rāmakrishna was already widely regarded as a saint by the time of his death in 1886, and some considered him an *avatāra* on a par with Caitanya or Krishna himself. His disciples did not disband at his death, but formed themselves into a monastic order to continue Rāmakrishna's teachings. One of the leading disciples, Vivekānanda (1863–1902), came to America in 1893 to attend the worldwide Parliament of Religions in Chicago and stayed on for extended lecturing and teaching. When he left America in 1896, he left behind a permanent group of followers and a new organization: the Vedānta Society of New York. When he returned to India he organized the disciples and devotees of Rāmakrishna into an official body, the Rāmakrishna Mission. A Rāmakrishna Order of monks was established to guide the teaching and service activities of the Mission. New centers were set up throughout India from the original base in Calcutta, and centers in London and San Francisco were started by Vivekānanda on a second visit to America. By the time of Vivekānanda's death in 1902, a new phase of Hindu development was under way.

The significance of this development is the new interaction between traditional Hindu religious life and Western intellectual traditions. Rāmakrishna was an authentic Hindu saint of a type that goes back to the Āḷvārs and Nāyanārs and the devotional poet-saints of later India. Keshab Candra Sen was a brilliant English-educated intellectual, an activist social reformer, and an internationalist in his religious views. Vivekānanda was educated to fit the new British India as the son of an attorney of the Calcutta High Court and as a student of law himself at the time he first met Rāmakrishna. The combination was powerful, and has occurred not once but several times in modern India.

Mohandas K. Gandhi (1869–1948) and Aurobindo Ghosh (1872–1950) are perhaps the best known and most influential representatives of this pattern in the twentieth century. Before he became active in India, Gandhi spent three years in England studying law and twenty-one years in Africa championing the cause of Indian settlers against economic and social discrimination. He returned to India in 1915 and soon became a leading figure in the Indian National Congress, the major organization working for Indian home rule and eventual independence.

Gandhi's great contribution as a nationalist leader was his merger of political protest with Hindu religious ideals. He interpreted his work in terms of the *Gītā*'s *karma-yoga,* active involvement in the world with an attitude of selflessness and dispassion. He held up as a goal for all Indians the ideal of *svarāj,* "self-rule," by which he meant first and foremost personal self-control. Indian nationalist leaders before Gandhi had been British-educated intellectuals who discussed freedom and justice in terms of constitutional law and Western liberalism. Gandhi put on a loincloth, the daily dress of Indian peasants, and carried the message of freedom and self-rule to the masses in terms of their own traditions, the Hindu gods and scriptures.

Gandhi became more saintly over the years. Intensely self-analytical and highly self-disciplined, he sought to eliminate in himself all passion and self-interest. His guide was the *Bhagavad Gītā,* which he constantly quoted in his writings and continually studied for his own spiritual development. He led an ascetic personal existence of poverty and continence combined with a buoyancy of spirit that gave him great popular appeal. He was widely regarded as a saint and was given the title Mahātma, "great-souled one," in recognition of his saintly qualities.

Gandhi turned his energies outward in the life of a *karma-yogin.* Aurobindo Ghosh turned inward to a life of yogic meditation. Aurobindo's entire early life was spent in the context of Western learning. He began his education in a European convent school in India and at the age of seven was sent to England for fourteen years to complete his studies. He was a gifted student of classics at Cambridge University, proficient in Latin, Greek, French, German, and Italian. His aim was a career in the Indian Civil Service, the highly prestigious bureaucracy of British rule in India. He passed the Civil Service examination, but was disqualified for failure to take the riding test. He then shifted to a career in teaching at an Indian college, where he studied Sanskrit and other Indian languages.

Aurobindo joined the Indian nationalist movement in 1902, started two nationalist publications, and joined in protest movements against the British. He was arrested and tried for sedition in 1908 and served a year in prison. A year after his release he was again under prosecution, but escaped to the French colony of Pondicherry south of Madras. There he withdrew from politics and spent the rest of his life as a Tantric yogin.

Aurobindo began his study of yoga during his year in prison. After his escape to Pondicherry he founded an *āśram* or "retreat" for the study of yoga and published a number of scholarly religious studies. In *Essays on the Gita* and *The Life Divine* he defined his position as "Integral Yoga," based on the Tantric principle of total integration of all of life in the union of Śakti and Śiva.

In his new identity as Śrī Aurobindo, he became widely known as both a scholar and yogic saint. His later years were lived in almost total exclusion from the world in the practice of meditation. Disciples gathered at Pondicherry to be near the Master, and the Aurobindo Āśram there has continued after his death to be a vital center of religious life. The Āśram is now headed by his long-time female companion who is known as "The Mother," the embodiment of Śakti.

Modern Indian religious life is of course not limited to these or other saints and their movements. The normative forms of Indian religious life are still to be found in the continuation of the Smārta tradition, in popular devotion within and outside the theistic sects, in temple *pūjā* and festivals, in pilgrimages to holy places, in household life in accordance with rules of *varṇāśrama-dharma,* in the austerities of *sannyāsins* and wandering ascetic *sādhus,* in art and music, and in the variety of forms which Tantra and yoga have taken as guides to the inner life.

The saints still remain, however, as they have always been, the generating centers of Hindu religion. It is notable that the most important saints in modern India are not those who remained outside the forces of modernity but those who faced these forces and overcame them. Even more significant, perhaps, is the new missionary zeal evident from the time of Vivekānanda to the present. The Rāmakrishna Mission has continued to grow in influence not only in India but throughout the world. The number of Vedānta Society centers in America has grown, and the Vedanta Press has become a major outlet for Hindu publications in America.

More recently, Swami A. C. Bhaktivedānta has started a rapidly growing devotional movement in America as an outgrowth of the Bengal Caitanya movement. Known as the Society for Krishna Consciousness, it has brought the devotional and ritual practices of Bengal Vaishnavism into American cities, has attracted numerous full-time disciples, and has influenced a much larger number of devotees who chant the sect's *Hare Krishna* mantra as a form of meditation. The Spiritual Regeneration Movement founded by Maharishi Mahesh Yogi is another highly successful transplantation of Hindu forms into the West, in this instance from the base of the *advaita* philosophy of Śankara and the tradition of *advaita* meditation. The main teaching agency of the Maharishi's organization, the Students' International Meditation Society, has initiated thousands of Americans into the practice of Transcendental Meditation in the past few years and has encouraged the development of college courses and research projects to study meditation and its effects.

Other movements in India and America could be added to expand this list, but the basic point is clear: the Hindu religious tradition is alive and well. Perhaps not in all its parts, for it never has been—nor has any other religious tradition. But there are centers of vitality and new growth, new efforts to engage the world or help men face its anxieties, new forms to meet new circumstances. We cannot point to any one feature of the tradition for special credit in this; the tradition has grown in many strands that have constantly interacted, from the Vedic ritual tradition and Brahmanical world view to the latest devotional movements and the saints today who carry the tradition forward. But if anything is certain, it is that the truths revealed in all the millennia of its existence will continue to be true, and will have in the future as in the past the power to shape men's lives.

OUTLINE OF THE DEVELOPMENT OF VEDIC WRITINGS

Mantra Saṃhitās	Vedic schools represented by separate collections	Brāhmaṇas	Early Upanishads (–500 B.C.)	Later (Verse) Upanishads (500 B.C.–200 B.C.)	Late Upanishads (200 B.C.–200 A.D.)
Ṛig	Aitareyin	Aitareya	Aitareya (4)[b]		
	Kauṣītakin	Kauṣītaki	Kauṣītaki (5)		
Sāma	Tāṇḍin	Pañcaviṃśa			
		Chāndogya	Chāndogya (2)		
	Talavakāra	Jaiminīya (Talavakāra)	Kena (6)		
Yajur	Kāṭhaka	Kāṭhaka (B)[a]		Kaṭha	
	Kapiṣṭhala-Kaṭha	(B)			
	Maitrāyaṇīya	(B)			Maitrī
	Taittirīya	Taittirīya (B)	Taittirīya (3)	Mahānārāyaṇa	
	Vājasaneyin (?)	Śatapatha	Bṛihadāraṇyaka (1)	Īśa Śvetāśvatara	
Atharva		Gopatha (Late)		Muṇḍaka	Praśna Māṇḍūkya

PARALLEL DATES

			Buddha (563–483 B.C.)	Pāṇini (ca. 350 B.C.) Alexander (326 B.C.) Candragupta Maurya (322–298 B.C.) Aśoka (269–232 B.C.)	
			Epics as Popular Poems (600–300 B.C.)		Epics as Vaishnava Didactic Poems (200 B.C.–200 A.D.)

[a] (B) indicates a text of the Black *Yajur Veda* (mantras and Brāhmaṇa intermingled)
[b] numbers in parentheses indicate the approximate order of formation of the texts

A SCHEMATIC DIAGRAM OF THE HINDU RELIGIOUS TRADITION

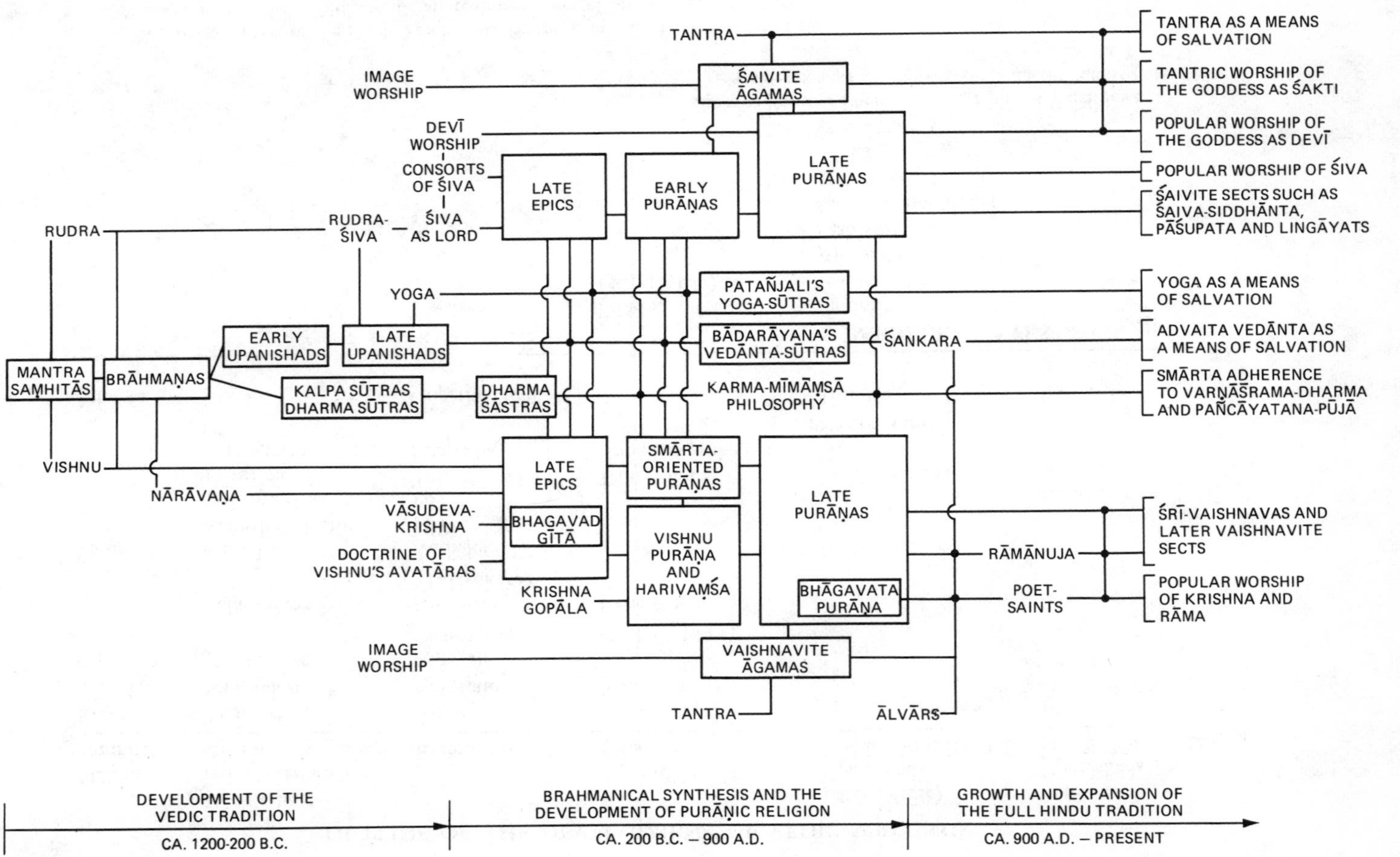

Selected Readings

GENERAL

Basham, A. L., *The Wonder That Was India.* New York: Grove Press, 1959. The best available introduction to the development of classical Indian culture from the Indus Civilization to *ca.* A.D. 1000. Combining clear presentation with scholarly authority, the book has become a modern classic.

Bhattacharyya, Haridas (ed.), *The Cultural Heritage of India,* Vol. IV: *The Religions.* Calcutta: The Ramakrishna Mission Institute of Culture, 1956. A valuable collection of over forty articles by a wide range of Indian scholars and religious leaders. Includes material on Hindu sects, Hindu and Buddhist Tantra, the lives and teachings of numerous saints, and descriptions of religious rituals, festivals, and popular practices.

Dasgupta, Surendranath, *A History of Indian Philosophy.* Cambridge: Cambridge University Press, 1952–55, 5 vols. (Vols. I–IV reprinted from the original editions published 1921–1949.) A comprehensive and detailed survey of Indian philosophical systems and their development from the Vedas through medieval scholastic and sectarian writings. Includes the six orthodox *darśanas,* Buddhist and Jain philosophy, and the philosophical positions of various Purāṇas and theistic sects.

Embree, Ainslie T. (ed.), *The Hindu Tradition.* New York: The Modern Library, 1966. An excellent collection of primary sources illustrating Hindu religious and cultural development from Vedic to modern times. The selections are arranged chronologically with brief introductions to interpret their contents and explain their place in the tradition.

Farquhar, J. N., *An Outline of the Religious Literature of India.* Delhi: Motilal Banarsidass, 1967. Reprint of the Oxford University Press ed. of 1920. An invaluable guide to the contents and chronology of Hindu, Buddhist, and Jain writings from the Vedas to *ca.* A.D. 1800. Writings are arranged by schools and systems of thought within historical periods to show the stages in Indian religious development.

Majumdar, R. C. (ed.), *The History and Culture of the Indian People.* London: G. Allen and Unwin, 1951–. A multivolume survey of Indian history and culture from Vedic times to the present by specialists selected from the best of modern Indian historians.

Majumdar, R. C., H. C. Raychaudhuri, and K. Datta, *An Advanced History of India.* London: Macmillan, 1963. A comprehensive survey of Indian political, social, economic, and religious history from prehistoric times through Indian independence.

Radhakrishnan, Sarvepalli and Charles A. Moore. *A Source Book in Indian Philosophy.* Princeton: Princeton University Press, 1967 (paperback ed.). A wide-ranging selection of primary sources from the major periods and systems of Indian philosophy, with brief introductions by the editors.

Sacred Books of the East, translated by various oriental scholars and edited by F. Max Müller. Oxford: Clarendon Press, 1879–1910. This fifty-volume series contains translations of many basic texts, including numerous Hindu texts unavailable elsewhere, with introductions and notes. The series has been reprinted in the U.S. by Dover Press in paperback and in India by Motilal Banarsidass.

Chapter One

The Indus Civilization

Gordon, D. C., *The Prehistoric Background of Indian Culture.* Bombay: N. M. Tripathi, 1958. A rather technical study of archaeological data from early Indian cultures, but with valuable interpretations of material from the Indus cities and other Indus sites.

Piggott, Stuart, *Prehistoric India.* Baltimore: Penguin Books, 1961. A very readable survey of the Early Stone Age and Bronze Age village cultures of western India, the Indus Civilization, and the coming of the Aryans, authoritatively interpreted by a leading modern archaeologist.

Wheeler, Sir Mortimer, *The Indus Civilization.* Cambridge: Cambridge University Press, 2d ed., 1960. A report and interpretation of discoveries at the principal pre-Indus and Indus sites, by one of the leading archaeological investigators.

———, *Civilizations of the Indus Valley and Beyond.* New York: McGraw-Hill, 1966. A more general and readable survey than *The Indus Civilization,* with valuable additional material on post-Indus developments up to the time of the Mauryans and many excellent photographs of Indus and Ganges excavations and artifacts.

The Aryans and Early Vedic Religion

Bhattacharji, Sukumari, *The Indian Theogony.* Cambridge: Cambridge University Press, 1970. An excellent recent study of the changing pattern of Indian gods, tracing their evolution from the early Aryan and pre-Aryan deities to the gods of the late Purāṇic traditions.

Keith, A. Berriedale, *The Religion and Philosophy of the Veda and Upanishads.* Cambridge: Harvard University Press, 1925. (Harvard Oriental Series, v. 31, 32.) An often technical survey of the gods, rituals, and philosophical concepts of the Vedas, from the early Vedic hymns through the Brāhmaṇas, Āraṇyakas, and Upanishads. An authoritative study by one of the great scholars of the past generation.

Kosambi, D. D., *Ancient India.* New York: Pantheon Books, 1965. A study of early Indian history, with emphasis on the merger of Aryan and non-Aryan cultures and the resulting civilization in Mauryan and post-Mauryan times.

MacDonell, A. A., *The Vedic Mythology.* Varanasi: Indological Book House, 1963. Reprint of the 1897 ed. A detailed compendium of Vedic mythology that brings together the scattered descriptions and fragments of myth for each of the Vedic gods.

Muir, John, *Original Sanskrit Texts on the Origin and History of the People of*

India, Their Religion and Institutions. Amsterdam: Oriental Press, 1967, 5 vols. Reprint of the rev. ed. of 1872–74. A useful collection of Sanskrit texts (and English translations) relating to selected topics. Sources range from the Vedic hymns to the Purāṇas and scholastic commentators, including much material not easily found elsewhere.

Chapter Two

Blair, Chauncey, *Heat in the Rig Veda and Atharva Veda.* New Haven: American Oriental Society, 1961. An important study of the Vedic concept of *tapas.*

Bloomfield, Maurice (trans.), *Hymns of the Atharva Veda.* Delhi: Motilal Banarsidass, 1964. Reprint of *Sacred Books of the East,* v. XLII. Introduction and translations of the most important hymns of the *Atharva Veda* by one of the best American Sanskritists of the nineteenth century.

Dasgupta, Surendranath, *Hindu Mysticism.* New York: Frederick Ungar, 1967. Reprint of the 1927 ed. See especially Lecture I, "Sacrificial Mysticism."

Edgerton, Franklin, *The Beginnings of Indian Philosophy.* Cambridge: Harvard University Press, 1965. Reflections on the origins of Indian philosophy by a great American Sanskritist, valuable for the careful translations of selected Vedic hymns and passages from the early Upanishads and the *Mahābhārata,* with scholarly notes and cross-references.

Eggeling, Julius (trans.), *Śatapatha Brāhmaṇa.* Delhi: Motilal Banarsidass, 1966, 5 vols. Reprint of *Sacred Books of the East,* v. XII, XXVI, XLI, XLIII, and XLIV. A translation of the most important of the Brāhmaṇas, with a valuable introduction by the translator.

Kane, P. V., *History of Dharmaśāstra.* Poona: Bhandarkar Oriental Research Institute, 1930–62, 5 vols. A masterpiece of dedicated scholarship and a gold mine of information on Vedic and classical Indian society and religious practices. Traces the development of Hindu teachings on *dharma* with extensive quotations and references to primary sources.

Keith, A. Berriedale, *op. cit.* Important material on the theory and practice of the various types of fire sacrifices.

———, *Rig Veda Brāhmaṇas: The Aitareya and Kauṣītaki Brāhmaṇas of the Ṛigveda.* Cambridge: Harvard University Press, 1920. Translations of the Brāhmaṇas of two *Ṛig Veda* schools, with introduction and notes by the translator.

Renou, Louis, *Religions of Ancient India.* London: The Athlone Press, 1953. A scholarly and perceptive discussion by one of the best modern Indologists, especially valuable for the insights it gives on the performance of the fire sacrifice.

Chapter Three

Hume, Robert Ernest (trans.), *Thirteen Principal Upanishads.* London: Oxford University Press, 1958. Reprint of revised 2nd ed. of 1931. Careful scholarly translations of thirteen complete Upanishads, with explanatory notes, a list of parallel passages in the principal Upanishads and the *Bhagavad Gītā,* and an excellent introductory essay. This is still probably the best and most usable translation of the major texts.

Mascaró, Juan (trans.), *The Upanishads*. Baltimore: Penguin Books, 1965. Clear translations of seven Upanishads and portions of five others, with a good general introduction to the religious and humanistic significance of Upanishadic thought.

Prabhavananda, Swami and Frederick Manchester, *The Upanishads*. Hollywood, Calif.: The Vedanta Press, 1947. Good literary translations of nine complete Upanishads and the most important sections of three larger ones, interpreted on the basis of Śankara's *advaita* (monistic) philosophy.

Radhakrishnan, Sarvepalli (ed. and trans.), *The Principal Upaniṣads*. London: George Allen and Unwin, 1953. Complete Sanskrit texts of eighteen Upanishads, with excellent translations, explanatory notes, and historical/philosophical introduction by India's best-known modern philosopher.

Chapter Four

Banerjea, Jitendranath, *The Development of Hindu Iconography*. Calcutta: The University of Calcutta, 1956. A detailed scholarly history of Hindu iconography, with numerous descriptions and illustrations.

Kane, P. V., *op. cit.* See Vol. II, Part II, pp. 708–712 for a discussion of early Hindu images and image worship.

Lee, Sherman E., *A History of Far Eastern Art*. Englewood Cliffs, N.J.: Prentice Hall, 1964. A general survey of early Buddhist and Hindu art, with many illustrations.

Rahula, Walpola, *What the Buddha Taught*. Bedford: The Gordon Fraser Gallery, 1967. A systematic presentation of basic Buddhist teachings, by a contemporary Theravāda Buddhist scholar.

Robinson, Richard, *The Buddhist Religion*. Belmont, Calif.: Dickenson, 1970. An excellent introduction to the origin and development of Buddhism in India and beyond.

Rosenfield, John M., *The Dynastic Arts of the Kushans*. Berkeley: University of California Press, 1967. A detailed study of developments in North India before and during the rule of the Kushans, with important information on early representations of Hindu gods.

Rowland, Benjamin, Jr., *The Evolution of the Buddha Image*. New York: The Asia Society, 1963. A concise discussion, with illustrations, of the development of images of the Buddha.

Thomas, E. J., *The Life of the Buddha as Legend and History*. London: Routledge and Kegan Paul, 1924. A careful evaluation of Buddhist texts to determine the historical facts of the Buddha's life and teachings.

Chapter Five

Apte, V. M., *Social and Religious Life in the Grihya Sutras*. Bombay: The Popular Book Depot, 1954. Reprint of the 1939 ed. A comprehensive survey of the conditions of Indian life from the time of the *Ṛig Veda* through the period of the Gṛihya Sūtras.

Banerjee, S. C., *Dharma Sutras: a Study in Their Origin and Development.* Calcutta: Punthi Pustak, 1962. A careful study of the textual background of the Dharma Sūtras and a survey of their contents.

Basham, A. L., *op. cit.* See especially Chapters V and VI on "Society: Class, Family and Individual" and "Everyday Life: The Daily Round in City and Village."

Bühler, Georg (trans.), *The Laws of Manu.* Delhi: Motilal Banarsidass, 1967. Reprint of *The Sacred Books of the East,* v. XXV. An early (1886) but valuable translation, with extensive introduction and a synopsis of parallel passages in other *dharma* texts.

Kane, P. V., *op. cit.* The principal sourcebook for data on the development of *dharma* teachings and texts. See v. V, Part I, pp. 486–603 for a discussion of astrology.

Taimni, I. K., *The Science of Yoga.* Wheaton, Ill.: The Theosophical Publishing House, 1967. A detailed modern commentary on Patañjali's *Yoga Sūtras,* with a careful description and explanation of the mental phenomena involved.

Wood, Ernest, *Yoga.* Baltimore: Penguin Books, 1967. A thorough introduction to the practical and theoretical aspects of traditional Indian yoga.

Chapter Six

Bhattacharji, Sukumari, *op. cit.* Valuable descriptions of the great popular gods of Purāṇic religion and their origins.

Farquhar, J. N., *op. cit.* Concise descriptions of the variety of religious positions recorded in the epics and Purāṇas.

Hazra, R. C., *Studies in the Purāṇic Records on Hindu Rites and Customs.* Calcutta: University of Dacca, 1940. An essential study. The only comprehensive analysis and interpretation of the contents of the major Purāṇas, their relationships to each other and to other texts, and their chronological development.

Pathak, V. S., *Śaiva Cults in Northern India From Inscriptions.* Varanasi: Ram Naresh Varma, 1960. A compilation and interpretation of available archaeological and textual data on Śaivite sects from *ca.* A.D. 700 to A.D. 1200.

Sanyal, J. M. (trans.), *The Srimad-Bhagavatam.* Calcutta: Oriental Publishing Company, 1952, 5 vols. Reprint of 1929–39 ed. The only readily available complete translation of the *Bhāgavata Purāṇa.*

Wilson, H. N. (trans.), *The Viṣṇu Purāṇa.* New York: B. Franklin, 1969. Reprint of the 1840 ed. An early landmark study by a great Sanskritist, with a complete translation of the text and references to related passages in other Purāṇas.

Zimmer, Heinrich, *Myths and Symbols in Indian Art and Civilization.* New York: Harper, 1946. A brilliant and readable presentation of major themes and symbols, with emphasis on the Purāṇas and Hindu art.

Chapter Seven

Banerjea, Jitendranath, *op. cit.*

Bharati, Agehananda, *The Tantric Tradition.* Garden City, N.Y.: Doubleday Anchor, 1970. An important study of Tantric thought and practice with explanations of many basic Tantric principles.

Bhattacharyya, Haridas, *op. cit.*

Daniélou, Alain, *Hindu Polytheism*. New York: Pantheon Books, 1964. (Bollingen Series, v. LXXIII.) A collection of traditional myths and symbols associated with the major Hindu gods, with selected Sanskrit texts and numerous illustrations.

Dimock, Edward C. and Denise Levertov (trans.), *In Praise of Krishna: Songs From the Bengali*. Garden City, N.Y.: Doubleday, 1964. Beautiful translations of some of the best Bengali songs expressing the love relationship of Krishna and Rādhā.

Farquhar, J. N., *op. cit.*

Hazra, R. C., *op. cit.*

Kane, P. V., *op. cit.*

Pratyagatmananda, *Japasūtram: the Science of Creative Sound*. Madras: Ganesh, 1961. A discussion of the creative power of sound and mantras in the Vedic and Tantric traditions.

Radhakrishnan, Sarvepalli and Charles A. Moore, *op. cit.* Representative texts from the major philosophical schools, including the Vedānta positions of Śankara and Rāmānuja.

Raghavan, V., *The Great Integrators: the Saint Singers of India*. Delhi: Ministry of Information and Broadcasting, 1966. A wide-ranging selection of translations from the songs of Indian poet-saints, with an historical introduction and evaluation of their contributions.

Suryavanshi, Bhagwansingh, *The Abhiras: Their History and Culture*. Baroda: University of Baroda, 1962. A survey of the available information on early Ābhīra history and movements and Ābhīra cultural characteristics.

Thibaut, George (trans.), *The Vedānta Sūtras of Bādarāyana with the Commentary of Rāmānuja*. Delhi: Motilal Banarsidass, 1962. Reprint of *Sacred Books of the East,* v. XLVIII. Rāmānuja's classic critique of Śankara's monistic position and his statement of a theology based on "qualified non-dualism."

——, *The Vedānta Sūtras of Bādarāyana with the Commentary by Śaṅkara*. New York: Dover, 1962, 2 vols. Reprint of *Sacred Books of the East,* v. XXXIV and XXXVIII. Śankara's major work in which he develops a position of absolute monism.

Zimmer, Heinrich, *op. cit.*

Chapter Eight

Bhaktivedanta, A. C., Swami, *The Bhagavad Gita As It Is*. New York: Macmillan, 1968. A translation and interpretation of the *Gītā* by the spiritual leader of the Krishna Consciousness movement in America.

——, *The Teachings of Lord Chaitanya*. New York: International Society for Krishna Consciousness, 1968. The devotional teachings of the Caitanya movement and the major early Caitanyite theologians, based on the *Caitanya Caritāmṛita,* the sectarian biography of Caitanya.

Bhattacharyya, Haridas, *op. cit.*

Farquhar, J. N., *Modern Religious Movements in India*. New York: Macmillan, 1924. Religious and reform movements in modern India up to the end of the nineteenth century.

Gandhi, Mohandas Karamchand, *Gandhi's Autobiography: My Experiments with*

Truth. Washington: Public Affairs Press, 1948. Gandhi's appealing account of the personal failures and achievements of his early years.

Ghosh, Śrī Aurobindo, *The Life Divine*. New York: The Greystone Press, 1949. Śrī Aurobindo's most comprehensive statement of his philosophy.

———, *Essays on the Gita*. New York: Dutton, 1950. Reprint of the original two volumes of 1921–1928. Studies and reflections on the *Gītā* from the viewpoint of Integral Yoga.

Maharishi Mahesh Yogi, *The Science of Being and Art of Living*. New York: Signet Books, 1969. The philosophical principles and practical effects of Transcendental Meditation as taught by the Maharishi.

Nikhilananda, Swami (trans.), *The Gospel of Sri Ramakrishna*. New York: Ramakrishna-Vivekananda Center, 1952. The profound yet warmly human teachings of Śrī Rāmakrishna, as recorded by one of his disciples.

Rishabhchand, *The Integral Yoga of Sri Aurobindo*. Pondicherry: Sri Aurobindo Ashram Press, 2d ed., 1959. A systematic interpretation of Śrī Aurobindo's teachings by one of his disciples.

Singer, Milton (ed.), *Krishna: Myths, Rites and Attitudes*. Chicago: The University of Chicago Press, 1968. Scholarly studies of various aspects of the Krishna tradition from the *Bhāgavata Purāṇa* to modern times.

Index

Nārāyaṇa, 89, 99, 109
Nārāyaṇiya (portion of *Mahābhārata*), 99, 102, 103
Nāthamuni, 118, 122
Natural powers, 7–8, 11
Nature (Prakṛiti), 66, 67, 70, 71, 91, 92 (*see also* Prakṛiti)
Nāyanārs, 117, 118, 125, 137
Nirguṇa (devoid of qualities), 119
Nirvāṇa, 55, 56, 57
Non-Aryans, 3, 16, 53, 60
North India, 52, 53, 55, 59, 125, 131
Nyāsa (ritual placing of gods or powers in the body), 115, 116, 127, 130

Offerings in *pūjā,* 110, 111
Oṃ, 29, 38, 71, 72, 73, 97, 114, 116, 127
One, the, 20, 21, 25, 37, 42, 43, 44, 45, 66, 69
Ouranos, 12
Outcastes, 126 (*see also* Untouchables)

Pañca Mahāyajña ("Five Great Sacrifices"), 15–16
Pañca-makāra ("five m's"), 128
Pañcarātra sacrifice, 89
Pāñcarātras, 99, 112, 113, 116, 118, 122 (*see also* Sects, theistic)
Pañcāyatana-pūjā (worship of the five shrines), 120–121 (*see also Pūjā and* Smārtas)
Pāṇḍavas, 90, 94, 102
Pāṇini, 62
Parjanya, 12
Parthians, 59
Pārvatī, 88, 114, 126
Paśu, 128, 130
Pāśupatas, 97, 98, 99 (*see also* Sects, theistic)
Paśupati (Lord of Creatures), 69, 97 (*see also* Lord of Creatures)
Pāṭaliputra, 57, 108
Patañjali, 67
Patna, 57
Persian Empire, 52, 57, 58, 60–61
Phallus, 7–10, 88, 98 (*see also Lingam*)
Pilgrimages, 111, 112, 125, 139
Piṅgalā (channel on the right side of the body), 128
Poet-priests, 14, 28 (*see also* Priests)
Poet-saints, 118, 124–126, 132, 133–134, 136, 137
Pondicherry, 138–139
Portugese, 132
Prahlāda, 102
Prajāpati, 32, 33, 37, 39, 41, 49
Prakṛiti (Nature), 66, 67, 68, 70, 71, 91, 92, 97, 100, 101, 114, 126
Prāṇas, 32, 40, 41, 65 (*see also* Breaths)
Prāṇāyāma (breath restraint), 65, 68
Prasāda (food offered in *pūjā*), 111
Pratyāhāra (withdrawal of the senses), 65, 68
Preservation of world, 100, 109
Priests, 14, 15, 24, 25, 26, 27–30, 31, 32, 34, 36, 37, 38, 49, 50, 51, 63, 73, 76, 77, 80, 81, 87, 89, 111, 136 (*see also Brāhmaṇas,* Brāhmaṇas, Brāhmans, *and* Poet-priests)
Primary Matter, 100, 126 (*see also* Prakṛiti)
Pūjā (worship), 110–112, 113, 114, 115, 120, 121, 123, 129–130, 139
Purāṇas, 95–97, 99, 101, 103, 106, 107, 108, 109, 110, 112, 117, 118, 120, 123, 124, 125, 135
Purī, 111, 136
Purification, 10, 48, 55, 116, 117, 129–130 (*see also* Purity)
Purity, 5, 9, 10, 31, 34, 55, 77, 82, 83, 124
Purohit (family priest), 1
Puruṣa (the self in the *sāṃkhya* system and in Patañjali's yoga), 68
Puruṣa (Person), 22–25, 32, 37, 40, 94, 100, 101
Puruṣa Sūkta (hymn to Puruṣa), 22–25, 116
Pūṣan, 12
Pūtanā, 104

Rādhā, 125, 136, 137
Raghavan, V., 125
Rājanya, 24 (*see also* Kṣatriyas)
Rajas (passion, one of the three *guṇas*), 66, 100, 128, 129
Rāma, 102, 125, 133
Rāmakrishna, 1, 118, 136–137
Rāmakrishna Mission, 1, 137, 139
Rāmānanda, 133
Rāmānuja, 122–123, 124
Rāmāyana, 87, 95, 96, 102
Rammohan Roy, 134, 136
Rāsa-līlā, 105, 106
Rebirth (transmigration), 34, 41, 42, 43–44, 45, 47, 50, 51, 52, 54, 56, 64, 73, 75, 78, 80, 81, 82, 85, 91, 92, 119
"Redeath," 34
Reform, social, 132–136, 137, 138
Release from rebirth, 41, 44, 45, 46, 47, 50, 51, 54, 55, 56–57, 66, 70, 71, 73, 74, 78, 82, 83, 85, 97, 107, 119, 121, 122
Renunciation (*see Sannyāsins*)
Rig Veda, 11, 13, 14–15, 17, 18, 20, 21, 22, 23, 24, 25, 26, 29, 30, 32, 49, 69, 73, 79, 84, 116
Rig Veda Saṃhitā, 14–15
Ṛishis (*see* Seers)
Ṛita (order, rightness), 12, 25
Rohinī, 103
Roman Empire, 59, 61
Rosary, 116